Authority in Islam

Authority in Islam

From the Rise of Muhammad to the Establishment of the Umayyads

Hamid Dabashi

Transaction Publishers
New Brunswick (U.S.A.) and London (U.K.)

Library of Congress Catalog Number: 88-36467
ISBN: 0-88738-288-6
Printed in the United States of America

Library of Congress Cataloging-in-Publication Data
Dabashi, Hamid 1951-
    Authority in Islam: from the rise of Muhammad to the establishment of the
Unmmayads / Hamid Dabashi
        p.   cm.
    Bibliography: p.
    Includes index.
    ISBN 0-88738-288-6
    1. Authority (Islam)—History of doctrines. 2. Islam—History.
I. Title
BP165.7.D33   1989   88-36467
306'.6—dc19

For my wife Afsaneh,
who makes it all possible,
and for our children,
Kaveh and Pardis,
who make everything else worthwhile

Contents

Acknowledgments

A remote, almost unrecognizable, version of this book was my doctoral dissertation "presented to the faculties of the University of Pennsylvania in partial fulfillment . . . ," etc. But I have been with this text for almost five years beyond my doctoral duties. We have grown together, you might say. But I still consider it my duty to thank the distinguished members of my dissertation committee who helped me organize my ideas into this work.

First and foremost I would like to thank my mentor for five years and beyond, Philip Rieff, for his untiring care in my intellectual growth. What I gave him, in that memorable first sitting with Max Weber's *Politics as a Vocation* in the autumn of 1980, was a confused potpourri of disjointed fragments I called my mind. What he gave me, after five years of relentless guidance into the vast maze of Weber phrases, Kierkegaard sentences, and Nietzsche paragraphs, was the ability to reach the pinnacle of my limited abilities, in order to work out what I can safely call my thought. For that, and for much more, I am most grateful to Philip Rieff. Whatever I write for the rest of my academic life, I will feel him looking over my shoulder.

Samuel Z. Klausner read my initial chapters with care and scrutiny. His comments, always precise, made me work these pages into readable passages. Gerhard Bowering, with his high standards, demanded the best that I could offer. That I occasionally failed to meet these standards to the best of his expectations, has made me rework entire sections of the book. If there are improvements, they are to his credit. If deficiencies persist, they are all mine.

S. H. Nasr paid exceptional attention to my academic life and work, for which I am grateful. E. Digby Baltzell provided a fresh theoretical look that forced me to keep the text sociologically relevant. Willy De Craemer and Rene Fox provided many valuable comments.

Although not members of my dissertation committee, Harold Bershady and Victor Lidz always read portions of my manuscript with more than professional interest. My understanding of Weber is much indebted to their guidance and instructions.

If I have said something in this book worth knowing about the historical working of the Weberian theory of authority, or about the formative phase of Islam, I owe that to the collective teachings of these distinguished scholars with whom I have had the honor of working. If errors of theoretical judgement, mistakes in historical accuracy, or flaws in causal explanations persist, they are all mine.

Finally, let me thank publicly, now that I keep failing to do privately, my dear wife Afsaneh for coping with much beyond the duties of a wife married to an absent-minded man who is either not there at all, or if there, only partially so. Without her moral and intellectual support, deeply as she is involved in her own academic career, this, among my other vanities, would not have been possible. If not by dedicating this book to her and to our children, how else can I tell her how much I cherish having her by my side.

Preface

When one of our most eminent historians [Edward Meyer] feels impelled to give an account to himself and his colleagues of the aims and methods of his scholarly work, this must necessarily arouse an interest far beyond the limits of his special discipline because in doing so he passes beyond the boundaries of his special discipline and enters into the area of methodological analysis.

—Max Weber

The primary purpose of this study is to examine the question of authority in Islam—its nature, organization, initial changes, vicissitudes, and transformations—from the immediate background of Muhammad's prophetic movement, through his successful mission, and into the formation of the paradigmatic patterns of the Sunnite, Shiᶜite, and Kharijite modes of authority. By centering on a crucial turning point of a society, this study attempts to see both the continuities and the disruptions inherent in a vast religious revolution.

Extensive descriptive accounts of the particular units of this study—that is, pre-Islamic Arabia, the life and mission of Muhammad, and the emergence of the Sunnite, Schᶜite, and Kharijite branches of Islam—already exist in abundance. But Muhammad's charismatic movement as expressed against the traditional Arab order and as later institutionalized into the tapestry of Islamic political culture is taken here as a specific case study primarily for its theoretical implications in the sociology of authority.

Of primary concern to me is to see how the emerging paradigm of a new religious culture is expressed and established. No culture supersedes another completely. Muhammad's charismatic authority, the needs of the emerging cultural paradigms, surpassed the pre-Islamic Arab traditional order. Yet in the process of its institutionalization, it interacted with the reemerging Arab order; and the synthetic results were the Sunnite, Shiᶜite, and Kharijite divisions within Islam. Those divisions then, in turn, constituted separate cultural paradigms within the confinements of which only certain potentialities could be realized and others could not. At this stage, the primary objective is not how these paradigms actually develop in history but, rather, how they were paradigmatically envisioned and construed initially.

My central theoretical problem is to see what particular modalities of culture were developed incipiently after the originating messaage (*risalah*) of Muhammad who sought and succeeded in leading a revolution in the established modalities of authority in his time.

The following seven purposes control this study: First, to discern the prevailing leitmotifs of authority in pre-Islamic Arab society. Second, to see the pre-Islamic Arab culture as an operating system of social actions upon which the Muhammadan charismatic movement is imposed. Third, to follow Muhammad's prophetic revolution as a phenomenon *sui generis*, introducing a forceful change in the fabric of pre-Islamic culture, so that the paradigmatic patterns of a new culture are established. Fourth, to realize the continuity and change of both pre-Islamic and Muhammadan cultural paradigms—centered around the element of authority—in the post-Muhammadan consolidation of the Islam. Fifth, to observe the formation of the Sunnite, Shi'ite, and Kharijite branches of Islam as specific expressions of deep cleavages within the general Islamic political culture. Sixth, to consider the formation of these early three branches of Islam as the dialectical outcomes of interactions between pre-Islamic motifs of authority and those of the Muhammadan charismatic movements. And seventh, to suggest that the obvious political divisions within the early Islamic community, deep-rooted as they were in the clash between the pre-Islamic and Muhammadan modalities of authority, manifested the formation of fundamental patterns of authority that would ultimately shape, in dialectical interaction with other external historical factors, the course of Islamic civilization.

Thus to discern the most general patterns of authority that emerged from the clash between the pre-Islamic and Muhammadan alternatives and, in turn, molded both the unity and the multiplicity of the Islamic political culture is the main objective of this study.

Weber's typology of "charismatic authority" will be employed as a model for this investigation of a particular historical case. The elements of this typology will be translated carefully into the Islamic case to render it not only applicable to Muhammad but also helpful in understanding his mode of authority. It should always be borne in mind, as Weber reminded repeatedly, "that none of these three ideal types . . . is usually to be found in historical cases in 'pure' form" (1978a, 216). Muhammad's is a particular historical case that Weber's typology of charismatic authority illuminates and which should be further elaborated and extended. The very typology of charismatic authority was developed by Sohm and extended by Weber through an empirical observation of historical Christianity. Historical Islam, the argument warrants, can improve on both its theoretical elaboration and its empirical verification. Muhammad's authority is as much illuminated by the typology of charismatic authority as the latter is empirically tested by the former.

Obviously not every particular aspect of historical cases is considered or assimilated into a typology. "The idea," Weber pointed out, "that the whole of concrete historical reality can be exhausted in the conceptual scheme about to be developed is as far from the author's thoughts as anything could be" (1978a, 216). Yet within the frame of reference established by the "ideal type," all of the peripheral historical aspects of the phenomenon can be properly addressed and assimilated into the general picture drawn by the typology. Thus, in investigating Muhammad's charismatic authority, Weber's typology is both a model and a point of departure. There will be occasions, consequently, to refer to and analyze the particular cases of discrepancies between Weber's formulation of an aspect of charismatic authority and the historical case of Muhammad. These occasions will be studied closely in order to draw theoretical conclusions warranted by the discrepancies.

Weber formulated the particular way in which a sociologist is interested in historical data:

> Sociology seeks to formulate type concepts and generalized uniformities of empirical process. This distinguishes it from history, which is oriented to the causal analysis and explanation of individual actions, structures, and personalities possessing cultural significance. (1978a, 19)

The "empirical process' here is the early history of Islam on which there are abundant data. The "type concepts" and "generalized uniformities" are those that would be utilized toward the theoretical construction of the major thesis that this study seeks to expound.

This work is not after critical verification of historical events. So long as a critical Western scholarship has established the validity of a historical report, it will be taken as truth. Occasionally references will be made directly to primary sources which are obviously religiously oriented and doctrinally molded. But such references will always be verified by critical scholarship. Even among Western scholars, there will not be total reliance on one or another source. A variety of perspectives shall be examined so that a more reliable picture of an historical event might emerge. Western scholarship has produced a remarkable body of literature that elucidates various periods of Islamic history. The principal difference among these analyses is the particular selection of historical events that are taken as causes for a set of effects.

Roth has outlined a Weberian approach to theoretical sociology:

> While Weber rejected master keys to history, he was interested in a "master theory" of Western history, of which the various secular theories constituted so many building blocks—in principle, a never-ending task of construction. (1979, 125 n. 10)

With that "never-ending task of construction" in mind for Islamic history, this study seeks merely to suggest a "building block."

1

Battle of the Old and the Charismatic

> *There arise from time to time men who bear to the moral condition of their age much the same relations as men of genius bear to its intellectual condition. They anticipate the moral standard of a later age, cast abroad conceptions of disinterested virtue, of philanthropy, or of self-denial that seem to have no relation to the spirit of their time, inculcate duties and suggest motives of action that appear to most men altogether chimerical. Yet the magnetism of their perfections tells powerfully upon their contemporaries. An enthusiasm is kindled, a group of adherents is formed, and many are emancipated from the moral condition of their age.*
>
> —W. E. H. Lecky

The emergence of Muhammad as a charismatic prophet in the early seventh century, the establishment of his personal authority against the traditional Arab order, and the variety of ways in which this authority was sought to be continued after his death all provide a unique historical situation in which the Weberian theory of authority, particularly the two modes of traditional and charismatic, can both illuminate the case study and, in turn, be illuminated by it.

Three major forces became active simultaneously upon the death of Muhammad, subsequently giving rise, out of their interactions, to the formation of three responses to the loss of the Muhammadan charismatic authority.

The most important and dominant force was the charismatic legacy of Muhammad and its strong propensity to be established permanently. As Weber recognized, if a charismatic movement is not to be a passing phase in the traditional mode of a given society, then it seeks to imprint itself permanently on its historical course (1978a, 246). In all domains of public and private life, the legacy of the charismatic movement seeks to establish and perpetuate the

1

particularities of its order of authority. Weber considered this entire process under the rubric of *routinization*. The particular case of Muhammad's charismatic authority, and the variety of ways in which it was sought to be institutionalized, makes the very use of this term—routinization— problematic. Weber sought to elaborate all of the possible ways in which the initial charismatic movement might be institutionalized; yet all such possibilities, for Weber, share this element of routinization. In the case of post-Muhammadan developments, the use of this term is problematic for two fundamental reasons: first, in the diversity of modes in which Muhammad's charismatic authority was sought to be institutionalized; and second, in the particular case of the Shiʿites, which was essentially an attempt towards the perpetuation of this mode of authority.

Generally, the extent and nature of pressure that the charismatic authority itself exerts in the postcharismatic period, once established in the form of an alternative, is determined by the particular formulation of (1) the qualities and attributes of the charismatic figure, that is, how extensive and comprehensive this authority is; (2) the mode of relationship between the charismatic figure and his ultimate and higher source of legitimation, God; and (3) the mode of the relationship established between the charismatic figure and his followers. More specifically, in the case of Islam this pattern consisted of the hierarchical structure of authority between Allah and his messenger, Muhammad, and that between Muhammad, as the Messenger of God (*Rasul Allah*), and the Islamic community (*ummah*). Allah's authority over this world is considered to be omnipotent; Muhammad's authority, too, consequently, was comprehensive and all-inclusive. From the other side of the command/obedience nexus, the total life of a Muslim, in all its diversity, is subject to this authority.

The omnipotence of Allah, the charismatic authority of Muhammad, his relationship with Allah, and the supremacy of Allah-Muhammad over the *ummah*, as well as individual Muslims, are all best represented in the following Qur'anic verse:

> Say (O Muhammad): O mankind! Lo! I am the messenger of Allah to you all—(the messenger of) Him unto whom belongeth the Sovereignty of the heavens and the earth. There is no God save Him. He quickeneth and He giveth death. So believe in Allah and His Messenger, the Prophet, who can neither read nor write, who believeth in Allah and His words, and follow him that haply ye may be led aright. (VII:158)

Through the agency of messengership, the omnipotence of Allah was translated into the comprehensive authority of Muhammad; and the complexity of the Allah-Muhammad relationship weighed heavily on the immediate post-prophetic period.

While this process gained momentum, a second simultaneous force was activated. A charismatic movement does not occur in a social vacuum; it is generally expressed against a traditional mode of authority. Various elements of that tradition seek either to reestablish themselves or, if unsuccessful in eradicating the charismatic experience altogether, to salvage some of their strongest traits.

Muhammad launched his charismatic movement against the traditional patrimonial mode of Arab tribal authority, the various elements of which first bitterly resented the Prophet and fought to eliminate his threat to their continuous existence but finally yielded to his power and sought to reestablish themselves, to whatever degree possible, in the institutionalization process of the prophet's charismatic authority. Yet the forceful pressure of this mode of authority for recognition was constantly countered by the charismatic force of Muhammad's spiritual, if not physical, presence as well as by what may be termed the metaphysical superiority of Islam over the Arab paganism. A complete return to the traditional mode of authority was impossible because of the successful establishment of Islam as the "religion of truth," mitigated by the Muhammadan legacy. Yet the physical pressure to salvage some moments of that "eternal yesterday" in Islam's today and tomorrow was constantly present.

To complicate these two simultaneous processes further, Muhammad's compound, but interrelated, authority began, after his death, the inevitable process of its disintegration. Muhammad's charismatic authority was, by definition, his personal quality. Recognized as the last Prophet to be sent by Allah (*Khatim al-nabiyyin*), he was not to be followed by a similar figure of authority. The process of his personal charismatic authority being disintegrated into various domains was inevitably added to the former two developments. This process of disintegration, to whatever degree it was realized, manifested the complexity of authority that the Islamic community had inherited after the death of its founding figure. This mode of sweeping personal authority was alien to the Arab collective memory. Attempted answers to this vital question, and Muslims coming to terms with either the comprehensive preservation or the disintegration of Muhammad's authority, added yet a third course of development that further complicated the institutionalization process that the legacy of this authority assumed.

These three simultaneous, forceful, and interacting processes, which may be visualized as three horizontal lines moving along early Islamic history, are then cut across by three vertical lines, known historically as the different branches of Islam. Each of these branches (vertical lines) will have a particular position vis-à-vis those forceful trends (horizontal lines), which were already independently and yet interconnectedly in process.

In what would later be known as Sunnite Islam there are pressures for the institutional preservation and continuation of the faith as the prophet's legacy. This tendency toward institutionalization and perpetuation of Islam is, however, characterized most emphatically by the routinization of the social/ economic life back to what Weber called a more "normal" situation. It is an inherent tendency of charisma, he noted, whenever it is institutionalized, to become either traditionalized or rationalized. There was a persistent and obvious tendency in the postcharismatic period to leave the Muhammadan experience behind as a "historical" event and arrange the Muslim community so it could resume a "stable" life.

The criterion for such an institutional arrangement is the unquestionable sacred authority of the Qur'an (as a revealed book) and Hadith (the exemplary conduct of the Prophet) over both the daily life of all Muslims and their universal metaphysical system of belief. This tendency was revealed particularly in the famous statement attributed to Abu Bakr, the first Sunnite caliph, upon the death of the Prophet: "If anyone worships Muhammad, Muhammad has died; but if anyone worships God, God is living and does not die." The death of the Prophet marked the end of an era—a charismatic and necessarily tumultuous era—which had to be put in the background so that the Muslim community could resume a more stable daily routine.

The massive attempt of the majority of Muslims, later to be called the Sunnites, towards a stable life was a direct response to the tumultuous experience of the Muhammadan prophetic period. Moreover, among this group of Muslims there was the strongest penetration of pre-Islamic traditional Arab forces for recognition and accommodation within the new Islamic organization. The emergence of these traditional elements, urging a resumption of daily routine life, had its concomitant economic relevance and significance.

Abu Bakr's most influential constituency consisted of the Meccan merchant establishment, a group most anxious to resume a routine economic life. Despite the continuation of Islam as the legacy of the Muhammadan charismatic movement, and despite its establishment as a strong and all-inclusive religion among the majority of Muslims, some major pre-Islamic Arab traditions found their way into the political and social developments of early Muslim history. In the same branch of Islam there also occurred the most fundamental disintegration of the Muhammadan charismatic authority into various spheres. Political authority, in the figures of the first four caliphs and others, was the first form to be separated from the total body of the Muhammadan charismatic authority. Subsequently, the religious (the formal, external, organizational, or exoteric), spiritual (the inner, devotional, or esoteric), legal, and military dimensions were further isolated and objectified into distinct and different modes; figures, and institutions of authority.

All three of these fundamental characteristics that identified the Muslim majority were manifested not only in the selection process of the first four caliphs, but also to a considerable degree in the Umayyad and ᶜAbbasiyd leaders as well, whereby in an essentially traditional, pre-Islamic Arab mode of selecting a tribal chief by the council of the elders and his subsequent recognition by other notables of the tribe (*bay^c ah*), the leaders of the Muslim community were selected and ascribed primarily temporal (political) authority. The honorific title "Vicegerent to the Messenger of God" (*khalifah rasul Allah*) signified essentially political, as opposed to religious, authority.

In what would later be identified as Shi^c ite Islam, however, there was an attempt towards the preservation and institutionalization of the prophet's charismatic authority. The same criteria of the universal and sacred authority of both the Qur'an and the Hadith are applicable here too. For the small group of ^c Ali's partisans Islam was the ultimate monotheistic religion, Muhammad was the last divinely ordained prophet, and the Qur'an was the very word of God revealed to his most honored servant. These beliefs constituted the most fundamental doctrines upon which Islam, as both a devotional faith and a communal organization, was to be founded. There is, however, a major distinction between the preservation and institutionalization of the Muhammadan charismatic authority as demonstrated in these two groups of Muslims—the future Shi^c ites and Sunnites.

In the case of the first force—the strong assertion of the charismatic movement to be institutionalized and perpetuated—among ^c Ali's partisans there was a persistent propensity to maintain and uphold the sanctity and universality of Islam as well as a growing tendency to encapsulate and preserve the very charismatic ambience experienced during the lifetime of the Prophet. This made the post-Muhammadan development of Shi^c ite Islam, in all its dimensions and magnitudes, an episode in the *perpetuation* of charisma, not its *routinization*. The Shi^c ite Imams constituted genuine charismatic figures with all the particularities of this Weberian typology. Of course, in the Shi^c ite hierarchy of authority, the Imams were located lower than the Prophet; however, the mode and nature of their authority were personal and charismatic. But while the Prophet's charismatic authority was defined, legitimated, or "authored" by Allah, the Imams' authority came from the Prophet. The later Shi^c ites' refusal to accept the authority of the first three caliphs, as well as their recognition of ^c Ali as the only legitimate heir to the prophetic authority, reflected their basic belief that the sacred task of designating a leader of the community, with simultaneous political and religious authority, should not be left to the community or, through a reversal of the political culture, to the established procedure of pre-Islamic Arab customs. This argument was obviously not so articulated in early Shi^c ite history; neither was it emphasized in the later theological and political developments. However, every doctrinal position of the Shi^c ites that marked the supremacy of the Imams as the true successors of the Prophet was a simultaneous departure from the prevailing pre-Islamic Arab practices.

As Shi^c ite Islam developed, there was also the strongest resistance to the emergence of traditional Arab elements into the total fabric of Islam, despite the fact that some such influences were actually detectable. At the highest level there is, of course, an unconditional and devotional submission to the supreme authority of Allah, His Book, and His Prophet, both spiritually and organizationally. In mind and body, the two being irrevocably interconnected, the Muslim community, according to the later Shi^cite doctrine, had to be Islamic; the spirit of the Muhammadan message, which had invigorated a particular span of time and place with a sacred force, had to be breathed into the body of the Muslim community and thus shape and mold it into an integral part of Islamic universality.

As to the complexity of Muhammad's charismatic authority, the Shi^cites gradually articulated a theology that held it intact and transferred it from the Prophet to the Imams, who participated in the same "light" that constituted Muhammad as the messenger of God. The Imams' authority, however de jure rather than de facto it might have been, was comprehensive and all-inclusive.

These positions vis-à-vis the three major forces that shaped the early history of Islam were manifested most clearly in the recognition of ^cAli as the political, religious, and spiritual (that is, charismatic) leader of the Islamic community, increasingly believed to be divinely ordained and personally designated by the Prophet. The charismatic nature of the Shi^cite Imams and their opposition to the traditional elements were inherently interconnected. "In its pure form," Weber pointed out, charisma "is the polar opposite of formal and traditional bonds, and it is just as free in the face of the sanctity of tradition as it is in the face of any rationalist deduction from abstract concepts" (1946, 250).

The Kharijites too had particular stands vis-à-vis the three major criteria that precipitated and identified the Islamic divisions. In fact, they were the first Muslims who asked some seminal questions about the nature of Islamic faith and community. Politically, it is important to realize that from the very beginning the Kharijite movement appealed, as will be demonstrated later, to the disinherited and discontented classes of Muslims, both Arab and *mawali* (non-Arab Muslims who had become "clients" of an Arab tribe), who were disenchanted with both political organizations and doctrinal positions of the Muslim majority. This historical fact is important for understanding the characteristic positions of the Kharijites towards the three forces that have been identified.

The Kharijites advocated the preservation and continuation of Islam as the universal expression of the Muhammadan charismatic legacy. They were among the most pious Muslims and initially the staunchest advocates of ^cAli. As a movement that represented the aspirations of the disinherited classes, Kharijite Islam supported the institutionalization of Islam, especially in its must fundamental tenets of Muslim brotherhood and equality. Within the traditional structure of Arabian society, the Arab Kharijites were the most socially and economically deprived classes who now had been given an equal standing with other Muslims in the social context of Islam. The establishment of this faith as the new spiritual and social order was strongly advocated by these pious Muslims. This tendency was further animated by a persistent urge to keep alive the revolutionary spontaneity of the Muhammadan period. Unlike the majority of Muslims who were seeking an immediate routinization of the charismatic period, the Kharijites advocated a form of permanent revolution against what they perceived to be an unjust social system. But whereas the partisans of ᶜAli tended to uphold the charismatic spontaneity of the Muhammadan period in an institutionalized mode of authority, the Kharijites failed to establish, either doctrinally or practically, any particular institutional form within which that authority could survive.

The Kharijites had a negative attitude towards the reemergence of traditional Arab elements into the total fabric of the post-Muhammadan authority without, however, being totally resistant to it. Any intrusion of traditional Arab elements, so far as it revived their former lower social status, would be resisted by the Kharijites. This was true not only for the Kharijite Arabs with less than glorious tribal ancestry but also for the *mawali*, who were attracted to the slogans of the Kharijites because of their opposition to the social and economic hegemony of the Arab caliphate. Non-Arab Muslims, who were denied an equal standing with their Arab conqueror-brothers, embraced the Kharijite version of Islam principally on the same grounds of its egalitarian and democratic ideals. Kharijite Islam thus basically recruited its zealot advocates from among the malcontents and the disillusioned Muslims who saw in both the pre-Islamic social conditions and the post-Islamic faith of the majority two disagreeable alternatives. They consequently opposed any reversal to the old Arab ways. Their famous motto that anyone, even an Abyssinian slave, could become a caliph quite emphatically attested to, among other things, their total rejection of both the traditional aristocratic criterion adopted by the Muslim majority and the charismatic quality believed to be present in the Shiᶜite Imams. In a few other instances, however, when, for example, they deemed some measure of stability to be inevitable if they intended a degree of political continuity, they did resort to pre-Islamic motifs, as will be demonstrated later.

Their view towards the segmentation of the Muhammadan charismatic authority, to whatever limited degree this materialized historically, went along the majority lines. They preferred its being broken down into various segments, with the political authority, stripped of any significant sacred or metaphysical significance, as the sole attribute of any Muslim leader. They attached neither a traditional Arab significance nor a charismatic particularity to the position of their leader; in the former they opposed the Muslim majority,

in the latter the partisans of ^cAli. Here again, their famous motto clearly
defied any traditional or charismatic criteria as the prerequisite of Islamic
leadership. This political authority, furthermore, was severely limited and
thus made precarious by the radical "democracy" of the Kharijites, according
to which their leaders were under continuous public supervision. This made
the assertion of any meaningful authority highly dubious.

The charismatic authority of the Prophet, and the various ways in which it
was sought to be institutionalized, overshadowed, to a considerable degree,
the rest of Islamic history, which may be considered as a continuous effort to
come to terms with the Prophetic authority of Muhammad. The legacy of this
authority, in its institutionalized forms, has been among the most vital and
energetic forces that have shaped the course of Islamic cultural history. The
growth and dynamic amplitude of the Muhammadan charismatic authority in
the course of history has embodied different modes of institutional order.

The institutional ordering of the Muslim society differed, to a considerable
degree, from one doctrinal formulation to another, depending on their understanding of the Islamic community (*ummah*). According to the general Islamic perspective, stipulated in the Constitution of Mecca drafted by Muhammad (Watt 1968a, 130), the *ummah* was a religious community, that is,
a community whose raison d'être was constituted in belief in a religious
brotherhood, the quality of every Muslim in Allah's presence and a universal
recognition of Allah's sovereignty and Muhammad's Prophethood. It was
particularly religious in its juxtaposition against the traditional Arab conception of tribal affinity, in which only blood relations constituted communal
solidarity. As Shi^cite Islam gradually developed, it maintained that a religious
community, because of its sacred nature, had to be led by a divinely inspired
and infallible Imam; the majority of Muslims, however, did not hesitate to
adopt traditional Arab concepts of leadership in the aftermath of Muhammad's charismatic experience and thus chose its leader through tribal council
and general communal consent (*bay^cah*); the Kharijites attempted a popular
and rather democratic approach to the question of post-Muhammadan authority, an abandonment of the Arab tribal tradition, and a utilization of Islam as
a doctrine of political and social emancipation. This latter form failed to
survive as a major religious tradition because it failed to develop an institutionalized mode of authority. Shi^cite Islam survived, despite the ambivalence
inherent in the institutionalization of charisma in its original anti-institutional
form, due primarily to the establishment of a particular mode of authority in
the figures of the Imams. The majority of Muslims, or the Sunnites, persisted
organizationally by institutionalizing and routinizing the Muhammadan charismatic experience into a chiefly traditional mode of authority.

In the general Islamic world view regulated in the Qur'an, all authority
belongs to Allah; He is the Omnipotent, the Omniscient, and the Omnipres-

ent. All other human authorities somehow must be derived from this source. Prophets (*anbiya'*) are chosen by Allah to lead humanity to His way. This divine inspiration is the source of legitimacy of all prophetic/charismatic authorities. "Where the idea of God has already been clearly conceived," Weber wrote, charismatic leaders "have practiced their arts and ruled by virtue of this gift (charisma) and . . . by virtue of the divine mission lying therein" (1946, 246).

Adam, Noah, Abraham, Moses, Jesus, and Muhammad are considered as these *anbiya'*. This belief is encapsulated in the concept of *nubuwwah*, that is, the necessity of God's sending prophets for guiding mankind. According to this general perspective, Muhammad was the last Prophet (*Khatim al-nabiyyin*) to be sent by God; there would be no other prophet, in the sense of having direct communication with Allah, after him. All early Muslims, whether identified as Sunnite, Shi^{c}ite, or Kharijite, accepted these general and fundamental doctrines of authority.

Following this line of authority, the majority of Muslims, under the influence of the reemerging traditional Arab motifs, considered the *Khalifah*, who was "elected" through a council of elders, as the legitimate heir to the authority of Muhammad, and who was, by virtue of this position, considered, more or less, as a "tribal chief." The partisans of ^{c}Ali, on the other hand, believed that after *nubuwwah*, Allah preordained *imamah*, that is, the legitimate authority of ^{c}Ali and his subsequent male descendants, as the rightful successors to the Prophet. The Shi^{c}ite Imams were further considered, as opposed to the caliphs, to possess personal charismatic authority over all aspects of Muslim life. In the Shi^{c}ite hierarchical structure of authority there are the following components: Allah, *nubuwwah*, and *imamah*. The Kharijites, opposing such views, maintained that after Allah and the Prophet, it was the prerogative of the Muslim community to "elect" their political leader "democratically" and depose him if he committed a sin. This perspective made the leadership, even in its mere political sense, extremely volatile. Neither traditional custom nor charismatic qualities sanctified the authority in the Kharijite case.

Consequently, the legitimacy of the ultimate figure of authority in the post-Muhammadan era assumed different patterns in the various branches of Islam: Among the majority, the traditional order of Arab patrimonialism determined to a considerable degree the particularities of the mode of selecting a leader for the Islamic community. The fact that he had to be a pious Muslim did not alter in any significant way the essentially traditional nature of his legitimacy. As the clearest indication of this traditional resurgence into postcharismatic developments, the supremacy of the Quraysh tribe, as a totally traditional and thus un-Islamic criterion, should be noted, as it was manifested in their exclusive claim to the office of the caliphate. The authority of Abu Bakr was consequently legitimated both by his being elected through the tribal council at the famous gathering of *Saqifah Bani Sa^cidah* and by his prominence in the Quraysh tribe. The fact that he was a pious Muslim and a close companion of the Prophet did not play as significant a role in the traditionally formed *Saqifah* as his Quraysh qualities, perceived and honored. ^cAli's authority, on the contrary, was considered to be legitimate by his followers on essentially charismatic criteria. He was believed to have been appointed by the Prophet as his successor; as such, his claim was further substantiated by his membership in the Prophet's household. The grounds of his legitimacy were rooted in the Muhammadan charismatic experience and its Islamic legacy. The Kharijites, finally, elevated the Islamic community to the highest position of authority, and anyone who was to be their leader had to derive and legitimate his authority from this source.

This general pattern was reflected in the view of the different Islamic branches toward the first four caliphs. The majority of Muslims considered Abu Bakr, ^cUmar, ^cUthman, and ^cAli as the four "rightly guided caliphs" (*al-Khulafa' al-rashidun*) because of their close association with the Prophet. They were *elected* through the traditional custom of tribal council. Their title was "caliph" with no considerable religious significance attached to it. The partisans of ^cAli, however, considered the first three caliphs—Abu Bakr, ^cUmar, and ^cUthman—as the usurpers of ^cAli's legitimate right and believed the latter to be the rightful heir and successor to the charismatic authority of Muhammad. ^cAli and his male descendants were called, as the successors to Prophet Muhammad, "Imams" with significant religious authority. The Kharijites considered Abu Bakr and ^cUmar as the legitimate successors to the Prophet, not because they were elected by a council but because of the popular consent to their authority. The Kharijites believed ^cUthman deserved to be murdered and accepted ^cAli's authority until he yielded to the "arbitration" in his battle against Mu^cawiyah. From that point on they did not consider him the rightful leader of the Islamic community. They did not attach any religious significance to their political leaders whom they believed should be pious, courageous, and elected by *all* Muslims regardless of ethnic or tribal background.

The recognition of the three major forces—(1) the charismatic legacy of the Prophet seeking permanent institutionalization and perpetuation (with various degrees of the loss or preservation of its spontaneous and dynamic nature); (2) the defeated and superseded traditional order remobilizing its forces,and, in the absence of the original charismatic figure, bidding for recognition and reestablishment; and, finally, (3) the segmentation or preservation of the comprehensive nature of the charismatic authority, as a major forceful issue to be reckoned with—along with the formation of three predominant positions, later to be recognized as the three branches of Islam, demonstrated the complexity and multidimensionality of the process Weber characterized very broadly as "routinization" of charismatic authority. He covered all the various contending forces involved in this process under one general term and sought to explain the inevitability of *routinization* in essentially economic terms. But as this historical case demonstrates, particular forces move in specific directions and thus steer the course of this routinization. Once a charismatic movement, as a unique and singular event in the traditional course of a society, is manifested and established, how does it fare with other contending forces—such as the precharismatic tradition—when the most emphatic enforcer of this movement, its presiding figure, is no longer present to assert and execute his authority?

Weber maintained that for a charismatic movement to be more than a transitory phenomenon and be institutionalized, it had to be routinized. But the forces surrounding the aftermath of a charismatic movement and the various modes of their particular interaction are so complex that a very broad and concealing concept such as routinization could not do justice to its intricacies. As the examination of the partisans of ᶜAli will reveal (see chapter five), a charismatic movement can be institutionalized and perpetuated without necessarily being routinized.

More important than the routinization of charismatic authority is the translation of its moral precepts—that is, what constitutes the ethical particularities of the charisma—into motifs of social relationship. "Every system of moral demands," according to Rieff, "must operate within some social order" (1966, 235). Shiᶜite Islam gradually established the foundation of such a social order, without being routinized in the Weberian understanding of this term.

The growth and development of the major Islamic branches in the early period may be considered as the external manifestations of the inner conflict between the two prevailing modes of authority competing and contending for exclusive supremacy. The charismatic authority of the Prophet Muhammad and the traditional Arab mode of patriarchal authority against which it was expressed were the two major contending forces. A given culture cannot function with two contending moral demand systems; only one uniquely integral hierarchical structure of interdictory, remissive, and transgressive motifs can regulate the social and moral life of a community. The cultural tension surrounding the Muhammadan charismatic event had to be resolved emphatically, one way or another, before the Islamic community and its individual members could resume a "normal" course. This tension was further complicated by the process of disintegration to which the prophetic authority was potentially subject.

The complex process that Weber covered under the general rubric of routinization must be unpacked in order to reach for the complexities of the postprophetic period. The two modes of authority prominent in the wake of the Islamic political culture constantly interacted, and the outcome of this interaction was instrumental in the outcome of the charismatic event. The ultimate extent and the end result of this confrontation was the formulation and formation of distinct religious orders otherwise known as the *sects* of Islam. As the most fundamental and essential religious identities of these various branches, the seminal positions that Sunnite, Shiᶜite, and Kharijite Islam gradually assumed became one set of crucial elements that shaped the course of the Islamic political culture.

Weber underestimated the doctrinal force of the revealed faith and, conversely, overestimated the economic forces necessitating the routinization of daily life. What grew to become Sunnite Islam verified Weber's assessment that normal social and economic factors immediately routinize charisma. There was a persistent pressure from the economic necessities towards routinization of daily life. But even here Weber identified such forces as basically economic, whereas for the Muslim majority the pressure for economic routinization followed simultaneously, or was at least disguised in, traditional motifs bidding for recognition against the predominance of purely charismatic social relationships. But, more importantly, the gradual development of Shiᶜite Islam posed a serious question for the ultimate inevitability of routinization and opened a new set of possibilities for the continuation and permanence of the charismatic movement in a charismatic way, that is, in a personal, devotional, dynamic, nonrational (as rationality is understood in the Weberian modality), and spontaneous manner.

The positions maintained by the different branches of Islam vis-à-vis the prevalent post-Muhammadan forces of authority subsequently defined, identified, and shaped the total spiritual, religious, social, and political character of these religious orders. Each of these orders subsequently constituted a cultural entity with various degrees of success. This success was determined ultimately by the intensity of tension between their constituent motifs of interdiction and remission.

Based on their fundamental positions, these three Islamic branches moved in the course of history and determined, with a host of other sociologically significant factors, the type of political culture that was most congenial with their primordial *weltanschaung*. The interplay among these three trends, in their historical progression, molded and shaped the general character of each of these branches of Islam; and since various combinations of these forces came to be established as different Islamic branches, then particular political cultural motifs were formed across the Islamic lands and along the Islamic history. They, in turn, became the hierarchical structures within which multitudes of Muslims regulated and conducted their lives. Thus, for the Muslim majority there was a particular combination and integration of these three forces, a different one for the partisans of ᶜAli, and, in the case of the Kharijites, the defeated attempt of yet another coordinate.

These three branches of Islam generally have been considered as different sects out of the main Sunnite "orthodoxy." Muslim heresiographers were first to establish this "orthodoxy-heterodoxy" dichotomy. Goldziher offered the following account of this question:

> There was a tradition that declared, in praise of Islam, that Islam had seventy-three virtues, as against the seventy-one of Judaism and the seventy two of Christianity. The tradition was misunderstood, and the virtues were turned into seventy-three branches. This error prepared the ground for the enumeration of seventy-three sects, each of them bound for Hell except the one "group that will escape" [al-firqa al-najiya] the only one that leads to salvation—which is to say the one that conforms to the requirements of the *sunna*. (1981, 167)

A host of social, political, ethnic, and religious causes have been identified for such "schisms." It is important to note, however, that "sect" stands for the legitimation of the "orthodoxy," and no believer would consider his faith a "sect" and still remain faithful. A particular formulation of a given religious tradition has a genuinely total claim on the universality of its theological legitimacy. These Islamic branches are yet to be studied as different expressions that the charismatic authority of Muhammad assumed in its process of institutionalization, forms of coming to terms with the death of a sole figure of authority. The formation of these various branches, however, should start from the moment that this authority was established and, in the absence of the Prophet, sought to be institutionalized. Thus the early segmentations in Islam should be considered as different attempts, with varying degrees of success, at solidifying and institutionalizing the authority/obedience nexus established between a figure of authority (Muhammad) and his followers (Muslims).

Most of the studies of the Islamic sects can be categorized very broadly as external examinations of the various branches of Islam. These studies, whether by early Muslim heresiographers or by Orientalists of different persuasions, usually have taken the exterior manifestations of the various tendencies in Islam as realities *sui generis* and then attempted to formulate a plausible set of motives and incentives, religious or otherwise, which are believed to have caused these historical phenomena. These external manifestations are always the starting point of the analytical investigation that usually leads, given the particular theoretical or ideological perspective of the observer, to a set of religious or political causes.

Under this broad category there are the medieval observers of the various dimensions of Islam, whether Muslim or Western, who have attributed religious causes to what they considered to be "sectarian" or "heretical" movements within Islam. In the case of the Muslim heresiographers, any particular formulation of Islam other than the author's own affiliation was invariably

labeled as *firqah* (sect), *bid °ah* (innovation), *ghuluw* (exaggeration), *zindiq*
(Zoroastrian, particularly Manicheism, heresy), *Ilhad* (disbelief), or *kufr* (blas-
phemy). The Orientalists also attributed similar religious causes to the formation of different Islamic "sects." Islam itself was considered by medieval
Christians as a "heresy." Von Grunebaum pointed out that

> John of Damascus, who treats Islam as a Christian heresy, tells how in the days
> of the Emperor Heraclitus, a false prophet [*pseudo-prophet*] arose among the
> Arabs. His name was Mamed. He became acquainted with the Old and New
> Testaments and later, after discussing with an Arian monk, "established his own
> sect." (1946, 43)

The same sorts of ideas were also presented by Theophanes Confessor (d.
817), Bartholomew of Edessa (thirteenth century), Eulogius of Cordova (d.
859), and Guibert of Nogent (d. 1124), etc. (43f).

With the advent of the Renaissance and the prevailing modes of rational-
ism, these religious explanations seemed superfluous to the Orientalists. More
objective causes were sought to explain the course of both European and
Islamic history. This perspective gradually led to the nineteenth-century ideas
of liberalism and nationalism which were believed to underlie any religious
movement or schism. Finally, with the advent of the Marxist philosophy of
history, a host of studies sought to demonstrate the economic causes of all of
these religious movements in terms of concepts such as "class conflict,"
"clashes of interests," and changes in the economic status of various societies
(Lewis 1953, 43-63).

These studies and perspectives have examined extensively the various dimensions of these branches from a variety of perspectives. So far, the Weberian "interpretative sociology" in general and his theory of authority in
particular have not been applied in a systematic way to an understanding of
the transitional period from the traditional Arab to the Muhammadan charismatic modes of authority. Among the sociologists, Turner (1974) has made
use of several Weberian theoretical categories in understanding some particular aspects of Islam, mainly the old question, "why did capitalism not
develop in Islam?" In neither the major thesis expounded nor the particular
Islamic questions addressed does Turner's work coincide or overlap with this
study. Watt (1961), among the contemporary Islamicists, has formulated the
two concepts of "charismatic leader" for the Shi°ite Imams and "charismatic
community" in the case of the Kharijite view of the Muslim community.
There will be occasion in the following chapters to refer to these two Weberian concepts which have not been extended very carefully by Watt into an
Islamic context.

The previous studies sometimes, in their unilateral determinism, have mis-
construed some essential aspects of the various branches within Islam. Shi°ite

Islam, for example, invariably has been considered as a basically "political" rather than religious stand. Whether Shi^{c}ite or Kharijite Islam were political or religious in their quintessential nature is, first of all, a totally misconstructed question in an Islamic context, and second, even if such a false categorization is adopted, it is of secondary importance. This is a false dichotomy in Islam both doctrinally and historically. Watt has pointed out that during this period "religious doctrine was at the centre of the intellectual life of the whole community, including its political life" (1973, 7). Goldziher, too, has verified this position, dialectically:

> In the foreground are not questions of religion but, it appears, questions of the state. In a community based on religion, religious considerations will, however inevitably, pervade political questions and political questions will take on the form of religious issues that give their own coloring to political strife. (1981, 168)

The primary question is what set of forces, dynamically active at the moment of the first expression of these branches, gave rise to the very need for such positions and stands. The gradual appearance of Shi^{c}ite, Kharijite, and Sunnite Islam may be compared to the formation of scattered islands on the surface of a running river. What the constituent elements of these islands are, and their various compositions and positions, is a set of distinct and secondary questions. The fundamental and primary question is what particular underlying forces, currents, tides, and waves gave rise to the initial formation of these islands. In identifying these underlying forces, first the very fabric of the pre-Islamic social structure and its mode of authority must be ascertained, and then the emphatic and forceful expression of the Muhammadan charismatic authority being pronounced against that background should be considered. It is, then, through an analysis of the interaction between these two forces, along with the particular changes that the charismatic authority may be forced to undergo, that the essence and raison d'être of these various branches of Islam may be detected. These branches later will function as religious/cultural structures within which the various shades of Islamic life and civilization were constructed. The particular mode of authority, coming into being out of the forceful and simultaneous interaction among the above forces, subscribed to by each of these branches, both constituted and indicated the specific cultural order whose interdictory, remissive, and transgressive motifs would govern the minds, the souls, and the bodies of Muslims and Muslim communities for ages to come.

A charismatic movement is generally expressed against a traditional mode of authority. It is, in fact, due to this forceful imposition as well as juxtaposition that charismatic figures have a fundamentally revolutionary character. In more than only social and economic terms, a charismatic movement revolutionizes the very fabric of a traditional society: It seeks to transform and charge afresh the very ethical foundations of that society, forming a new hierarchical structure of interdictory, remissive, and transgressive motifs.

The charismatic authority of Muhammad was asserted and established against the traditional order of Arab society. Before any examination of the particular ways in which the various modes of authority in the post-Muhammadan period developed, it is important to recognize that both the traditional Arab authority prior to Islam and the powerful superimposition of Muhammad's authority were of central importance. Based upon these two modes of authority—traditional Arab and charismatic Muhammadan—two essentially different world-views were constructed. For the elements of authority to be operative within the realm of a given society, only one mode of legitimacy can prevail as the most dominant. Once these two come into direct confrontation, as happens any time a charismatic movement challenges traditional authority, ultimately one will supersede the other by establishing its particular interdictory, remissive, and transgressive motifs. But this "triumph" in the Islamic case was not a unilateral victory of one over the other. Out of the fierce confrontation between the two visions of the highest authority, a variety of patterns—three significant ones—emerged in each various degree of persistence and can be detected from one or the other mode of authority.

2

Traditional Arab Authority: An Established Order

Authority will be called traditional if legitimacy is claimed for it and believed in by virtue of the sanctity of age-old rules and powers. The masters are designated according to traditional rules and are obeyed because of their traditional status (Eigenwurde).

—Max Weber, *Economy and Society*

In an ex post facto explanation of the emergence of Islam, many Islamicists have argued explicitly or implicitly that the "corruption" of Arab society gave rise to a religious movement that offered a more "just" alternative (Hodgson 1974; Petroshevsky 1976, Watt 1961)—a particularly untenable argument because of the continuity of such practices as slavery from the pre- to post-Islamic periods. Considering the Muhammadan movement as a social rebellion against an "unjust" system is an anachronistic reading of the phenomenon. The fundamental reorientation of pre-Islamic Arab culture by and through Muhammad's revolution was plausibly much more pervasive and comprehensive than a singular, monocausal and unidirectional approach would render it. Specific and even pervasive modifications within Arab society could have been, and in fact were, realized—in economic, social, political, and religious domains—without a cataclysmic revolution essentially and organizationally changing its cultural identity. The Muhammadan charismatic movement inevitably should be seen as a total expression of a new cultural order that challenged the Arab traditional system in its homogeneous entirety and as a complete cultural paradigm and not in its specific social mandates—some of which Islam, in fact, adopted.

Traditional Arab culture had the entire pre-Islamic millenia as its temporal context. However, of that extended pre-Islamic cultural history, only that limited period immediately preceding the emergence of Muhammad and Islam shall be considered here. The cultural milieu within and against which

Muhammad pronounced his new faith and cultural order was inseparable from the specifics of the Qur'anic message. As the last Prophet of Allah, Muhammad initiated a new religion that constituted the doctrinal foundation of Islam. This religion initially was juxtaposed against and then superceded pre-Islamic Arab traditionalism. Of all those infinite foregone years prior to Muhammad only those will be recalled that, in their constituting an "eternal yesterday" for Arabian society and character, legitimated the customs, mores, and habits— a uniquely organized set of limitations—of that culture.

The cultural peculiarities of Arabia prior to Islam should be sought primarily within Arabia, with the least possible outside influence. Commenting on the Semitic originality of the Arabs, Hitti has observed that

> the reasons which make the Arabians Arabs, particularly the nomads, the best representations of the Semitic family biologically, psychologically, socially and linguistically should be sought in their geographical isolation and in the monotonous uniformity of desert life. Ethnic purity is a reward of the most ungrateful and isolated environment, such as Central Arabia affords. (1970, 8)

It is essentially against this cultural homogeneity that Muhammad's charismatic authority would later be expressed. This homogeneity continued despite the Jewish and Christian presence in North and South Arabia. Although Judeo-Christian traits were recognizable in Muhammad's message, Arabian traditional culture was devoid of such or similar influences and represented something of a peculiarly Semitic, geographically isolated, and homogeneous nature.

The derogatory notion of *Jahiliyyah* (ignorance) that post-Islamically was attributed to pre-Islamic Arab culture should be read as an exclusive Islamic term of distinction to establish its own inclusiveness. Pre-Islamic Arabs were ignorant of Islam as the coming order of their communal life. But there was nothing ignorant about the validity and operative intelligence of the Arab character in the pre-Islamic Arab culture. Major shifts from one modality of command-obedience to another, traditional to charismatic in Weber's stipulation, does entail, but does not warrant, labeling of ignorance and barbarism. It is the inclusive nature of all religious cultures to exclude past paganisms and future sectarianisms in the name of a permanently present and valid orthodoxy.

The vitality of the Arab culture prior to the rise of Muhammad formed the necessary background against which the Islamic revolution assumed momentum. The presence and continuity of both formal and substantive elements of authority from the pre-Islamic culture, through the Muhammadan charismatic movement, to the initial formation of divisions within the Islamic culture, must be detected by an examination of the structure of authority in the Arabia of Muhammad's birth. From the time of the immediate predecessors of Muhammad, Qusayy, Hashim, etc., to his immediate successors, Abu Bakr, ᶜAli, etc., the nucleus of the transformation of the Arab culture into the Islamic culture was patently manifested.

The ancient customs continuously regulated both the daily life and the identity of the tribal Arab. They were "mores sanctified," as Weber called them, that established the guidelines upon which the ancient Arabs conducted their lives and perpetuated their tradition. Tribes and clans became the most obvious social expressions of pre-Islamic Arab authority.

The significance of genealogies, according to which the legitimacy of a particular clan or chief is authenticated, points to the perpetual continuity of the past in the present. "Pride of descent is strong among the tribesmen, who carry in their heads long and complicated genealogies . . . (Saunders 1965, 4). The authority of the past is made relevant by being personified and symbolized in aristocratic figures of authority who can claim descent from an illustrious ancestry. Authority of the past, emphatically yet tacitly expressed in the genealogies, is as natural to an Arab as the physical existence of his father. One necessitates and legitimates the other.

The most important factor that connected the tribal Arabs together and established a lasting bond among them was the blood relationship. Of migrating Arab tribes, Brockelmann pointed out that

> since this breed can only be cared for by migration through widely extended regions, any political organization based on fixed dwelling places is impossible for the Bedouins. Blood relationship alone traces the orbit of their lives, it binds families into clans, and clans into tribes. Even the great tribal federation still traces their descent through an ostensible blood relationship, grouping the whole people together into a genealogical system. (1948, 4)

Blood relationship is another physical and natural expression of traditional authority. Here, the authority of the past became as natural and as abiding as the physical presence of a father or the flow of blood in the veins. Under the particular circumstances of a tribal life, in which all expressions of social solidarity are in a state of flux, these two symbols of traditional authority guarantee a measure of continuity and permanence in an otherwise transitory life.

The structure of traditional authority in pre-Muhammadan Arabia was expressed nowhere more emphatically and explicitly than in the hostilities between the two clans of Banu Hashim and Banu ᶜAbd Shams. The essence and complicated intricacies of this authority were best crystallized and symbolized in the various manifestations of hostility.

To be obliged to express hostility is the most emphatic form of membership in a moral demand system. This, in turn, testifies to and validates the legitimacy of the system. This legitimacy—compelling as much affinity as hostility—sustains the relationship of authority.

Within the context of the pre-Muhammadan tribal configuration, Banu Hashim and Banu ᶜAbd Shams were the two major clans of the Quraysh tribe. This tribe had assumed political, social, and religious ascendancy in Mecca, the major cosmopolitan area of the Arabian Peninsula, during the life of Qusayy, the great-great-great-grandfather of Muhammad. Qusayy was a member of the Quraysh tribe. He lost his father when still a child. Qusayy's mother, after the death of her husband, married a man from the tribe of Banu Qadaᶜah and left Arabia for Syria (*Sham*). Qusayy grew up in Syria but came back to Mecca and married the daughter of the prince (*Amir*) of the Khazaᶜi tribe. After the death of his father-in-law, who was the head of the Khazaᶜi tribe, he united the different clans of his own tribe, the Quraysh, with those of his stepfather's tribe, the Banu Qadaᶜah, and defeated the Khazaᶜi, the ruling tribe of Mecca, and consolidated his political, social, and religious authority in Mecca. This authority traditionally was manifested in the guardianship of the sacred house of Kaᶜbah, which had religious significance for the pre-Islamic Arabs.

Qusayy settled the Quraysh tribe around the city of Mecca and established a chamber of deputies (*Dar al-Nadwah*) to preside over their tribal affairs. He himself had the most important religious/political positions of the time; he held the key to Kaᶜbah and he provided its pilgrims with water and other necessities. These were the seminal religious and political positions of al-Hijaz. Whoever held these positions maintained the highest authority in Mecca.

When Qusayy died, disputes arose among his family as to who was to succeed him in his range of authority. His son ᶜAbd al-Manaf, the great-great-grandfather of the Prophet, assumed these positions. He had four sons, the eldest of whom was a certain ᶜAbd Shams who did not succeed his father, apparently because of his constant travels. Instead, another son, Hashim, the great-grandfather of Muhammad, despite his young age, succeeded his father in occupying these important positions.

ᶜAbd Shams died quietly, but his son, Umayyah ibn ᶜAbd Shams, claimed the authority of these positions for himself and did not yield to his uncle. This dispute between Hashim and Umayyah over the leadership of the Quraysh tribe and occupancy of the most important religious and political offices of the time led to an arbitration by a *Kahin* from the Khazaᶜi tribe. The *Kahin* gave his opinion in favor of Hashim and against Umayyah. Consequently, Umayyah was forced into exile, from Mecca to Syria (*Sham*), for ten years. This was the first manifestation of hostility between the two clans of the Quraysh tribe, Banu Hashim and Banu ᶜAbd Shams. (al-Tabari 1879-1901, 3:1088-99; Ibn al-Athir, 1851-76, 2:16-22).

This episode affords a rare glimpse of the traditional pattern of authority in pre-Islamic Arabia. Tribal solidarity constituted the most significant cohesive element of both the social structure and the cultural order. Within the context of tribal solidarity, the tribal council in the form of *Dar al-Nadwah*, formed by the elders of the tribe, established the main body of authority; its functions were both normative and executive. Furthermore, a clear juxtaposition of religious and political authority was manifested in the figure of the "key-holder" to the house of Ka{c}bah. This juxtaposition continued to pronounce itself in the course of Islamic history.

Another figure of authority in whom the traditional Arabian order manifested itself was the *Kahin*. Even in its earliest meanings, the *Kahin* referred to the possessor of the function of "offering of sacrifices in the name of the group before the deity, the interpretation of the will of the deity, and in addition the anticipation of the will of the deity, and in addition the anticipation and communication of his wishes" (Gibb et al. 1979, s.v. *Kahin*). The *Kahin* personified, or at least represented, the supreme deities, and as such was the "agent of the official cult." However, because of "the predominance of nomadism, . . . it was usually the head of the family or tribe who offered sacrifices, after the manner of the patriarchs in the Old Testament, and in which frequent migrations prevented the establishment of an official form of worship and fixed places of worship. . . ." While the nomadic form of Arabian society prevented the office of the *Kahin* from being developed into an organized established priesthood, the advent of Islam aborted its further development. Of importance was the predominance of age, tribal genealogy, blood relationship, tribal customs, and religious functionaries as the most important factors for prescribing the mode of traditional authority in Arabia.

The hostility between Hashim, the Prophet's great-grandfather, and Umayyah continued to demonstrate itself during the earlier part of Muhammad's mission. When Muhammad started his preachings, Abu Sufyan, the grandson of Umayyah, launched the most persistent attacks against him. Abu Sufyan, at the time, was one of the prominent figures of the Quraysh and, after the death of Abu Talib, the Prophet's uncle, one of its leaders. In this position, Abu Sufyan did all in his power to try to prevent Muhammad from accomplishing his mission. Abu Sufyan's hostility toward Muhammad, who was from the Banu Hashim branch of the Quraysh, must be understood in the context of this tribal hostility.

The fact that the roots of some of the decisive conflicts in Islamic history go back to pre-Islamic tribal hostilities testifies to the vitality of the Arab culture even after the Islamic victory. It was against the background of persistent tribal customs and conflicts that Muhammad launched his prophetic movement. This movement changed the essential nature and composition of authority in Arabia and introduced a new religious order that defined authority anew in its hierarchical universality.

To realize the severity and the degree of identification with these tribal conflicts, it is important to note that they surfaced again in the hostility between Mu^cawyiah, Abu Safyan's son, and ^cAli, the Prophet's cousin and a son of Abu Talib, who was one of the leaders of the Quraysh before Abu Sufyan. This conflict, which was one of the contributing political factors in the formation of the Shi^cite branch of Islam, indicated the continuing presence of a number of major traditional elements in the post-Muhammadan developments. Tribal affinities, as well as hostilities, continued to play major roles throughout Islamic history. However, after the successful assertion of the Muhammadan prophetic authority, they were not the primary determining factors of the mode of authority in post-Muhammadan Arabia.

Perhaps exaggerating a bit the traditional mode of life in Arabia, Hitti has characterized the nomad as a type who

> is today what he was yesterday and what he will be tomorrow. His culture pattern has always been the same. Variation, progress, evolution are not among the laws he readily obeys. Immune to the innovation of exotic ideas and manners, he still lives, as his forebearers did. (1970, 23)

Although certain modalities of change and alternation were, in fact, introduced and tolerated in the context of the Arab cultural order, homogeneity and consistency were the chief characteristics of the traditional mode of authority. Generations are the living blood fused into already established veins; the direction of movement and life is relatively predetermined. Through a persistent repetition of cultural traits, since time immemorial, the traditional mode of Arab life had assumed both its validity and vitality. Muhammad's charismatic movement should be seen as a major attempt to disrupt this repetition and establish a new modality of command and obedience. His religious revolution set up a radical discontinuity with the Arab past and simultaneously established a new cultural pattern with its specific interdictory-remissive motifs.

The traditional mode of tribal authority was operative in the Arab culture much more extensively than merely in the collective consciousness of its members. Every aspect of the social structure, political organization, commercial network, etc. reflected this mode of authority.

The traditional Arab authority was expressed in a stratified social structure, of which the master-slave relationship was the most immediate manifestation. At the bottom of the social structure, as the counterpart of the *pariah* in the Indian caste system, were the *qinn* and their offspring, the *muwalladun* (Lammens 1924, 237). Captured in war or purchased at the market, the *qinn* provided menial services to their masters. A set of normative behaviors governed the master-slave relationships. A slave could purchase his freedom. On the other hand, through the religious practice of *sadaqah*, masters freed slaves on a regular basis. *Sadaqah,* which was later extended into the Islamic religious culture, was on oath through which an individual pledged to do a certain thing, such as free a number of slaves, as an expression of his prosperity. *Sadaqah* sanctioned previous success and guaranteed future prosperity.

The emerging commercial stratification manifested the organization of traditional authority in its own structured way. Below the sayyids, as merchant capitalists of the Arab trade economy, were free tribesmen who engaged in commerce on behalf of the mercantile class, occupying various skills and professions (Wolf 1951, 359ff.). There was a close tribal loyalty between the sayyids and their professional affiliates, indicating that the emerging economic structure was fused into the existing tribal organization. It is true that the merchant capitalists of diverse tribes constituted a distinct social/ economic class; yet this commercial affinity, because of its roots in Arab customs, was not at the expense of the validity and continuity of the tribal structure.

Lower than the free tribesmen in the commercial/tribal structure were the *mawali*, or clients of specific tribes. To benefit from membership in the specific tribes, the *mawali* were connected to either the *sayyids* or their free subordinates. At the bottom of the social/economic structure, they closed the communal/tribal organization of authority. The *mawali* were not necessarily of non-Arab origins; there were Arab and non-Arab *mawali*. The organizational legitimacy of the Arab social/economic structure could not assimilate all of the positions within it.

The social/economic organization of authority was dynamic, and mobility was, to a certain extent, tolerated. A member of the *mawali* could purchase his own freedom and change his status into a *halif*, or ally. This possibility, again engineered through specific channels of Arab customs, from *mawla* to *halif*, further advanced both the legitimacy and the perpetuity of the expressed organization of authority in pre-Islamic Arabia. The organization of traditional authority was stable; mobile were the specific individuals who manned it. The possibility of upward mobility, from a *mawla* to a *halif*, and from that to a *sayyid*, a merchant capitalist, provided the organization of authority with a constant flow of rejuvenating forces. To be sure, oligarchical tendencies within the Arab society, as in the case of the Quraysh, maintained some degree of aristocratic permanence and continuity. That, however, was an expression of the tribal structure of authority rather than the juxtaposed commercial stratification. Upper mobility was more permissible and attainable in the latter than in the former. However, given the close affinity between the two, mobility in one was honored almost equally in the other.

Divisions within the tribal structure often centered around major institutions of authority. The dispute between Banu ᶜAbd al-Dar and Banu ᶜAbd Manaf over the institution of *wilayat al-bait* resulted in the major division in the Quraysh tribe: Al-Ahlaf supported ᶜAbd al-Dar, and al-Mutayyabun supported ᶜAbd Manaf. This institutional split indicated the simultaneous vitality of the cohesive elements of authority, in conjunction with the genealogical/ tribal nexus of affinity and obligation. The institutions of authority had economic force and communal validity *sui generis,* regardless of the tribal structure.

As the extended genealogies of the Arab tribes suggest, succession to authority in this patrimonial society was primarily, but not exclusively, through primogeniture. In the Banu Hashim clan of the Quraysh, Hashim had succeeded his father, ^cAbd Manaf. After Hashim his son, Abd al-Muttalib, and after him his son, ^cAbd Allah, had succeeded him. This brought the line of Banu Hashim down to Muhammad. The same rules of succession were true for the Banu ^cAbd Shams branch of the tribe.

The succession of ^cAbd al-Dar, Qusayy's eldest son, to occupy the positions his father had institutionalized indicated the introduction of some form of oligarchy against the background of Arab gerontocracy. Qusayy was perhaps the most important reformer in the pre-Islamic Arab culture who both consolidated and renovated a number of crucial religious and commercial institutions. Despite their traditional nature, these institutions were intimately related to the character of Qusayy himself. His nomination of his eldest son, ^cAbd al-Dar, as his successor was directly related to his own assumption of a supratraditional status. Such pre-Islamic events were of crucial significance for the detection of the cultural traits most congenial to the rise of Muhammad in the seventh century. But of more immediate and obvious interest was the significance of such primogeniture antecedents for the principal doctrine of the Shi^cite self-understanding of succession to Muhammad's authority.

Hashim, Muhammad's great-grandfather, became the custodian of *siqayah* and *rifadah* once ^cAbd Shams abdicated these offices to him because of his constant business trips. The towering figure of Hashim in the Quraysh tribe could not be totally inconsequential in Muhammad's prophetic career. Although institutionally based on a set of different cultural parameters, Hashim's prominence in the pre-Islamic Meccan domain was, on a smaller scale quite similar to Muhammad's later authority.

Within the general context of traditional patrimonialism, the pre-Islamic Arab culture gave rise to and sustained individual figures of authority who, in turn, became the primary custodians of the dominating culture but did not alter its essential character in any way. In figures such as Qusayy there were clear indications of how extensive the inner developments of the pre-Islamic Arab culture could have been without a drastic change essentially altering its predominant character. Far from being a static modality of simple repetitions, the Arab culture was perhaps at the peak of its vitality—however confined by its own political limitations—prior to the Islamic movement. The existence of the malcontents—slaves, *mawali,* etc.—did not warrant, in the general scheme of the Arab cultural order, the coming of a revolution. The Qur'anic injunctions against usury or its admonition of certain ethics in the pre-Islamic culture were not drastically crucial in the overall scheme of the social order to consider Islam a mere "religious ideology" for otherwise economic/social concerns.

A charismatic movement can be as much a response to what Weber called social or psychological crisis as an initiator of totally new social, political, economic, or purely metaphysical concerns. The mere ethical saturation or thematic exhaustion of a cultural order may invite the revolutionary outburst of a new paradigmatic pattern of authority. In superseding the old order, the new paradigm inherits the past in digesting it. But this digestion is not uni-directional; the old habits simply die hard, if ever.

While individuals personified the traditional Arab culture, historically val-idated institutions imbued it with its most effective endurance. Many such institutions were detectable in the pre-Islamic social order.

Dar al-Nadwah, initiated by Qusayy, constituted perhaps the most impor-tant institution that expressed the pre-Islamic Arab political culture. This house was built adjacent to the sacred precinct of Ka^cbah as both Qusayy's residence and the center of political leadership (al-Maqdisi 1899, 4:126). The institutionalization of *Dar al-Nadwah*—so close to the emergence of Islam—indicated an organizational development of Arab cultural mores to the point where they needed a bodily expression in which to persist. It may also have reflected a process of rationalization in the context of Arab traditionalism. At any rate it institutionally manifested what culturally had been operative for quite some time. Centralizing the political authority of the elders, *Dar al-Nadwah* was the most immediate expression of the Arab gerontocracy.

Dar al-Nadwah was built adjacent to Ka^cbah. As the most visible mani-festation of a political institution, it could not be separated from the sacred precinct and still hold measures of legitimacy. Sacred ground in pre-Islamic Arabia complemented sacred ancestry. Although any figure from the father of a family to the chief of a clan claimed authority by virtue of the blood in his veins—living testimony of his ancestral authority—the establishment of *Dar al-Nadwah* next to Ka^cbah extended the traditional manifestation of authority into a new level. The sacred ground motif of pre-Islamic Arabia as a major constituent element of the culture surpassed the Muhammadan revolution and continued into the Islamic period.

The central significance of *Dar al-Nadwah* was extended into social, po-litical, economic, and civil domains. Other than being the residence of Qusayy, *Dar al-Nadwah* was also the site of tribal meetings. Marriage ceremonies and other such events were performed here as well (al-Tabari 1879-1901, 2:260). Such ceremonial and practical extensions of an institution of authority into routine life substantiated its cultural relevance. *Dar al- Nadwah* as the center of ceremonial life survived in the institution of the mosque and as the headquarters of political administration in the caliphal court. The intermediary institution between these two phases was the Prophet's house in Medina that functioned as both a mosque and a political/administrative center.

There were also religious functions associated with *Dar al-Nadwah* that had important social, political, and economic ramifications. A number of responsibilities—and thus authorities—were related to *Dar al-Nadwah*: *hijabah* or *wilayat al-bait* (general maintenance of Kaᶜbah), *siqayah*, (providing the annual pilgrims with water), *rifadah* (providing the annual pilgrims with food), *liwa'* (standard of war), and *ᶜushr* (collecting taxes from the merchants) (al-Azraqi 1857, 107). The pattern that emerged from these authorities/responsibilities indicated the widespread expansion of the institution of *Dar al-Nadwah* into the fabric of the pre-Islamic Arab culture. An elaborate process of rituals, concentrated on Kaᶜbah and *Dar al-Nadwah*, unified and defined the collective consciousness of the Arabs. By the authority they manifested, *Dar al-Nadwah* and its ancillary institutions rendered the Arab culture and character expressions of each other. The dynamism of the pre-Islamic Arab culture, so prevalent in such institutions and yet so totally concealed under the post-Islamic accusation of *Jahiliyyah*, is of utmost significance in understanding the nature and organization of the Islamic Political culture.

The vitality of the pre-Islamic culture was also manifested in its ability to expand and accommodate new situations. During Hashim ibn ᶜAbd Manaf ibn Qusayy's tenure as the leader of the Quraysh tribe, the exhaustion of the internal Meccan market economy necessitated its commercial expansion into the Syrian and Yemenite trade. This necessity, supported by the political and commercial crises of the Himarites, gave rise to the institutions of *'ilaf* and *khafarah* introduced by Hashim. According to an agreement (*'ilaf*) between the Quraysh and other tribes along the trade route in Western Arabia (Najd), the Meccan trade caravans were given safe passage (*khafarah*) to commute between the Syrian and Yemenite trade centers. This improvisation of a new pattern of normative contract was an indication of the vitality of the pre-Islamic Arab commercial culture only four generations before the rise of Islam. (Hashim was Muhammad's great-grandfather.) It is important to note later that Muhammad's attacks on the Meccan caravans were a direct charismatic negation expressed against a normative pattern of Arab culture just recently institutionalized.

Consequently, the nature and organization of a charismatic movement must always be assessed in terms of its expressed patterns of authority against an established modality. There is neither a complete break with nor a mere repetition of the established paradigms that constitute a charismatic revolution. It is always a dialectical interaction between the two competing orders of authority that ultimately determines the emerging paradigm of authority.

What is constant, as Rieff has pointed out, is the permanent order of authority in its interdictory, remissive, and transgressive motifs (1981, 226). The content of these motifs, "what is" and "what is not" to be done, distinguishes one cultural paradigm from another.

Perhaps nowhere is the authority of tradition expressed more emphatically than in circumstances involving human life. One of the most remarkable practices in Arab commercial life was the ritual suicide known to Arabs as *i*ᶜ*tifad*. In case of bankruptcy, an Arab separated himself and his family from his tribe, and they all starved to death. This honorable suicide was directly related to the intolerable shame of financial insolvency and becoming a burden on one's clan. Invocation of shame, as the most potent ingredient of a thriving culture, was perhaps the most important expression of an interdictory code of honor that characterized the pre-Islamic Arab culture. As a self-inflicted punishment, *i*ᶜ*tifad* was an indication of the transferral vehicle of culture and character. Through such practices the inculcation—or engraving—of a sacred order into a character becomes evident. Character or personality, here as elsewhere, is culture personified and rendered alive. There is nothing stagnant, corrupt, or ignorant about a culture that can still invoke guilt and shame or enforce its codes of honor in ritual suicide. The condescending and concealing expression of *Jahiliyyah* should be understood only as an expression of Islamic self-understanding, very similar to other distinguishing and excluding factors such as *kafir* or *mushrik*. The significance of Muhammad's charismatic revolution, in fact, is understood more clearly if it is seen as expressed against a thriving culture rather than against an empty desert, as Islamic self-understanding would have it, or against a corrupt society, as some Islamicists have argued.

The pre-Islamic Arab culture was normatively thriving and organizationally innovative. When Hashim ibn ᶜAbd Manaf ibn Quasayy saw the destructive nature of *i*ᶜ*tifad,* he established a new organizational arrangement of Arab commerce, *mudarabah*, through which merchants engaged in joint or collective ventures, thus minimizing their risks and maximizing their profits. *Mudarabah*, as an indigenous Arab enterprise, set their commerce on a new scale enabling them to exploit the Syrian-Yemenite commercial potentials. The essential purpose of every culture is civilized survival, not self-destructiveness. The degeneration of cultural mores into empty dogmas is the most important indication of corruption and decline. Far from being corrupted or bankrupt, the pre-Islamic Arab culture thrived on its old institutions as well as on its ability to change and meet new material demands.

As a material indication of a thriving culture, the economic prosperity of Arabia on the verge of Islam is particularly striking. It is also important to realize that this economic prosperity was directly related to certain indigenous Arab institutions. Through contractual agreements (*'ilaf*) with non-Qurayshite tribes, Hashim not only secured the safe passage of Meccan caravans on the trade route but also incorporated other Arab tribes who provided armed protection (*khafarah*) to Meccans in the emerging commercial organization. As a result, partnership (*mudarabah*) unified the Quraysh merchants into a full commercial force, prevented ritual suicide of the bankrupts (*iʿtifad*), paved the way to geographical (market) expansion through *'ilaf* and *khafarah,* and ultimately established the sound institutional basis of a full-fledged trade economy. This close affinity between cultural institutions and the conduct of commerce was a major characteristic of pre-Islamic Arabia that was also present in the Islamic commercial culture.

The reorganization of Arab commerce, through the innovative mobilization of traditional institutions, successfully launched the Meccan capital into the international markets of Syria, Iraq, Yemen, and Abyssinia and through the Red Sea into other parts of the world.

Two other institutions complemented *mudarabah* and *'ilaf*, and together they comprised a confederation of alliances and associations that held the Arab commercial culture together. *Hilf* was an alliance between the Quraysh and any other tribe not already in the *'ilaf* confederation. It was directed at those tribes who were not located on the trade route, yet their commercial partnership was helpful in joint ventures. Usually a marriage between the Quraysh and these tribes intensified the *hilf* alliance. The institution of *jiwar* served as a neighborly alliance between the Quraysh and all of its surrounding tribes. More than just a geographical expression of solidarity, it had extended commercial ramifications, especially through the period of pilgrimage to Mecca.

What held all of these institutions together, as the symbolic center of the Arab culture, was Kaʿbah. As a living institution of authority Kaʿbah had its occasions for rejuvenation. When Abrahah's attempt to capture Mecca catastrophically failed, the incident was taken as a sign of divine intervention and Kaʿbah assumed new institutional significance. By extension, the Quraysh tribe was further elevated in social prestige and, as the custodians of Kaʿbah, received the honorific title of the *Ahl-Allah* (the people of God). The unique position of the Quraysh as an aristocratic tribe was connected intimately to their functions as the guardians of the sacred precinct, *haram*. Events such as the Abrahah's aborted invasion further strengthened both Kaʿbah's and the Quraysh's authority.

The institution of *Muhrimun* was made more exclusive after Abrahah's aborted invasion of Mecca, when the significance of Kaʿbah increased considerably. Gradually, the Quraysh and its closest tribal allies in the vicinity of Mecca further concentrated the exclusive authority of the Meccan tribal/ commercial establishment. It is important to realize that the formation of the institutions of authority had always been an outcome of external political and/or commercial developments interacting with the inner dynamics of Arab tribal customs.

The most thriving commercial center of pre-Islamic Arabia was the $^{c}Ukaz$ market, where elaborate expressions of the traditional culture were manifested. This market, which attracted merchants/pilgrims from all over Arabia, was much more than an intertribal commercial fair; it was a cultural, religious, political, social, and economic event of central significance. Here merchants traded their goods, poets recited their poetry, pilgrims performed their rites, tribal chiefs consolidated their power, clans substantiated their solidarity, and above all the Qurayshite Meccans exercised their authority. Ka^{c}bah grew in significance by incorporating Arab deities other than those of the Quraysh and their immediate allies. It grew into a full-fledged pantheon of Arab deities. $^{c}Ukaz$ was the most eminent expression of the Quraysh's religious and political authority. It was also the microcosm of the pre-Islamic Arab culture.

There were remarkable similarities between the mechanisms through which the Quraysh aristocracy consolidated its authority in pre-Islamic Arabia and those that Muhammad employed to establish his prophetic mission. When Mecca was growing in religious and commercial significance, its most important urban rival was Hira. Around 580, the Meccan establishment launched a series of attacks, known as the Fijar Wars (al-Baghdadi 1965, 185-211), against Hira and its central Arabian allies. These wars began with an attack on the annual trade caravan of the Lakhmids and eventually led to the downfall of Hira and the supremacy of Mecca in central Arabia. Through the same procedure Muhammad later paralyzed the Meccan economy. These elements of continuity from pre- to post-Muhammadan periods point to a common repertoire of cultural traits that the traditional and charismatic modes of authority mobilize.

The same continuity of common symbolics was also evident in such aspects of traditional Arab culture and the Muhammadan mission as the supremacy of Allah as the highest authority, the centrality of Ka^{c}bah, the Meccan pilgrimage, etc. Although in its nature charismatic authority is essentially and organizationally different from traditional modalities of command and obedience, within a given cultural setting they both employ a given set of common symbolics. This was true about Christ in the Jewish tradition, about Buddha in the Hindu faith, and about Muhammad in the pre-Islamic Arab culture.

Ka^{c}bah was the center of authority; all other parts of Arabia under its jurisdiction extended into the periphery from this point of gravity. Even the Quraysh, who under Qusayy were the chief custodians of the sacred precinct, were divided into two groups according to their physical distance from Ka^{c}bah:

The Quraysh al-Bata^cih settled closest to the *haram,* and the Quraysh al-Zawahir in its vicinity. This distinction was a criterion of social and religious privilege. With the commercial and political ascendancy of Mecca and especially the Quraysh tribe, Ka^cbah assumed an increasingly central sacred significance in pre-Islamic Arab life. The concomitant concentration of the sacred in Ka^cbah and commerce in Mecca worked towards the ascendancy of Mecca in Arabia. This ascendancy was later of such central significance that Muhammad, perhaps for other reasons too, abandoned altogether the idea of selecting Jerusalem as the direction of prayer, *qiblah,* for the early Muslim community. The adoption of Mecca, or more especially Ka^cbah, as the center of gravity for Islam and its sacred House of God (*Bayt Allah al-Haram*) is a clear indication that the primary elements of a cultural revolution must necessarily be derived from the incumbent culture. Jerusalem was too distant a symbol to command the obedience of tribal Arabs.

As indicated earlier, perhaps the most important office of traditional authority in Arabia was *wilayat al-bayt,* physically demonstrated by holding the key to Ka^cbah. During the time of ^cAbd Manaf, a major rivalry emerged between the two factions of the Quraysh to possess this office. The tribe was thus divided into al-Ahlaf, the supporters of ^cAbd al Dar, and al-Mutayyabun, the supporters of ^cAbd Manaf. This confrontation was finally settled with the *Mutayyabun* receiving the offices of *siqayah* and *rifadah* while the *Ahlaf* maintained their office of *wilayat al-bayt, riwa',* and *Dar al-Nadwah* (al-Baghdadi 1965, 331). Institutions of authority such as *wilayat al-bayt* were loci of tribal rivalries between the contending factions.

Both intra- and intertribal conflicts were settled through the institution of *munafarah* (arbitration). The two tribal adversaries conceded to the authority of a third party, usually from a neutral tribe, to arbitrate in the matter of their dispute. Thus the dispute between Harb ibn Umayyah and ^cAbd al-Muttalib, both from the Quraysh, over the murder of a Jewish merchant was referred to a *hakam* from Banu^cAdiyy. Another dispute over a piece of land, between ^cAbd al-Muttalib and Nawfal ibn ^c Abd Manaf, was settled similarly through *munafarah* (al-Baghdadi 1965, 80).

One of the varieties of communal association was *munadamah* or close friendship. This tie established a means of obligation between two clans. One incident regarding this institution was reported by al-Baladhuri: ^cAbd al-Muttalib, Muhammad's grandfather, was in a *munadamah* with a Jewish merchant whom Harb ibn Umayyah had murdered (al-Baladhuri 1916, 1:73). The *munadamah* obligated ^cAbd al-Muttalib to seek compensation for his murdered friend. This incident also indicated that such associations were transtribal and, in fact, superimposed upon tribal obligations.

Munadamah was not the only institutional form of transtribal association and obligation. Alienated from the Banu Umayyah faction of the Quraysh tribe, ʿAbd al-Muttalib approached both Banu al-Najjar of Yathrib and Banu Khazaʿah of Mecca for alliance. The latter accepted his bid, and a coalition between Banu Hashim and Banu Khazaʿah was superimposed against the natural tribal affinity of the Quraysh.

All these institutional expressions of the pre-Arab culture were the nuclei of its permanence, relevance, and legitimacy. In both their stable and evolving dynamisms, they regulated daily routine life within the boundaries of a moral demand system, which, as a whole, was traditionally legitimated. The operational relevance of these institutions, as both cultural motifs and social organizations, precluded any characterization of pre-Islamic Arabia as chaotic or "corrupt." Within its own specifically stipulated cultural order, sustained by both figures and institutions of authority, pre-Islamic Arabia was, for all practical and illuminative purposes, an operating social order.

Two contrasting/complementing symbolics regulated the social organization of the pre-Islamic Arab cultural order around the principle of *haram*. Those who adhered to the sacredness of both the Kaʿbah precinct and the specific months were known as *al-muhrimun* (those who believe in and maintain the sacred), and those who did not were called *al-muhillun* (those who consider permissible what *al-muhrimun* regard as transgressive). These two symbolic categories, corresponding to the realities of the Arab culture, did not contradict but complemented each other. They were the constituting elements of the major tension within the Arab culture. The principle of *haram* at once unified and dialectically complemented.

Within the sacred space of Kaʿbah, *al-muhrimun* were the interdictory figures of authority, the personifications of "thou shalt nots," while *al-muhillun* were the opposing transgressors. As in all cultures, the two modalities of interdictions and transgressions held their tension and thus animated the culture. A culture holds itself together insofar as these two constituent elements do not take over each other completely (Rieff 1972b, 92–100).

The supreme symbolic of authority, *haram* was central to the Arab culture. When, for commercial reasons, the Quraysh intended to purchase the fertile lands of Wadi Wajj in Taʿif and were resisted by the Banu Thaqif, who, as the chief tribe of Taʿif, had ancestral claims over the land, all the Quraysh had to do to threaten the Banu Thaqif was indicate that they would be denied access to *haram*. This threat, supported by the possibility of a military confrontation, facilitated the Quraysh's bid to acquire the property (al-Baghdadi 1965, 28). The sacred significance of *haram* for the Arabs was further substantiated by the infusion of its consecrating power into commercial activities. *Haram* was the sacred space on which the Arab merchants engaged in commerce. This at once made commerce tantamount to a religious ritual and extended the metaphysical significance of *haram* into the domains of economic life. Out of this interpenetration of the metaphysical/physical the Arab culture both legitimated and sustained itself.

As a sacred, inhibitive space, *haram* also provided haven for anyone seeking protection. After the battle of Yaum Dhat Naqif (al-Baladhuri 1916, 1:75), in which the Quraysh inflicted heavy losses on the Banu Laith, the defeated tribe escaped from the battleground and ran into *haram*. There they were spared their lives. As a symbolic of authority, *haram* regulated the degree of violence that the Arab culture could tolerate collectively. Such symbolics were expressive of specific mechanisms through which the Arab culture perpetuated itself. Sacred space is authority visibly manifested. As a center of gravity it holds a culture together. Violence is central, as Weber pointed out, to any form of political life. But legitimate violence ideally eliminates itself. Inhibitive spaces, such as *haram*, counter violence by rendering it impermissible within their confinements. While political life within any cultural order necessitates violence, inhibitive spaces, stipulated by that culture, keep it in control.

Through specific figures, institutions, and symbolics of authority, the traditional Arab culture was the thriving force of a traditional order of life. As a trajectory of common symbolics, it sustained itself through its specific paradigmatic expressions from a traditional culture inculcated in the Arab collective consciousness. These paradigms, moreover, were present and operative simultaneously in every dimension of life. Politically they regulated the relations of command and obedience within the tribal structure; commercially they established and subjected to renovations the normative patterns of transactions, collaborations, and joint ventures; and religiously they required certain repetitive annual rituals that brought Arab physical life and metaphysical concerns into a close harmony.

Yet within this same harmony the notes of the coming revolution were being tuned. Before I examine the specifics of Muhammad's charismatic authority—as it was expressed against the traditional Arab culture—this Weberian conceptualization must first be stipulated within a specifically Islamic context.

3

Muhammad's Charismatic Authority: Towards an Equivalent Islamic Typology

> *I profess that there is no god save God,*
> *And I profess that Muhammad is His Messen-*
> *ger.*
>
> —Muslim Profession of Faith

Applied to Muhammad, the Weberian typology of charismatic authority requires a careful consideration of this mode of legitimate domination within the Islamic (Qur'anic) context. This chapter is devoted to a formulation of an equivalent Islamic typology that would specifically characterize Muhammad's charismatic authority.

Although "charismata" is, and shall remain, an essentially Christian phenomenon, the Weberian conceptual categorization of "charismatic authority," as a "neutral" sociological designation of a mode of authority, directs attention to other "similar" modalities of command and obedience. This direction and the theoretical implications it entails are the only justification for trying to locate the Islamic context within which Muhammad's authority over both his immediate disciples and the later Islamic community can be considered as charismatic. The purpose of this hermeneutic designation is not simply to state that Muhammad's authority was charismatic but to see in what specific way it was charismatic and how that specific way was important for the course of post-Muhammadan developments of the Islamic political culture. The uniqueness of Muhammad's central authority and the particular mode of its legitimacy were essential to the very nature and organization of authority in the future formation of the Islamic political culture.

Within a sociological context, "charisma" is

> applied to a certain quality of an individual personality by virtue of which he is considered extraordinary and treated as endowed with supernatural, superhuman, or at least specifically exceptional powers or qualities. (Weber 1978a, 241)

Belief in such qualities on the part of the followers constitutes a nexus of authority/obedience within which the commands of the charismatic leader are obeyed as if they were the wishes of the followers. For this relationship to be operative, Weber stipulated two particular conditions of "inner justification" (*inneren Rechtfertigungsgrunde*) and "external means" (*ausseren Mittel*) (1946, 78). "Inner justification" is the interactive process between the leader and the led, inseparable from the mode of domination through which an authority is considered to be legitimate. The "external means" is the political apparatus of domination appropriated by the figures of authority.

One major factor distinguishing this mode of authority from the other two—traditional and rational/legal—is the belief on the part of the followers in "supernatural, superhuman . . . or exceptional powers" with which the charismatic leader is considered to be endowed. Once a charismatic authority is established, the existing social relationships, whether traditional or rational/legal, are fundamentally challenged and superseded by a new "nonrational" mode of social relationships. Thus, charismatic leaders usually launch a revolutionary movement that seeks to alter the status quo and establish a new order.

A charismatic revolution initiates an essential, yet never a total, break with the authority of the past through the agency of a charismatic figure who, while deconstructing the old order, constructs a new one—always simultaneously. The construction of the new order is usually infused with powerful characterizing elements of the superseded order. Communities follow these charismatic figures because they perceive qualities in them that "are not accessible to the ordinary person, but are regarded as of divine origin or as exemplary (Weber 1978a, 241). The "divine origin" of charismatic domination is a common motif that legitimates this form of authority. Furthermore, whatever may be understood by this concept in various social/religious settings, it puts the source of charisma "out of" human reach, as it were. Consequently, the charismatic leader does not derive his authority from either the community he rules or the "office" he occupies. His is a purely "personal" authority; followers obey him because of what he "personally" possesses. However, this "personality" is considered to be divinely ordained. By obeying the charismatic leader, "salvation," whatever it may convey to a particular religious community, is secured.

If a charismatic figure comes to exercise specifically political authority, like Muhammad and unlike Buddha or Jesus, then the acceptance of his legitimacy raises the question of submission to the ruler. This is the other significant part of the command/obedience nexus. "It is recognition on the part of those subject to authority," Weber pointed out, "which is decisive for the validity of charisma" (1978a, 242). A charismatic leader does not derive his authority from his followers, as Weber made clear. The sole source of this authority is "metaphysical," above and beyond the social/physical. It is, in fact, the follower's belief in this metaphysical source that legitimates the authority of the charismatic figure.

Prophets are among the chief figures whom Weber included in his typology of charismatic authority. He also included "in the field of politics . . . the elected warlord, the plebiscitarian ruler, the great demagogue, or the political party leader" (1946, 79). "What is a prophet," Weber said,

> from the perspective of sociology? . . . We shall understand "prophet" to mean a purely individual bearer of charisma, who by virtue of his mission proclaims a religious doctrine or divine commandment. (1978a, 439)

He added further that "the prophet's claim is based on personal revelation and charisma" (439). More specifically, Weber considered Zoroaster, Jesus, and Muhammad as prophets whose followers were attracted to them for their personality, that is, their charismatic authority. Weber contrasted these three prophets, whose authorities were personal, with Buddha and the prophets of Israel, whose followers were attracted to the doctrines they put forward (439).

The particular nature of Muhammad's charismatic authority, that is, the way his authority was charismatic, provides the Weberian typology with a specific case to observe the constituent elements of a rising charismatic movement.

Within the Islamic context, Muhammad's "charisma" or "charismatic authority" has been identified by two terms—*karāmah* and *wilāyah*—both of which pose difficulties as equivalents of the Prophet's "charismatic authority." An exposition of these difficulties should also clarify the principal content of the Islamic concept that best corresponds to "Muhammad's charismatic authority."

In the *Shorter Encyclopedia of Islam*, Macdonald (1953) confirmed Gardet's suggestion of "*Karama*" as the proper equivalent of "charisma." Gardet stated that "in the technical vocabulary of the religious sciences, *karama* . . . assumes the sense of 'charisma,' the favor bestowed by God completely, freely, and in superabundance." He further stated that

> the word comes to denote the "marvels" wrought by the "friends of God," '*awliya*' . . . which God grants to them to bring about. These marvels most usually consist of miraculous happenings in the corporeal world, or else of predictions of the future or else of interpretation of the secrets of hearts, etc. (1979)

Allowing for the technical meaning of this Islamic/Arabic term, the etymological root of the word seems to substantiate the equation of "charisma" and "*karāmah*." Gardet maintained that "*karāmah*" "seems very likely to have come about through phonetic assimilation to the Greek χαρίσματα," which is the etymological root of the Christian "charisma." Macdonald developed this apparent similarity further:

> The coincidence in sound, in derivation, and in meaning between these *karamat* and the χαρίσματα of the early Christian church (I Cor. XII) is most striking and can hardly be accidental. The religious phenomena behind both are the same; but the verbal link is not clear; the Syriac church called the χαρίσματα simply "gifts," *mauhebhatha*, in Arabic *mawahib*, which indeed occurs in this sense; it is possible that the Greek word taken over into Syriac may have suggested to users of Arabic their own karamat. (1953)

Whatever its merits as a proper equivalent of "charisma," "*karamah*" will have substantial difficulties maintaining the theoretical requirements of Weber's concept of "charismatic authority."

Within the Islamic context, any expression that identifies Muhammad's charismatic authority must be specific to him and to no one else. It should refer to some particularity in Muhammad's self-understanding that no one else shares within the Islamic social and theological limits. This principle is understood from the Weberian stipulation that charismatic authority is a "personal" quality. Weber pointed out that

> the "natural" leaders in moments of distress . . . [are] the bearers of specific gifts of body and mind that were considered "supernatural" (in the sense that not everybody could have access to them). (1978a, 1111-12)

Moreover, in defining charismatic authority he said that

> there is the authority of the extraordinary and personal *gift of grace* (charisma), the absolutely personal devotion and personal confidence in revelation, heroism, or other qualities of individual leadership. (1946, 79)

It is necessary that the Islamic term specify something peculiar to Muhammad and no one else. If the chosen term could be applied equally to other religious and spiritual figures in Islam, such as the ᶜUlamá, the Sufis, etc., then the unique and personal nature of his authority is not recognized and specified. Using the same argument, if ᶜAli's charismatic authority were to be identified, it ought to be applicable only to ᶜAli and his perception by the community of followers. Muhammad could not be referred to as a *Shaykh* (chief) or *Sayyid* (master), for example, because these are positions that were shared by many pre-Islamic Arab leaders; as a result, there would be no distinguishing factor constituting Muhammad's charismatic authority. But, drawing from the Weberian stipulations, the Islamic term should be applicable to Muhammad and only to him in the Islamic context. *Karamah* does not meet this qualification because it may be extended, theoretically, to almost all Muslims as long as they have received *barakah* (grace) from God. As a "divine gift," *karamah* is not the prerogative of Muhammad. Any righteous Muslim may achieve a level of piety to attain this status.

There is yet another difficulty with *karamah* as a concept identifying Muhammad's charismatic authority. In Weber's theory of authority the question of "domination" and "political community," whether in their primitive (sib) or modern (state) forms, are interrelated. In fact, Weber defined "state" in terms of "domination":

> Like the political institutions historically preceding it, the state is a relation of men dominating men, a relation supported by means of legitimate (i.e., considered to be legitimate) violence. If the state is to exist, the dominated must obey the authority claimed by the powers that be. (1946, 79)

The question of "authority" or "domination" is inseparable from "state" and the use of "legitimate violence." Both terms are translations of *Herrschaft*. Weber's original sentence, more forcefully connecting "authority" and the use of "legitimate violence," reads,

> Der Staat ist, ebenso wie die ihm geschichtlich vorausgehenden politischen Verbände, ein auf das Mittel der legitimen (das heisst: als legitim angesehenen) Gewaltsamkeit gestütztes *Herrschafts*verhältnis von Menschen über Menschen. Damit er bestehe, müssen sich also die beherrschten Menschen der beanspruchten Autorität der jeweils herrschenden *fügen*. (1980a, 507)

Gewalt may be translated as "power," "authority," "domination," etc.; *Gewaltsam* as "vigorous," "forcible," "violent," etc.; and *Gewaltsamkeit* as "violence" or "force."

Muhammad's establishment of Islam as a "universal," or metahistorical, religion was implemented through physical force and was simultaneous with the foundation of the Islamic state. Given the inherent connection of authority to violence, the term that identifies Muhammad's charismatic authority should have specific references to his ability to use physical force "justifiably." *Karamah* does not meet this requirement. As a *barakah* (gift) received from God, *karamah* does not legitimate the recipient's use of physical force. Consequently, there might be particular recipients of *karamah* who exercise no "political" domination over a multitude of people. For example, the most important figures who have been considered historically to possess *karamah*, that is, special favors from Allah, are the *áwlia'-Allah* ("the friends of God"). Major representatives of this type are the Sufi saints, who have been identified, both historically and ideally, with the image of the "perfect man" (*al-Insan al-kamil*).

Among the major Sufi theoreticians who have developed this concept was Azia al-Din al-Nasafi (d.c. 1290) who, in his *Kitab al-Insan al-Kamil (The*

Book of the Perfect Man), extensively developed the particularities of this ideal type. Despite all saintly virtues, such as good sayings, good acts, good conduct, and the knowledge of God, al-Nasafi argued,

> this perfect man has no power; and lives with his wishes unfulfilled . . . , in terms of knowledge and conduct he is Perfect, but in terms of power and [fulfillment of his] wishes he is imperfect. (1962, 7)

Since *karamah* conferred no right on Muhammad to use physical force in establishing his domination over a multitude of followers, it cannot render accurately the nature of his charismatic authority.

The next problem with *karamah* is that it contains no reference to the essential concept of "authority." If Muhammad was considered to have *karamah*, this by itself did not entitle him to exercise authority over and demand obedience from his followers. "Charismatic authority" in the context of the Weberian theory of domination is first and foremost a mode of authority. It refers to a

> situation in which the manifested will (*command*) of the *ruler* or rulers is meant to influence the conduct of one or more others (*the ruled*) and actually does influence it in such a way that their conduct to a socially relevant degree occurs as if the ruled had made the content of the command the maxim of their conduct for its very own sake. Looked upon from the other end, this situation will be called obedience. (Weber 1978a, 946)

If a particular "gift of grace" does not entitle its recipient to a position of authority, the charisma will remain an essentially "private" attribute recognized by a limited number of disciples. An artist, for example, may be considered to have received the "gift" of painting, a singer that of singing, and a Sufi that of Divine unity; yet these gifts do not demand the obedience of a multitude of people to a degree that is politically relevant. Nor do they entitle the charismatic figure to exercise authority. There must be something inherent in the nature of the "gift" received that endows authority and demands obedience. Therefore, the term that identifies Muhammad's authority must carry within itself "authority," that is, it must legitimate violence in establishing a political community.

It has also been suggested that *wilayah* is a proper equivalent of "Muhammad's charismatic authority" (Nuri ᶜAla' 1978, 21). The root of this word in Arabic is "WLY," meaning "to be in charge," "manage," "run," "administer," "govern," "rule." The argument for this equivalent is stated as follows: "Among the Islamic concepts we have to look for a term that conveys the idea of 'domination' (21). The Qur'anic verse that is offered as justification is XVIII:44, where all authority is stated as belonging to God. Pickthall's translation of this verse reads: "In this case is protection (*wilayah*) only from Allah, the True." Nuri ᶜAla' read *wilayah* in this verse as "authority," whereas Pickthall translated it into "protection." Both are among the dictionary definitions of the term. Both Arberry (1979) and Dawood (1956) translate *wilayah* in this verse as "protection." All authority in Islam must be legitimated in terms of this ultimate source. The prophet's authority, the argument continues, is legitimated through this very source. For this point Nuri ᶜAla' referred to V:55: "Your friend (*Waliukum*) can be only Allah; and His messenger and those who believe, who establish worship and pay the poor-due, and bow down in prayer"; and XXXIII:6: "The prophet is closer (*awlá'*) to the believers than their selves. . . ." *Again the root meaning of "WLY" makes "friend," "closer," "master," and "leader" all possible. The trilateral root in its general meaning makes all such interpretations plausible. Thus, wilayat al-nabawi* (the prophetic *wilayah*) according to Nuri ᶜAlá, is the Islamic equivalent of "Muhammad's charismatic authority" (Nuri ᶜAlá 1978, 22-23).

This formulation is addressed more directly to the Weberian typology and is a more sociologically developed concept. Yet it is equally problematic as an accurate equivalent for "Muhammad's charismatic authority" for two reasons: it is too general, and it is too vague.

It is true that the concept properly conveying Muhammad's authority must entail the idea of domination. In fact, this is one of the criteria with which *karamah* was evaluated. But *wilayah* is not specific or concrete enough to be applied as an equivalent of "Muhammad's charismatic authority." Under this category there are three essential problems with the term: (1) it has no particular reference to "charisma" as the "gift of grace," (2) it makes no reference to the legitimate use of physical force in establishing charismatic authority, and (3) it is not specific to Muhammad.

Wilayah has no inherent reference to a "charismatic" relationship between God and *wali*, on the one hand, and between *wali* and his possible followers, on the other. The appropriate equivalent of "charismatic authority" for Muhammad must indicate a "unique" and "personal" relationship between Allah and Muhammad and, at the same time, require the obedience of people to his authority by virtue of this relationship. The different variations of "*wilayah*" in the Qur'an all indicate Allah as the "protecting friend" (for example, II:120: "And if thou shouldst follow their desires after the knowledge which hath come unto thee, then wouldst thou have from Allah no protecting friend [*waliyan*] nor helper"), any "friend" in general, "devils as the protecting friends of unbelievers" (for example, VII:27: "Lo! We have made the devils protecting friends of those who believe not"), or "friends of Allah" (for example, X:62: "Lo! Verily the friends of Allah are [those] on whom fear [cometh] not, nor do they grieve"). Even in the last meaning, which refers to a mode of relationship between Allah and man, the term embraces almost all

Muslims and yet no man or group of men in particular. So far as all Muslims worship Allah and perform their other religious obligations, they are "friends of God" (for example, V:55: "Your friend can be only Allah; and His Messenger and those who believe, who establish worship and pay the poor-due and bow down [in prayer]"). But "charismatic authority" is a highly personal and exceptional quality, legitimated by the belief that it is bestowed upon a particular person. If the quality that identifies Muhammad's charismatic authority, within the Islamic context, can be shared by others, there remains nothing peculiar to him, in which case he will lose the source of his legitimacy.

In defining "the prophet" and distinguishing him from "the priest," Weber pointed out that

> the personal call is the decisive element distinguishing the prophet from the priest. The latter lays claim to authority by virtue of his service in sacred tradition, while the prophet's claim is based on personal revelation and charisma. (1978a, 440)

Even disregarding the diffused nature of *wilayah* and the multiplicity of its meaning, this term does not entail any particular element of "gift of grace" being initiated on Allah's part towards his "favored" servant.

Wilayah, to turn to the second problem in this category, carries no reference to the legitimate use of physical force for the establishment of charismatic authority. No authority, in a sociological sense, can be established without the "legitimate," that is, considered to be "legitimate," use of physical force. In none of its Qur'anic forms does *wilayah* entitle its bearer to use violence to enforce his authority. Even with the assumption that *wilayah* constitutes a "gift of grace" from God to his favored creature, an assumption rendered inappropriate through the last argument, it does not entitle the *wali* to use physical force to establish his authority. There are many references in the Qur'an to the use of physical force, usually associated with the two key words of *qatala* (to kill) and *jahada* (to fight). In no way is the concept of *wilayah* related to these "legitimate" uses of physical force. There are verses in the Qur'an in which both *qatala* (to kill) and *'awliya'* (friends) appear in exactly the opposite sense of a *wali* being entitled to use physical force, such as IV:76: "Those who believe do battle for the cause of Allah; and those who disbelieve do battle for the cause of idols. So fight the minions of the devil. Lo! the devil's strategy is ever weak." "Minions" was Pickthall's (1976) translation of *awaliya'*; "do battle" is not a totally accurate translation of *yuqataluna*, from the root *qatala*, "to kill," "to slay." *Yuqatalu* is the imperfect mode of the III form (*qatala*), and in this form the verb does indicate "to combat" and "to battle"; but the underlying significance of the command "to kill" is always present in all of the various verbal forms derived from the

I form. Only under specific circumstances and in reference to a particular attribute of the prophet is the command "to kill" or "to fight" issued; and *wilayah* is not related to these circumstances.

To turn to the third problem in this category, *wilayah* does not meet the "specific reference to Muhammad" criterion. There is nothing in this term that is uniquely related to the "Prophet." The Qur'anic verse offered as a justification for this term states that "Your friend (*waliukum*) can be only Allah; and His messenger and those who believe, who establish worship and pay the poor-due, and bow down (in prayer)" (V:55). Even if *wali*—the active participle of WLY—is read as the "master" and "leader" and not as "friend" in this verse—a justifiable interpretation of the word—it is immediately obvious that not only Muhammad but all those "who believe, who establish worship and pay the poor-due, and bow down (in prayer)" share this status with him. Thus *wilayah* is not a prerogative of Muhammad. In fact, all those who may possess *karamah* as a sign of "divine favor" may be and are addressed as *awliya'* (the plural of *wali*)-*Allah*, that is, the friends of God, those whom He favors. *Awliya'* appears as many as thirty-four times in the Qur'an; and each time it refers to "pious Muslims," "friends," or "protecting friends" whom men might choose to deify instead of God. For example, III:28: "Let not the believers take disbelievers for their *friends* . . ."; IV:76: "Those who believe do battle for the cause of Allah; and those who disbelieve do battle for the cause of idols. So fight the *minions* of the devil"; XLII:46: "And they will have no protecting friends to help them instead of Allah" (emphasis is added and denotes translations of *awliya'*; see also XXV:18, XXIX:41, XXXIX:3, XLV:10, et passim).

Following an extensive examination of the etymological and theological significance of *wali*, Carra de Vaux, in an article in the *Shorter Encyclopedia of Islam* under the same entry, maintained that "when used in a religious connection, *wali* corresponds very much to our title of 'saints'" (1953). Moreover, in its reference to traditional Islamic sources, "wali is equivalent to that of *ʿarif bi'allah*, 'he who possesses mystic knowledge,' 'he who knows God'" (1953). Again there is no exclusive reference to Muhammad and his unique personal qualities in this term. The spiritual state of *ʿarif bi'allah* is attainable, theoretically, by all pious Muslims. The equivalent of "Muhammad's charismatic authority" in Islamic terminology must be peculiar to Muhammad and no other Muslim.

To return to the second major problem with this term, *wilayah* carries a number of meanings, as has become evident now, and for that reason lacks the direct and emphatic vigor necessary to express the charismatic quality of Muhammad's authority. This vagueness arises from six distinct meanings and connotations, mentioned in the Qur'an into which the different uses of this term may be divided. The first meaning, in the form of *waliyukum* (your *wali*), denotes the friendship, the protective friendship, or the authority of Allah (V:55: "Your friend [*waliukum*] can be only Allah . . ."); the second, that of the Prophet (V:55: "Your friend [*waliukum*] can be only Allah; and His Messenger and those who believe . . ."); the third, that of all the believers (ibid.); the fourth, in the form of *'awliya'* (the plural of *wali*), the friends of Allah (X:62: "Lo! verily the friends [*'awaliya'*] of Allah are [those] on whom fear [cometh] not, nor do they grieve"); the fifth, those of the devils (IV:76: "Those who believe do battle for the cause of Allah; and those who disbelieve do battle for the cause of idols. So fight the minions [*'awliya'*] of the devil . . ."); and the sixth, in the form of *waliyan* (a *wali*), friends and friendship in general (IV:89: "So choose not friends (*waliyan*) from them till they forsake their homes in the way of Allah . . ."). A term with so many connotations, however interrelated, cannot be used to identify a particular attribute of Muhammad that ultimately constitutes his charismatic authority.

Based on the evaluation of these two terms, the equivalent Islamic concept for "Muhammad's charismatic authority" should be founded on the following five criteria, the validity of which have now been established: (1) It must directly convey the idea of "authority"; (2) it must identify the nature of this authority as "charismatic," that is, as a "personal gift" received from the source of legitimacy; (3) it must entitle the recipient of the "charisma," Muhammad, to use physical force in order to establish his authority; (4) it must be specific to Muhammad, so that no one else within the Islamic context can claim a similar "charismatic authority"; and, finally, (5) it must be a clear and distinct term, immune to oscillating interpretations and readings.

"What is a prophet," Weber (1978a, 439) asked, "from the perspective of sociology?" To this he answered, "We shall understand 'prophet' to mean a purely individual bearer of charisma, who by virtue of his mission proclaims a religious doctrine or divine commandment" (439). It is precisely "by virtue of his mission" that (1) the legitimacy of charismatic authority is established and (2) the charismatic figure is distinguished from others. Moreover, in distinguishing between "exemplary" and "ethical" prophets, Weber pointed out that the followers of a prophet may be "attracted to his person, as in the case of Zoroaster, Jesus, and Muhammad, or to his doctrine, as in the case of Buddah and the prophets of Israel" (440). Weber's references to the personal charisma were abundant: "For our purposes here, the personal call is the decisive element distinguishing the prophet from the priest," "the prophet . . . exerts his power simply by virtue of his personal gifts," etc. (440). Here, too, Muhammad's authority was associated with his personal qualifications and attributes.

The most essential characteristic with which Muhammad and only Muhammad can be identified in the Islamic context was his *risalah* (messengership), a distinctive quality which legitimated his personal authority and did so with

clear reference to his "divine mission." Muhammad's "charismatic authority" is best identified by this term. *Risalah* is from the root "RSL," meaning
in its various forms "to send out," "to dispense," "to send off" (form IV,
arsala); "to keep up a correspondence," "to send to one another" (form VI,
tarasala). In the form proposed here, *risalah* means "mission," "calling," or
"vocation." There are several Qur'anic references to this word in various
forms, with many prefixes and suffixes: in the form of *rusulun* (a messenger),
thirty-four times, among them II:87, II:253, III:144, VI:10, and XXXIX:71;
in the form of *rusuluna* (our messengers), seventeen times, among them
V:32,VI:61, XI:69, and XXXIX :31; in the form of *rasulun* (a messenger),
one hundred and sixteen times, among them II:87, III:32, IV:42,VII:61,
XXXIII:21, and XLVIII:12.There are many other forms. One of the most
significant Qur'anic references is VII:158:

> Say (O Muhammad): O mankind! Lo! I am the messenger of Allah (*rasul Allah*)
> to you all—(the messenger of Him) unto Whom belongeth the sovereignty of
> the heavens and the earth. There is no God save Him. He quickens and He
> giveth death. So believe in Allah and His messenger (*rasuluhu*), the unlettered
> prophet, and follow him that haply ye may be led aright.

All the essential elements of Muhammad's charismatic authority are con-
tained in this verse—along with the Qur'anic term that best identifies it as
such. According to this verse all authority belongs to Allah. He is "the
Sovereign of the heaven and earth." There is no God but Him, and all
authority must come from this source. He sends (*'arsala*), out of His own
volition, Muhammad as His messenger (*rasul*) to guide mankind. The only
source of "salvation" for mankind is to obey God through His messenger.
The authority of Muhammad is thus legitimated because of its being "authored" by Him "unto Whom belongeth the sovereignty of the heavens and
earth" and he is rendered charismatic by virtue of his personal attribute of
risalah (messengership).

The first principle according to which other suggestions were evaluated is
that the Islamic term "must directly convey the idea of authority." *Risalah* is
the sole source of Muhammad's authority. The verse just quoted clearly
indicates that men should obey Muhammad *because* he is the messenger
(*rasul*) of Allah. Obedience to Muhammad is always demanded because of his
messengership (*risalah*): "Therefore I shall ordain it for those who ward off
(evil) and pay the poor-due, and those who believe Our revelations; Those
who follow the messenger (*ar-rasul*)" (Qur'an VII:156-57). Or it is more
specifically indicated that: "Say: obey Allah and the messenger (*ar-rasul*).
But if they turn away, Lo! Allah loveth not the disbelievers (in his guidance)"
(Qur'an III:32). The Qur'anic verses that refer to Muhammad's authority
stemming from his messengership (*risalah*) are numerous, for example, II:143:

"And we appointed the *qiblah* which ye formerly observed only that we might know him who followeth the messenger (*ar-rasul*) from him who turneth on his heels"; III:53: "Our Lord! We believe in that which Thou hast revealed and we follow him whom Thou hast sent (*ar-rasul*)"; III:132: "And obey Allah and the messenger (*ar-rasul*), that ye may find mercy"; etc. In all such references, obedience to Muhammad is a direct consequence of his *risalah*, messengership of Allah, which becomes a connecting link between Allah and Muhammad. Through Muhammed the authority of Allah is sought to be established on earth, and through Allah the authority of Muhammad is legitimated. *Ar-risalah al-Muhammadiyyah* (the Muhammadan messengership) indicates the charismatic authority that Muhammad possessed as the messenger of Allah.

The second principle states that the Islamic term "must identify the nature of this authority as 'charismatic,' that is, a 'personal gift' received from the source of legitimacy." According to the Islamic doctrines, Muhammad was the seal of all the prophets (*Katim al-nabiyyin*) that Allah has sent to guide humanity. There shall be no other messenger after him. "Muhammad is the messenger of Allah and the seal of the prophets" (Qur'an XXXIII:40). Many messengers have been sent before Muhammad, such as Adam, Noah, Abraham, Moses, and Jesus; but to the Arabs of the seventh century, only one messenger was believed to have been sent, and that was Muhammad. According to the Qur'an, Allah "never sent a messenger save with the language of his folk, that he might make the message clear for them" (Qur'an XIV:4). This is a direct reference to Muhammad as an Arab prophet and to the Qur'an as an Arabic scripture. In the historical context Muhammad was believed to be the only messenger who received the "gift" of communicating between Allah and humanity. This *risalah* constituted the charismatic/personal nature of Muhammad's authority. "Muhammad is the messenger (*rasul*) of Allah," the Qur'an states (XLVIII:29). He was the sole recipient of this title, the only Muslim in such proximity to Allah, and this established his charismatic authority.

The third principle asserts that the Islamic text "must entitle the recipient of the charisma to use physical force to establish his authority." Throughout the Qur'an the divine command "to fight" and "to kill" is addressed to Muhammad as the "messenger." At the commencement of the battle of Uhud (625), Allah addressed Muhammad in the Qur'an: "And when thou settest forth at daybreak from thy housefolk to assign to the believers their position for the battle (*qital*), Allah was Hearer, Knower" (Qur'an III:121). Allah commanded the Prophet and his followers to fight and promised them victory: "O Prophet! Exhort the believers to fight. If there be of you twenty steadfast they shall overcome two hundred, and if there be of you a hundred (steadfast) they shall overcome a thousand of those who disbelieve, because they (the disbelievers) are a folk without intelligence" (Qur'an VIII:65). The use of physical force was granted to Muhammad in order to establish his authority and, through him, Allah's. "Warfare is ordained for you" (Qur'an II:216); "Come, fight in the way of Allah" (III:167); and "Fight in the way of Allah against those who fight against you" (II:190), Allah commands the believers. Such use of physical force is rendered legitimate because it establishes, ultimately, the authority of Allah. Since Muhammad was His messenger, the use of legitimate violence was permissible.

The fourth principle is that the Islamic term "must be specific to Muhammad, and no one else within the Islamic context could claim a *similar* charismatic authority." The argument presented for the "charismatic" and "personal" nature of Muhammad's authority, the second principle, is applicable here, too. Whereas both *karamah* and *wilayah* may be applied to any pious Muslim, *risalah* is the prerogative of Muhammad alone. No one among the Muslims can claim this status. Only Muhammad was chosen by Allah to be His mesenger; and this uniqueness was the source of "the messenger's" charismatic authority.

Finally, the fifth principle suggests that the Islamic concept "must be a clear and distinct term, immune to oscillating interpretations and readings." As opposed to *wilayah*, which has many connotations, the various forms of *risalah* are used consistently throughout the Qur'an to denote "the messenger" of Allah, either those before Muhammad, such as Moses and Jesus, or Muhammad himself. *Ar-risalah al-Muhammadiyyah* constitutes the charismatic authority that Muhammad possessed and exercised as the "last messenger of Allah" and which entitled him to use legitimate physical force to establish this authority.

The formulation of this Islamic concept introduces the Weberian sociology of domination—at its most relevant theoretical level—to the seminal period of Islam. But the typology of charisma and its precise conceptual transliteration into Islamic terminology is the starting point for applying the Weberian sociology of authority to Islam. It cannot but be considered the first step in a long process. A hermeneutic explication of the concept of charisma is only a prelude to a careful understanding of the cultural framing of this mode of authority. What must be recaptured, following Weber's own successful studies of different charismatic settings, is the whole texture of social relationships holding the original charismatic leader together with a vast, evolving, and singular community (*ummah*). But for the purpose of this study, the specific conceptualization of Muhammad's charismatic authority in the Islamic context will render the Weberian sociology of domination immediately accessible to the early period of the Islamic political culture. I will now examine the juxtaposition of Muhammad's "charismatic authority" (*risalah*) against the Arab traditional order as the necessary background of the later doctrinal/political movements in Islam.

4

Establishment of Muhammad's Charismatic Authority: Emergence of a New Order

> *O ye who believe! Choose not your fathers nor*
> *your brethren for friends if they take pleasure*
> *in disbeliefs rather than faith.*
>
> —Qur'an IX:23-24

Muhammad's charismatic movement was a revolution in the political culture of Arabia, in the full sense of the term. His success was not predicated on a corrupt or exhausted political culture. A revolution breaks with the political culture of the past by incorporating it into a new ordering of command and obedience. A defeated cultural order, moreover, is no indication of its corruption. There are as many continuities between the pre- and post-Islamic political cultures as discontinuities. The most important link between the two cultural structures is the essential modality of a hierarchical—interdictory, transmissive, and transgressive—order of authority which is atemporal and universal. But even in the construction of the new hierarchical order of authority, Islam, elements of the superseded order, the pre-Islamic Arab culture, were used.

The traditional Arab mode of authority could have continued or been internally modified without experiencing a fundamental reorientation. Muhammad's prophetic mission redesignated the source of authority from "the eternal yesterday" to an Omnipresent Supreme Deity, Allah, who authored legitimacy from "above" instead of from "behind." Allah's Omnipresence encompassed the "eternal yesterday." Not only all Arabs but all humanity, especially those to whom previous divine emissaries had been sent, came under the authority of Allah. As the mouthpiece of Allah, Muhammad redefined the Arab traditional order and established with Islam a new political culture.

The process of the establishment of Muhammad's charismatic authority was a complicated course of events and related revelations. In the period between 610, when Muhammad received the first Qur'anic verses, until his death in 632, an intricate interplay between divine revelations and political events gradually established his charismatic authority.

47

Among Muslim theologians there have been disagreements as to whether Muhammad's ancestors were "monotheists" (*muwahhid*) or "polytheists" (*mushrik*). Al-Mas^{c}udi (d. 957) reports that

> people have disagreed about ^{c}Abd al-Muttalib. Some have said he was a mono-theist and a believer, and neither he nor any other of the Prophet's (may God's Greetings and Benedictions be upon him) ancestors ever disbelieved the Al-mighty God, and that the Prophet descended from pure ancestry, and the same told that he [^{c}Abd al-Muttalib] was a legitimate and not an illegitimate son. Some others have said that ^{c}Abd al-Muttalib and all other ancestors of the Prophet have been disbelievers. And this question among the Shi^{c}ites, Mu^{c}ta-zilites, Kharijites, and Murji^{c}ites, and other sects . . . is a point of disagree-ment. (1977, 49)

This disagreement makes the expression of Muhammad's charismatic author-ity against the order of his forefathers emphatically clear.

Muhammad's authority was fundamentally different from the traditional authority of a tribal chief, whose position was legitimated by what Weber called the "eternal yesterday, i.e., . . . the mores sanctified through the unimaginably ancient recognition and habitual orientations to conform" (Weber 1946, 78-79). The position Muhammad occupied was not that of a tribal chief but of an Arab prophet, which was a totally new concept in seventh century Arabia.

Islam was the first genuine Arab religious event that the peninsula had experienced; but it was not the first religious experience, as such. Primitive local polytheism had long been experienced in the Arabian peninsula; in addition, Judaism, Christianity, Zoroastrianism, and Manichaeism had also been introduced into various parts of the peninsula. Shahid refers to

> a new force, namely religion, [which] enters into the dynamics of Near Eastern history, and continues to acquire momentum throughout the whole of this period from the fourth to the seventh centuries. The peninsula is now surrounded by vigorous, newly rejuvenated states, and each of the two contestants for suprem-acy, Christian Byzantium and Zoroastrian Persia, have definite religious and economic policies which operate to the disadvantage of southern Arabia. (1970, 12-13)

Yet despite this widespread presence of Christianity, Zoroastrianism, and Judaism, they had not penetrated enough into the fabric of the society to form an essentially religious order such as Zoroastrian Persia or Christian Byzan-tium. The decisive character of pre-Islamic Arabia remained fundamentally tribal patrimonialism with no particular religion, in the most systematic sense of the word, giving it a religious definition or purpose.

In the traditional order of pre-Islamic Arabia, tribal solidarity was the most significant form of social structure. This solidarity was manifested by such practices as a tribe collectively avenging a crime perpetrated on one of its members or a tribe's being held collectively responsible for a crime that one of its members had committed. This was, in fact, a form of brotherhood in blood. Thus, when a particular murderer was not killed to avenge his act, any other member of his tribe could be killed instead.

Muhammad's charismatic authority established a new order of social solidarity. It substituted brotherhood-in-faith for brotherhood-in-blood, which went against traditional Arab practices. In the reemergence of old Arab practices after the death of the Prophet, mainly among the Muslim majority, the traditional Arab solidarity most emphatically sought to reassert itself. In Abu Bakr's rise to power, in the subsequent election of the other three rightly guided caliphs, in the establishment of the Umayyad caliphate as a purely Arab dynasty, etc., traditional Arab practices of tribal solidarity found their most expressive manifestations. In certain aspects of the Shiᶜite and Kharijite movements, however, attempts were made to perpetuate the innovative Muhammadan doctrine of brotherhood-in-faith. Such dimensions of the Shiᶜite and Kharijite movements attracted, most obviously, the sympathy and active approval of non-Arab Muslims (*mawali*).

From the moment it was launched, the Muhammadan *risala* (divine mission) introduced a totally new political phenomenon in Arabia. In all of its particularities, as well as in the unique reformulation of some elements of its religious and cultural antecedents, Muhammad and his movement constituted a turning point in the history of Arabia. Yet, after the death of Muhammad, and once his charismatic authority started its course of institutionalization, some fundamentally strong pre-Islamic characteristics started to play major roles in determining the directions that Muhammad's charismatic authority would undergo in the process of its seeking to be permanently established.

A charismatic authority always strives to establish itself above and against a traditional society. In the process of its establishment, it may incorporate some of the major traditional elements, always with a new understanding, into its particular *Weltaanschaung*. The incorporation of Kaᶜbah, a sacred site in pre-Islamic Arabia, into Islam constituted a major expression of this general tendency. Those aspects of the tradition which are not incorporated into the charismatic authority and are strongly rejected in the new order will remain suppressed until time occasions their reemergence. Muhammad's prophetic authority superseded the traditional Arab authority in a most universal way. Despite incorporating some elements of traditional authority with new definition, the Muhammadan authority left no room for its predecessor to remain operative. The hierarchical structure of the moral demand system, in its interdictory, remissive, and transgressive levels, remained constant; changed were the particularities that constituted these motifs. There were still acts that Arabs, as Muslims, were proscribed from doing, as members of a "common symbolic" world. But these acts did not necessarily coincide with acts that Arabs, as "pagans," did not do before.

The nature of Muhammad's authority was all-inclusive. His mission, from the very beginning, was as political as it was religious, and ethical. Even the separation of Qur'anic verses into the Meccan (more religious) and Medinan (more political) tractates is arbitrary, because the very message of Islam is universal and thus includes both social and political aspects. As Watt has noted:

> from the first the religious message proclaimed by Muhammad had been ad-dressed to a *qawm* or *ummah*, a "tribe" or "community," that is, to a body politic of the type familiar to the Arabs. When Muhammad was accused of political aspirations, the Qur'an instructed him to reply that he was only a "warner"; but this warning was a warning to the whole community that such false attitudes as niggardliness and pride in their own power would lead to catastrophe, and in order to correct such attitudes something approaching po-litical activity would be necessary. The Qur'anic phrase (88.22) that Muham-mad is not a "controller" (= "overseer"—*musaytir*) over the Meccans may reflect the feeling among some of them that he was in danger of becoming so because he had access to a superhuman source of knowledge about what was good or bad for the community. This would indicate that the political relevance of his preaching was felt even by his opponents. (1968a, 27)

Watt's treatment, however, is too narrow. The universality of Muhammad's message, at this level, leaves no place for specifying his political authority. As the messenger of Allah, who is Omnipotent, he had command over all practical and spiritual aspects of the believers' lives.

In order to arrive at the Islamic theory of authority, the Qur'anic verse VII:158 should be considered carefully:

> Say (O Muhammad): O mankind! Lo! I am the messenger of Allah to you all—(the messenger of) Him unto whom belongeth the Sovereignty of the heavens and the earth. There is no God save Him. He quickeneth and He giveth death. So believe in Allah and His messenger, the Prophet who can neither read nor write, who believeth in Allah and His words, and follow him that haply ye may be led aright.

This verse must be read in the light of Weber's assessment that

> experience shows that in no instance does domination voluntarily limit itself to the appeal to material or affectual or ideal motives as a basis for its continuance. In addition, every such system attempts to establish and to cultivate the belief in its legitimacy. (1978a, 213).

Nowhere is this inculcation of belief present more strikingly than in the process of Muhammad's establishing his charismatic authority. In fact, the belief in the legitimacy of his charismatic authority gradually became so powerful that it survived despite occasional military and political defeats, such as the battle of *Uhud,* and not because of such victories as *Badr* or the Meccan conquest. The Qur'an as a whole is a testimony to the hardships endured by the early followers of Muhammad whose success in establishing his divine mission was as much, at least, the result of the belief of a pious and devoted elite as the result of his political and military successes. It is true that there is a fundamental difference between the Islam that Abu Bakr, ᶜAli, or ᶜUmar professed, on essentially religious grounds, and that which Abu Jahl, probably the staunchest enemy of Muhammad, or Khalid ibn Walid and ᶜAmr idn ᶜAs professed, essentially on material grounds.

Weber recognized that "loyalty may be hypocritically simulated by individuals or by whole groups on purely opportunistic grounds or carried out in practice for reasons of material self-interest" (1978a, 214). It is the overall and essential mode of obedience between a community and a leader that determines the existence and type of authority. The initial success of Muhammad during his lifetime aside, the continuing success of Islam as such was also determined not by sword alone but by the works of mind and heart. It is true that most conversions to Islam in its early phases took place in lands that were conquered by the Muslim armies and that there were social and economic incentives to become a Muslim. But the Arab armies of bedouin soldiers were followed by local armies of theologians, philosophers, and Sufis who won the minds and hearts of the nominal converts. Authority of an order is implemented, as Weber recognized, not only by "external means" but by "inner justifications" as well. Moreover, such considerations as whose obedience to Muhammad was genuine and whose false

> are not decisive for the classification of types of domination. What is important is the fact that the particular claim to legitimacy is, to a significant degree and according to its type, treated as "valid"; that this fact confirms the position of the persons claiming authority and that it helps to determine the choice of means of its existence. (Weber 1978a, 214)

"Obedience," Weber noted,

> will be taken to mean that the action of the person obeying follows in essentials such a course that the content of the command may be taken to have become the basis of action for its own sake. Furthermore, the fact that it is so taken is referable to the formal obligation, without regard to the actor's own attitude to the value or lack of value of the content of the command as such. (1978a, 215)

Muhammad's charismatic authority and obedience to it posed the question of whether it is possible to maintain the dichotomous assertion that "the command may be taken to have become the basis of action for its own sake" and doing so "without regard to the actor's own attitude to the value or lack of value of the content of the command as such." These two assertions create a tension, if not essentially contradicting each other. Obedience to a command is taken only if there is something compelling in the command itself when there is a genuine belief in its validity. "The actor's own attitude" is inseparable from the mode of authority to which he is a subject. In fact, the only guarantor of the perpetuity of any mode of authority, and particularly charismatic because of its lack of institutions, is this inner attitude or justification of legitimacy on the part of the follower. "Formal obligation" can rely on only two pillars—external means and inner justifications—as Weber himself recognized. There is no separation of form and content in this or any other case.

Another source of Muhammad's legitimacy was his knowledge of past events. Allah informed him of these events in order to establish a particular code of conduct and subsequently indicate to him that the source of his knowledge was divine inspiration (Qur'an III:44).

Of His own volition, God favors some of His creatures. This was not peculiar to Muhammad. Mary, for example, was chosen (*istafa*) and purified (*tahharah*) by God (Qur'an III:42).

In the case of other divinely chosen figures of authority, the Qur'an postulates the possibility of their reconstituting an existing moral demand system by releasing elements of its interdictory motifs (Qur'an III:50). This passage, which is related to Christ, serves as the historical antecedent of Muhammad's charismatic authority.

Perhaps the most revolutionary idea that was introduced to the Arab political culture through Muhammad's charismatic movement was the whole notion of prophethood. There are, of course, intrinsic cultural antecedents for prophethood in the Arab environment itself. At various levels of authority, *sha'ir, kahin,* and *hanif* have represented personal figures of authority. But judging from the Qur'an itself, Muhammad was a messenger (*rasul*) within the same category that Adam, Noah, Abraham, Moses, and Jesus were emissaries of God. Although a generally Semitic notion, with some parallels in the Zoroastrian tradition, prophethood as the human mouthpiece for divinity, or the Supreme Divinity, was immediately connected to the Judaic tradition of this archetype.

Abu al-Qasim Muhammad ibn ʿAbd Allah ibn ʿAbd al-Muttalib ibn Hashim, the prophet of Islam, was born in Mecca around 570. ʿAbd Allah, the Prophet's father, died before Muhammad was born. This common factor among the major prophetic figures is of particular importance insofar as the establishment of their charismatic authority is concerned. Moses, as the prototype of the prophetic figures, was "taken" from the Nile and never associated with a father; Jesus was "the Son of God," in his original Christological context, and thus never physically associated with an earthly father. The lack of a natural father facilitated the establishment of a direct relationship between the Prophet and the ultimate source of charismatic authority: God. This connection can assume any form from a father-son relationship, in the case of Jesus, to a common man-God relationship, as in the case of Muhammad. In such a situation, it becomes manifestly easier to be considered as bestowed with the *gift of grace*. Muhammad, according to the Qur'an (III:144; IX:128; X:2), was a common man.

Muhammad began his preaching at about the age of forty. One of the most important aspects of the early stage of the Prophet's mission was the support he received from his wife Khadijah who was extremely instrumental in the early stages of Muhammad's preachings. Undoubtedly, the course of the Prophet's life and mission would have been drastically different had it not been for the devotion, love, care, encouragement, sacrifice, and moral support (not to mention financial sponsorship) that she willingly offered her husband. Khadijah did not live to see the full flowering of Muhammad's mission and died three years before his migration from Mecca to Medina; but she saw him through the most trying years of his early preachings and the hostile persecutions by the Meccan establishment.

Muhammad's active mission began in 612 when he received the first revelations. His initial period of doubt and uncertainty was overcome, thanks to Khadijah's moral support and assurance. Between 612 and 615, there continued a series of revelations in which Allah proclaimed Himself to be the One and the All-Powerful, and the Meccans were warned of the day of judgment. There were few, yet significant, conversions to Islam. First Khadijah accepted Islam; subsequently Abu Bakr and ⁣Ali became the first Muslims. Because of Abu Bakr's position, a considerable number of Meccans accepted Islam as well. Ibn Hisham provided a full description of these early converts (1955, 115ff.).

After the "Abyssinian migration," in which a number of the Prophet's early supporters were sent to Abyssinia, Muhammad continued preaching until 619, when the severest blows to both his personal life and his mission occurred with the deaths of his wife Khadijah and his protective uncle Abu Talib. Khadijah's support not only kept his morale high but also made him financially independent and secure; and Abu Talib, as one of the leaders of the Quraysh, protected Muhammad from the Meccan hostility to a considerable extent.

On September 24, 622, following an invitation by a group of men from Yathrib, the future *Ansars*, Muhammad made a crucial move, migrating from Mecca to the city which later became known as *Madinah-al-nabi* (the city of the Prophet). The political pressure in Mecca had become intolerable; it is believed that there were plans to assassinate the Prophet and that, in fact, he managed to flee from the city in disguise. The Muslims of Mecca migrated with Muhammad to Medina, and they came to be known as *Muhajirun* (those who migrated). In Medina, Muhammad first managed to exemplify the most fundamental substance of his message, the brotherhood of man, by unifying the *Muhajirun* and *Ansar* in a sacred bond of brotherhood. This was a remarkable event in the early development of Islam because for the first time a new unit of social solidarity, the Islamic community, was created against the traditional tribal loyalty and bondage. The Prophet's charismatic authority began to exert itself most emphatically.

The next move for the Prophet was to consolidate his authority in Medina. This consolidation was best represented in the drafting of a document, now known as the Constitution of Medina, legitimating the new social and political order. The document begins:

> In the name of God! the Merciful, the Compassionate! This is a writing of Muhammad the prophet between the believers and Muslims of Quraysh and Yathrib (sc. Medina) and those who follow them and who crusade along with them. They are a single community distinct from other people. (Watt 1961, 94)

As the last sentence clearly indicates, Muhammad was concerned particularly with the distinctive character of this community. It is one of the major characteristics of charismatic movements that a simultaneous destructive and constructive process is pursued. While the most fundamental manifestations of the given tradition are superseded, a counterpart is simultaneously constructed. Keenly aware of the paramount importance of community solidarity, Muhammad was determined to build the edifice of his new religion on such a foundation. But tribal solidarity, as it existed in Arabia, not only presented a practical political problem for Muhammad's higher aspirations for Arabia but, on a more substantial level, contradicted the universal claims of Islam. Thus, the principle of communal solidarity was preserved while its definition changed. Now "Muhammad the prophet" defined this solidarity and not "the authority of the 'eternal yesterday'"; the bond was now "between the believers and Muslims" and not among the brothers of one blood.

The next phase in the Prophet's tumultuous life was a series of military encounters between the Muslims and the Meccan establishment. The most famous of these battles were known as *Badr, Uhud,* and *Khandaq.* During these and other battles, which occurred from 624 to 632, Muhammad was at the peak of his power. He countered the Meccan establishment with the obvious expression of his charismatic authority, that is, physical force. While gradually eliminating the Meccan opposition, these battles established and consolidated, ever more strongly, the Prophet's authority in the newly formed

Muslim community. The battles were seen as fights in the name of God (*al-Jihad fi sabil Allah*); victories were considered signs of Allah's favor, while defeats were understood as signs of His disappointment with the community.

The winning over of the Meccans, the ultimate test of Muhammad's supreme authority in Arabia, was simultaneously a process of the increase in Muhammad's power, in a range of different domains, and the decline of the Meccan supremacy in Arabia. The series of attacks on the Meccan caravans, trading between Syria and Mecca paralyzed the commercial nerves of the city, on the one hand, and provided moral and material support for the Prophet's mission and message, on the other.

Finally, on March 13, 628, Muhammad decided to go to Mecca for what is known as a lesser pilgrimage (*ʿUmrah*). With a force of 1,600 men he approached Mecca. The Meccans thought Muhammad's intentions were hostile and sought to prevent his approach militarily. The Prophet circumvented the Meccan army and at the outskirts of Mecca resided on the edge of the sacred territory of Mecca known as *al-Hudaybiyah*. The Meccans still insisted on countering Muhammad with force. Ultimately a peace treaty was signed between the two parties (now in equal standing), according to which Muhammad was to return to Medina and not perform the *hajj* that year, while the Meccans would evacuate their city the next year for three days so that the Muslims, headed by the Prophet, could come to the city and conduct their pilgrimage.

On January 11, 630, Muhammad, "the Prophet of Allah," triumphantly entered Mecca. Only one column of the Muslim forces, headed by Khalid ibn al-Walid, met any semblance of resistance. Muhammad did not seek revenge against the Meccans for the persecution to which they had subjected him, a revenge which in the cultural context of Arabia was his right. He declared a general amnesty and forbade the pillage of the city. The Meccans at last surrendered to Islam.

There were a few other battles after the conquest of Mecca, but the Meccan victory can undoubtedly be considered as the final stage of the consolidation of the Prophet's authority. This supremacy was achieved through a process in which religious doctrines and beliefs corroborated and sanctified the military and political actions of the Prophet from one direction and military and political successes authenticated and accredited the claims of prophetic authority from the other. The former worked for the Muslims of Medina and the latter for those of Mecca. But this dialectical mechanism of legitimation provided Islam, eternally, with a material/ideal continuum on the foundations of which Islam became a major world religion.

On Monday, June 8, 632, Muhammad died in Medina, having established the foundations of a universal religion; no more can be said of the extent to which his authority was manifested, nor of the material testimony to his charismatic authority. When Muhammad died, he had provided his community with a holy book, the Qur'an, to guide the most detailed aspects of their lives. He had also established a Muslim community, a new form of social solidarity unknown to pre-Islamic Arabia. With his message and through his charismatic authority, Muhammad consolidated and unified the peninsula religiously and politically, to an extent never before attained in its history. He provided the Muslims with the momentum to defeat and consequently absorb the most vital forces of the two major civilizations of the time, the Sasanids and the Byzantines, the former more than the latter. Muhammad's charismatic authority was manifested in a variety of ways: He was a military commander, a general for the Muslim soldier; he was the political leader of the administrative apparatus of Muslim society; he was the religious leader who intervened between the *ummah* and Allah; and he was the spiritual leader who inspired the minds and hearts of all the Muslim saints in the generations to come. The domains of his charismatic authority recognized no limits. He established this authority by appealing to the omnipotence of Allah. Allah legitimated his authority; no man could disobey him. He expressed and established, in less than twenty years, his charismatic authority against the traditional order of Arabia.

Muhammadan *risalah* launched a powerful momentum in the course of Arab social experience. From the beginning of Muhammad's active preaching in 610 to his death in 632, a pervasive and new phenomenon was injected into the normal and traditional course of Arab society. This powerful injection fundamentally altered the course of history not only in Arabia but also in all other societies which came under the religious and cultural hegemony of Islam. Pre-Muhammadan and post-Muhammadan Arabia were two essentially different societies. The former was regulated by an ancient tradition, and the latter was a genuinely religious community originating in a charismatic movement.

The Qur'an specifically indicates that Muhammad was the last prophet to be sent by Allah: "Muhammad is not the father of any man among you, but he is the messenger of Allah and the seal of the prophets; and Allah is ever aware of all things" (XXXIII:40). After Muhammad, no direct line of divine revelation would be established between God and humanity. This was the most crucial aspect of the Muhammadan legacy, because he had introduced a new political order—a facade of the sacred order he had established—that Arabs and other Muslims had to deal with thereafter. He formulated the doctrinal belief that he was the last prophet and thus created an authority vacuum, the occupation of which was the most crucial problem, both theoretically and practically, of the Islamic community. Who was to succeed Muhammad, the last prophet of God, in his multidimensional authority?

Due to the prophetic nature of Muhammad's authority, the type of solidarity that he created in the Muslim community was fundamentally different from any known to the Arabs. The Muslims were considered to be brothers in faith under one God, regardless of their tribal affiliation or social status. It is true that *ummah* was a functional equivalent of a tribe in terms of its characteristics, but it was different from a tribe in terms of its *raison d'être*. Transtribal and cross-familial solidarity in the Islamic *ummah* clearly indicated that it was founded on a distinct and unique criterion. The Constitution of Medina maintains that Muslims are "a single community distinct from other people" (Watt 1961, 94). This community was "distinct from other people" because it was defined differently. It was not defined in terms of blood relationships, as traditional tribes had been, but in terms of Muslim brotherhood under one God. This major theme of the Islamic *ummah* was one of the most significant characteristics of the Muhammadan legacy and continued to play an active role in the future course of Islamic history.

The legacy of Muhammad's charismatic authority was left to the Islamic community. If this community, as the external expression of the Islamic faith, were to survive, the authority of the Prophet and, through it, the authority of Allah had to be institutionalized. In a famous passage concerning the aftermath of a charismatic movement, Weber maintained that:

> in its pure form, charismatic authority has a character specifically foreign to everyday routine structures. The social relationships directly involved are strictly personal, based on the validity and practice of charismatic personal qualities. If this is not to remain a purely transitory phenomenon, but to take on the character of a permanent relationship, a "community" of disciples or followers or a party organization or any sort of political or hierocratic organization, it is necessary for the character of charismatic authority to become radically changed. Indeed, in its pure form, charismatic authority may be said to exist only *in statu nascendi*. It cannot remain stable but becomes either traditionalized or rationalized, or a combination of both. (1978a, 246)

Whether the character of the charismatic authority is "radically changed" or not, the institutionalization of the charismatic authority, in one way or another, is necessary. It is obvious that as a religious force that had dominated the society for a period of twenty-three years, appropriating all claims to authority, the charismatic authority of the Prophet could not be ignored.

The necessity of the institutionalization of charismatic authority is further complicated by the simultaneous problem of its being segmented into various domains. Charismatic authority, as such, is a complex set of different authorities. It consists of a number of domains of legitimacy, such as political, religious, or spiritual. Muhammad was not only considered the supreme head of the Islamic community but, as the Prophet of Allah, he was also the ultimate source of religious authority. He, for example, led the pilgrimage from Medina to Mecca as one expression of his authority and led the public prayers as another. As the obvious indication of his authority, in the profession of faith, immediately after acknowledging that "there is no God but Allah," one confesses that "Muhammad is His messenger."

Such charismatic leaders develop the nucleus of their initial authority, over a period of time, into a complex body of multidimensional authorities. A multidimensional charismatic authority, as such, becomes a prism that from one side receives the light of the original source of his authority (as from Allah in the case of Muhammad) and from the other side emanates a variety of specific and particular forms of legitimate authorities.

Initially starting, for example, from a "spiritual" authority over a limited group of individuals, Muhammad extended his authority, in due course, to encompass "political" and "religious" domains. By "spiritual," the reference here is to authority over nonmaterial, mental, intellectual, sentimental, or emotional aspects of an individual or a community. This should be distinguished from religious authority, which refers to Muhammad as the central figure of the institutionalized form of Islamic beliefs and rituals.

When Muhammad started his preachings, he had only a few devotees (members of his immediate family) who believed in and supported him: Khadijah, his wife; ᶜAli, his cousin; Abu Bakr, an influential Meccan; and a few others. But this devotion could not be said to be on any religious grounds because as yet there was no systematic form of belief, either formulated or established. Neither was it a devotion due to any political authority because not only did Muhammad at this stage not command any such authority, but he was even under persecution by the Meccan political establishment. At this stage the attraction and devotion of Muhammad's immediate followers could not but have been on primarily spiritual, nonmaterial grounds.

However, following Muhammad's migration from Mecca to Medina in 622, he gradually developed both religious and political authority as he maintained spiritual authority. In the process of developing and maintaining these authorities, the Qur'anic revelations continued to form a body of religious beliefs and precepts, while the initial groups of *Muhajirun* (the Emigrants) and *Ansar* (the Helpers) were extended into a large community; furthermore, by commanding a series of attacks on the Meccan caravans trading between Mecca and Syria, and arbitrating a number of tribal disputes among the Medinese, and a few other political maneuvers, Muhammad consolidated and established his religious and political authority. Finally, Muhammad's triumphant return to Mecca in 630 was the ultimate point in the development of his leadership into a complex body of political, religious, and spiritual authorities.

Such differentiation in the range of the Prophet's authorities, however, is basically intended for analytical purposes. The actual charismatic authority, at any given moment, is a complex web of different types of potential capabilities to enforce obedience. These capabilities are independent of one another and do not follow, necessarily, a chronological or logical pattern of realization. The distinction among these different forms of authorities is an analytical device to facilitate the initial penetration into the logic and mechanism of the charismatic authority.

The complexity and totality of charismatic authority, in all of its different dimensions, is not, nor can it be, maintained after the death of the charismatic leader. The absence of the charismatic figure, to embody all of these different dimensions, is the most immediate reason for the breakdown of his authority. This absence inevitably occasions the segmentation of charismatic authority into different domains. It is only in the figure of a charismatic authority, such as Muhammad, that all of these authorities could be accumulated, maintained, and commanded. The death of the charismatic leader creates a new situation in which no single figure can command unchallenged the same types of omnipotent authorities that the actual charismatic leader maintained. Although this segmentation of Muhammad's authority is evident in the general course of Islamic history, there has been an attempt in the Shiᶜite branch of Islam to maintain the totality of Muhammad's authority and infuse it into the figure of the *Imam*. The *Imam,* in the Shiᶜite view, maintains a level of totality in his authority which, although in a general hierarchical order below the level of the Prophet, is multidimensional and omnipotent. But this is a theme to be developed more fully later.

A crucial factor that influences this process of segmentation is the profundity and extent of the original authority as exercised by the charismatic leader. The more complex and multidimensional the nature of such an authority in its original form, the more diversified and intricate the network of its potential possibilities for the emergence of different domains and ranges of authority in the process of its institutionalization.

To examine this process one step further and specifically consider it in its Islamic manifestation, the depth and range of Muhammad's authority are to be seen essentially as reflections of the omnipotence of Allah, who is the ultimate source of this authority. Allah, according to the Qur'an, is the Omnipotent, Omniscient, and Omnipresent Supreme Being. "Truly, God is powerful over everything" is one of the major leitmotifs of the Qur'an. Thus, one of the most influential factors enriching the charismatic authority of Muhammad, extending the domains of its preeminence into a vast body of different social and personal spheres, and ultimately being manifested in the complications of the institutionalization process, is the Omnipotent Allah. It is Allah who has bestowed upon Muhammad the distinguished position of "messenger." Since Muhammad derived his authority from Allah's will, then this authority is a reflection of the Omnipotence of that Original Source and, subsequently, has a command over all the diversified domains of the Islamic community (*ummah*) and over all of the different activities of a Muslim as a member of this community.

The Omnipotence of Allah, the charismatic authority of Muhammad, his relation to Allah, and the supremacy of Allah/Muhammad over the *ummah* and individual Muslims are best represented in the following verse:

> Say (O Muhammad): O mankind! Lo! I am the messenger of Allah to you all—(the messenger of) Him unto whom belongeth the Sovereignty of the heavens and the earth. There is no God save Him. He quickeneth and He giveth death. So believe in Allah and His Messenger, the Prophet who can neither read nor write, who believeth in Allah and His words, and follow him, that haply ye may be led aright. (Qur'an VII:158)

Allah is also the "Lord of the Worlds" (I:2), "Owner of the Day of Judgment" (I:4). The Qur'an indicates that "knowest thou not that it is Allah unto whom belongeth the Sovereignty of the heavens and the earth" (II:107). This absolute authority is also manifested in His mastership of the universe: "Unto Allah belongeth whatsoever is in the heavens and whatsoever is in the earth. Allah ever surroundeth all things" (II:151).

Muhammad is the intermediary between Allah and the Muslims. He is a messenger, sent by Allah to guide people. Authority of the Prophet is thus legitimated by his being chosen by God. "Even as We have sent unto you a messenger from among you, who reciteth unto you Our revelations and causeth you to grow, and teaches you the Scripture and wisdom, and teaches you that which you knew not" (II:151).

Obedience to God and His Messenger are simultaneous: "And obey Allah and the Messenger, that ye may find mercy" (III:132). Also: "Say: Obey Allah and the Messenger. But if they turn away, Lo! Allah loves not the disbelievers (in His guidance)" (III:32). Obedience to Allah, manifested in the expression of love for Him, is considered as contingent upon obedience to His Messenger: "Say (O Muhammad, to mankind): If ye love Allah, follow me; Allah will love you and forgive you your sins. Allah is Forgiving, Merciful" (III:31). Both divine mercy and the salvation of man are contingent upon such obedience to the Prophet. Allah says in the Qur'an that "We sent no Messenger save that he should be obeyed by Allah's leave" (IV:64). The hierarchy of authority is from Allah to Muhammad to men; and the direction of obedience is from men to Allah through Muhammad. The omnipotence of Muhammad's authority is a reflection of the authority of Allah.

This is not a mere theological concern and is immediately translated into daily routine life. The whole structure of social action, in the Parsonian understanding of the term, is established on the basis of this hierarchy. In evaluating the Weberian conceptualization of charisma, Parsons realized that it is . . . not immediately related as such to action—it is a quality of concrete things, persons, acts, etc. But a hint of relation to action is given in the kind of attitude men make toward charismatic things or persons. Weber applies a number of terms, but two may be singled out. Applied to a person the charismatic quality is exemplary (*vorbildlich*), something to be imitated. At the same time recognition of it as an exceptional quality lending prestige and authority is a duty. (Parsons 1973, 622)

The "exemplary" and "authoritative" nature of charismatic figures regulates the social action according to the new moral demand system that it seeks to establish. Such attributes of a charismatic movement extend the Weberian assessment that it is essentially transitory into new domains. In its revolutionary spirit and while disrupting the traditional order, the charismatic movement seeks to establish a new order, that is, a new moral demand system, a restructuring of social action. In some significant ways this constructive aspect of charismatic movement may be in a nascent condition, but in many other ways, particularly in the case of Muhammad and Islam, it establishes the fundamental cornerstone of a new and permanent structure of authority.

In the interval between the death of the prophet in 632 and the establishment of the Umayyad dynasty in 661, a period of twenty-nine years, four caliphs ruled the Islamic community: Abu Bakr (632-634), ʿUmar (634-644), ʿUthman (644-656), and ʿAli (656-661). With the exception of Abu Bakr, who died naturally at an old age, the other three "Rightly-Guided Caliphs" met violent deaths. They were all brutally murdered in the tumultuous post-Muhammadan period of early Islamic history. This violence is a testimony to the difficult and transitional nature of this short and crucial period. The charismatic event itself is a crucial revolutionary experience in the political life of a people. The disappearance of the charismatic figure is a disruptive event that the society should endure successfully if that movement is not to pass as only a transitional event with no lasting effect.

Weber maintained that

for charismatic leadership, too, if it wants to transform itself into a perennial institution, the basic problem is that of finding a successor to the prophet, hero, teacher or party leader. This problem inescapably channels charisma into the direction of legal regulation and tradition. (1978a, 1123)

This inescapability assumes a different direction in the case of Islam. Charismatic authority and its legacy do not function in an authoritative vacuum. Inevitably they have expressed themselves against a rational/legal or traditional background. In the Islamic case, the traditional Arab mode of authority did not yield completely to the Muhammadan charismatic legacy. It reemerged to shape the post-Muhammadan period. Out of this confrontation, as we shall see in subsequent chapters, a variety of combinations grew. The case of Shi^cite Islam will demonstrate that it was fundamentally charismatic in its nature. It sought to perpetuate, in the figures of the *Imams*, the charismatic legitimacy in positions of authority.

Concerning the particular problems surrounding the succession of a charismatic figure, Weber believed that,

> given the nature of charisma, a free election of a successor is originally not possible, only the acknowledgment that the pretender actually *has* charisma. Hence, the followers may have to wait for the epiphany of a personally qualified successor, temporal representative, or prophet. Specific examples are the incarnation of Buddah and the Mahdis. (1978a, 1123)

Again, the case of Shi^cite Islam demonstrates that followers can try to perpetuate the charismatic legacy without necessarily or initially resorting to a Mahdi figure. The position of ^cAli was charismatic for his followers, not because he was believed to be a Mahdi but because of his proximity, in both physical and spiritual aspects, to the Prophet. To be sure, there were many movements in the first three centuries after the death of Muhammad which historically had been branded as *hululiyyah* (those who believe in "the incarnation of the soul") and could be considered as "Mahdi" movements (because they believed in the emergence of a savior), such as the group of *Bayaniyyah* who believed that the divine spirit was incarnated through the prophets, to a certain Bayan ibn Sam^can, or *mughayriyyah* who maintained the same thing about a Mughayrah ibn Sa^cid al-Jali, or many other such groups (al-Baghdadi 1954, 165-66). There was even one particular brand of Shi^cah, associated with an ^cAbdullah ibn Saba', who exaggerated the position of ^cAli to the point of divinity (a view not maintained by the *Imami* Shi^cites). Yet these instances were isolated movements, strong sometimes as they were, that did not constitute the main Shi^cite response, which, while it sought to perpetuate the charismatic mode of authority in the *Imams*, necessitated the continuity of the Islamic community.

So long as a charismatic leader is alive, he is the ultimate arbiter among his followers. He is the most immediate and imposing bonding factor that unites the supporters. Muhammad stood at the center of the newly formed Islamic community, and the social structure and spiritual unity of the Muslims were directly connected and related to him. Once he was physically removed from the center of this community, his charismatic legacy and the major contender for authority came into conflict with the defeated tradition that it had superseded.

The nature of this conflict is to be understood in terms of the two distinctly different modes of authority that they represented. Further, the intensity of this conflict is due to the "ethical" (the Weberian typology of prophets) nature of Muhammad's prophethood. Ethical prophets are always innovators of a new moral demand system, opposed to that of the traditional order. As Parsons pointed out:

> the ethical prophet feels himself to be the instrument of a divine will. As such a part of his mission is to give men ethical norms with which they are expected to conform. And by definition these norms are different from the existing traditional state of affairs . . . the source of the new norms, cannot be merely a manifestation of the imminent order of the world as it is. Only the conception of a transcendental personal God, concerned with, but not in His essence involved in, the existing cosmic and human order, can be adequate to ethical prophecy. (1973, 568).

In Islam, *Allah* is that transcendental, although not "personal," God that is ultimately the source of the "new norms." Muhammad as a charismatic leader was the earthly figure who, by "divine grace," was selected to lead men to the right path. Muhammad's authority was thus legitimated through this divine decree:

> He it is Who hath sent among the unlettered ones a messenger of their own, to recite unto them His revelations and to make them grow, and to teach them the Scripture and Wisdom, though heretofore they were indeed in error manifest, along with others of them who have not yet joined them. He is the Mighty, the Wise. That is the bounty [*Fadl*] of Allah, which He giveth unto Whom He will. Allah is of Infinite bounty. (Qur'an LXII:2-4)

Muhammad as a charismatic figure and Islam as his religious legacy sought to change, fundamentally, the entire Arabian traditional culture. This fundamental change, however, was the direct outcome of the interaction between the legacy of the Muhammadan charismatic authority and the traditional Arab order. The distinction made here between the traditional Arab order and Muhammad's charismatic authority is based essentially on the latter's introduction of a new set of interdictory, remissive, and transgressive motifs to legitimate the hierarchical structure of authority with which every society regulates its self-understanding. As such, the two modes are treated as "ideal types." Otherwise, many elements of Muhammad's "message" already existed in the Arab religious consciousness, although with a different significance. Here the Qur'anic reference that "we never sent a messenger save with the language of his folk, that he might make (the message) clear for them" (XIV:4) refers to more than just language in its semantic significance and includes the conceptual and symbolic frames of reference. Al-Mas^{c}udi reports, for example, that

> the Arabs in *jahiliyyah* [the pre-Islamic time] had many sects; some were monotheists and believed in God . . . and [believed that He] rewards the obe-

dience and punishes the disobedience. . . . Some believed in the creation of the
world and accepted the resurrection, yet they disbelieved in prophets. . . .
(1977, 485)

Shahid also has pointed out that

the term "pre-Islamic Arabia" is . . . a fortunate and a significant one, reflecting as it does, the decisive role which Islam played in changing its character,
both as a religion which appeared within its boundaries, and as a movement
which launched the Arabs on the path of world conquest. (1970, 3)

The most obvious, as well as the most important, aspect of this changed
character is the definition and location of political authority. As a new sacred
order, claiming universal atemporality, Islam introduced a specific set of
communal symbolics within which every mode of authority would have to
find and define its legitimacy.

The immediate aftermath of the death of a charismatic leader is, of course,
confusion and upheaval. It is the nature of a charismatic movement to be
totally dependent, for both its general direction as well as its minute daily
problems, on the figure of charismatic authority. In his character this figure
encapsulates all sources of authority. The universality of this figure of authority surpasses both time and space. In this universality the charismatic
authority assumes its overwhelming supremacy over an established traditional
order. Once this center of authority is absent, a vacuum is created that can be
filled only with the institutionalization of that original authority. The process
is long and elaborate; but the crucial force that leads to the assertive establishment of the institutionalized authority is the charismatic legacy itself.

The charismatic legacy of Muhammad was Islam. As a new sacred order it
had its metaphysical foundations in the revelatory language of the Qur'an.
Through the particular stipulation in the message of Muhammad, according to
which Allah was the Supreme source of authority, Islam could survive the
death of its Prophet. "Islam" was the name given to the religion by Allah
Himself. "This day," says Allah in the Qur'an, "have I perfected your religion for you and completed My favor unto you, and have chosen for you as
religion Al-ISLAM" (Qur'an, V:3). Islam, in this sense, was a religion even
before Muhammad.

What makes it eternal is the metaphysical foundation of Islam that supersedes Muhammad. There remains, however, the question of the particular
way in which the followers of the deceased charismatic figure, who are also
the believers in his established religion, formulate a theory of leadership
compatible with its general metaphysical statement.

When Muhammad died on June 8, 632, he was not survived by a son. As
a result, the possibility of problems related thereto never materialized in
Islam. His adoptive son, Zayd ibn Haritha, was killed in one of the Prophet's

campaigns. The rest of his children were all females. Even if Muhammad had been survived by a son, the nature of the problems of succession would not have been drastically different, because the Islamic doctrine that designated him as the last prophet sent by God had set the specific theme upon which certain limited variations could have been realized, and they mostly did materialize.

The events that immediately followed the Prophet's death were of crucial importance for the rest of the Islamic history. The detailed account of these events, preserved in the Islamic sources, indicated the immediacy of their relevance for the specific course of the Islamic political culture.

While ⁽ᶜ⁾Ali and Ibn Abbas were in the process of preparing the Prophet's body for the ritual washing (*ghusl*) and burial, the *Ansar* gathered in a place known as *Saqifah bani-Saᶜidah*. *Saqifah* in Arabic means "roof," "ceiling," or "arch." This apparently indicated that for each tribe there existed a particular "arch" or "ceiling" under which matters of general communal concern were discussed. *Banu Saᶜidah* is the name of a tribe, apparently chosen for this settlement because of its being a neutral party to the *Aws* and *Khazrahj*, the main antagonist parties among the *'Ansar*. This account has been reported in most Islamic historical sources, including al-Baghdadi's *al-Farq bayn al-Firaq* (1954), al-Shahrastani's *al-Milal wa al-Nihal* (1979), and al-Tabari's *Ta'rikh al-rusul wa al-muluk* (1879-1901). Saᶜd ibn ᶜUbadah, chief of the *Khazraj* tribe, was nominated to become the leader of the Islamic community. 'Asid ibn Hudayr, chief of the *'Aws* tribe, a tribe traditionally hostile to the *Khazraj* (the *'Aws* and *Khazraj* were the two major tribes of Medina who provided the Prophet from 621 on with protection while remaining tacitly hostile to one another), came to the *Muhajirun* and informed them of the intentions of Saᶜd ibn ᶜd ᶜUbadah and his *Khazraj* supporters. Abu Bakr and ᶜUmar, two of the Prophet's closest companions, in the company of a number of other *Muhajirun* came to the *Saqifah* and saw Saᶜd ibn ᶜUbadah, ailing and weak, sitting in a position of authority at the gathering while a spokesman described his and his tribe's virtues. Among these virtues the spokesman referred to the fact that while the Prophet's own tribe, the Quraysh, persecuted and forced him to depart from Mecca, the *'Ansar* welcomed him and embraced Islam. Thus, he argued, the *'Ansar* were, more than any other tribe, entitled to the succession of the Prophet's authority.

The formation and internal composition of this tribal council at this juncture was a remarkable phenomenon that revealed the immediate complexity of the postcharismatic anxiety. Initially it clearly indicated the persistence of the traditional mode of tribal procedure for the selection of a chief, as it had been practiced in Arabia since time immemorial, and the introduction of a new element, namely, the loyalty and obedience to the Prophet of Allah. This was the first and most significant instance in which the traditional Arab practices were reintroduced into a fundamentally Islamic event. The very formation of this tribal council constituted a fundamental antithesis to the new mode of authority that Muhammad as the Prophet of Allah, had introduced. As it was presented and established, Islam was a universal order that explicitly regulated the entire way of life of those under its authority. The crucial question of choosing the new leader of the Islamic community could not remain out of this jurisdiction. The reemergence of the tribal council in deciding the fate of the Muslim leadership was an immediate revival of the temporarily defeated traditional order, bidding for the recognition and reestablishment of its own mode of authority.

Saᶜd ibn ᶜUbadah's bid for leadership was challenged by 'Asid ibn Hudayr, chief of the 'Aws tribe. The hostility between the 'Aws and the Khazraj tribal divisions of the 'Ansar prevented them from attaining a unified position on who should succeed the Prophet. 'Asid ibn Hudayr informed the Muhajirun of the 'Ansar's intention to choose the next leader of the Muslim community. In response to the spokesman for Saᶜd ibn ᶜUbadah and the Khazraj tribe, basically an 'Ansar bid for power, Abu Bakr gave a speech praising the Muhajirun and defending their right to succession on the grounds of their being the first group of Arabs to embrace Islam and to yield to the Muhammadan authority in the most dangerous of all times. To this the 'Ansar responded with the famous statement of "a leader from us, a leader from you," which meant dividing the Muslim community into Mecca-Muhajirun and Medina-'Ansar segments.

Saᶜd ibn ᶜUbadah, chief of the Khazraj tribe, had a cousin, Bashir ibn Saᶜd, who was his rival in leadership over their tribe. Once Bashir ibn Saᶜd realized that the 'Aws were about to select Saᶜd ibn ᶜUbadah as the leader of the Muslim community, contrary to his tribal affiliation, he gave a speech in support of the Muhajirun and their initial right and supremacy over the 'Ansar in succeeding the Prophet. Furthermore, he argued that Prophet Muhammad was from the Quraysh tribe, and thus it was more appropriate for this tribe to choose his successor (al-Tabari 1879-1901, 4:1820-25).

Bashir ibn Saᶜd's argument, again, presented the persistence of traditional Arab ideas of tribal affiliation that, while totally alien to Islam as a claim to a universal sacred order, found their way into the most crucial moments of Islamic history. From a purely Islamic point of view, the Quraysh could not claim any position of authority simply because Muhammad happened to be from that tribe. Membership in the Quraysh tribe as a prerequisite for Islamic leadership constituted yet another element of Arab traditionalism emerging into the Muhammadan charismatic legacy.

Abu Bakr then argued for his case by maintaining that for the unity of the Islamic community and its survival in the future it was important that Muslims have only one leader and that he should be from the Prophet's tribe (the

Quraysh). He then nominated either Abu ᶜUbaydah ibn al-Jarrah or ᶜUmar ibn al-Khattab, two of the most prominent members of the *Mahajirun,* as the successor to the Prophet. They both refused to accept the responsibility and, in turn, asked (and thus nominated) Abu Bakr himself to succeed the Prophet. They argued that Abu Bakr was one of the oldest members of the *Mahajirun,* he had been among the first to embrace Islam, and he had accompanied the Prophet in his flight from Mecca to Medina. Abu Bakr, furthermore, had led the public prayers when Muhammad, due to some preventive reasons, could not do so. ᶜUmar ibn al-Khattab, Abu ᶜUbaydah ibn al-Jarrah, and Bashir ibn Saᶜd then took Abu Bakr's hand, a traditional sign of acknowledging the leadership of tribal chief, and proclaimed him the successor to the Prophet and leader of the Islamic community. Abu Bakr went to the Prophet's mosque, and subsequently the Muslims, *Muhajirun* and *Ansar,* rushed to acknowledge his authority (*bayᶜah*). Saᶜd ibn ᶜUbadah did not recognize the authority of Abu Bakr, nor did he recognize the authority of the Abu Bakr's successor, ᶜUmar. he went to Syria where he was later killed, probably at the instigation of ᶜUmar (al-Dinawari 1936-37, 1:2-10; al-Nawbakhti 1963, 6).

ᶜAli refused to pledge his allegiance to Abu Bakr. ᶜUmar's intervention to secure his *bayᶜah* was useless. Abu Bakr was so frustrated that he went to the mosque and asked to be relieved of his responsibility, to which people responded negatively. As long as Fatima, ᶜAli's wife and the Prophet's daughter, was alive, ᶜAli would not acknowledge Abu Bakr's authority, but once this symbolically most powerful connection of ᶜAli to the Prophet's family died, he extended his allegiance to Abu Bakr while still asserting his right to succeed the Prophet (Ibn al-Athir 1851-76, 2:325-32; al-Tabari 1879-1901, 4:1825-30; al-Yaᶜqubi 1883, 2:102-5.)

From the course of his prophetic career, it is quite evident that Muhammad recognized the uniqueness of his mission against the background of traditional Arab culture. He could not have remained indifferent to the fate of his community vis-à-vis the presence of traditional forces that had just been defeated and inevitably would have sought a renewal at a favorable opportunity. A Qur'anic verse suggests this concern: "Muhammad is but a messenger, messengers (the like of whom) have passed away before him. Will it be that, when he dieth or is slain, ye will turn back on your heels? . . ." (Qur'an III:144). He must have realized that the fate of his faith and the question of leadership of his community were ultimately inseparable. His remaining indifferent would have been but a negation of the entire "divine mission" that constituted the source of his legitimacy.

As Watt (1968a, 31) has indicated, however, the general Arab practice of the tribal council deciding on the fate of the leadership governed the process of finding a successor for the Prophet, and that is how Abu Bakr was elected. But the adoption of one traditional Arab custom, selecting a leader, was not an isolated phenomenon. It was a particular manifestation of a more general and fundamental trend in which traditional Arab tribal customs sought to reemerge in the post-Muhammadan era and to attain the lost grounds.

ᶜUmar died in 644. Before his death, he nominated a council of prominent Muslims to select the next caliph. This council consisted of ᶜAbd al-Rahman ibn ᶜAwf, ᶜAli, ᶜUthman, Talhah, Zubayr, and Saᶜd ibn abi Waqqas. ᶜUmar had willed that this council be responsible for choosing the next caliph by a majority vote within three days after his death. If there were a split decision among the members, the caliphate should go to the person selected by that group in which ᶜAbd al-Rahman ibn ᶜAwf was a member. If the opposing group did not yield, they would have to be executed. Apparently, the reason for this special privilege being given by ᶜUmar to ᶜAbd al-Rahman was the fact that he was the only member of the group who was not a candidate for the caliphate. The pre-Islamic traditional forces, at work after the death of the Prophet, were here being strongly manifested. The destiny of the Islamic community, inseparable from its leader and the process of his selection and legitimacy, once again was being determined not by an Islamically mandated decree but by councils and prominent members as prescribed by traditional Arab customs. Qualifications for candidacy were now being considered objectively: leadership qualities, political perspicacity, etc. The candidates were then being weighed against one another and the most suitable candidate selected. These were all specific manifestations of traditional pre-Islamic Arab customs finding their way back into the political and social life of post-Muhammadan Arabia.

ᶜAbd al-Rahman favored the caliphate of ᶜUthman and finally gave his vote of confidence to him. ᶜUthman was elected as the third caliph of the community, and the Muslims were urged to pledge their allegiance to him (Ibn al-Athir 1851-76, 3: 65-75; al-Shahrastani 1979, 1:18).

There are a number of immediate factors that precipitate the institutionalization of charisma into specific channels. Weber maintained that

> the routinization of charisma, in quite essential respects, is identical with adjustment to the conditions of the economy, that is, to the continuously effective routines of workaday life. In this, the economy leads and is not led. (1946, 54)

But routinization of charisma is not a spontaneous act necessitated only by the economic needs of a faithful community. The more general trend, which includes a secure economic continuity, is the whole traditional way of life that had been defeated and now seeks to reemerge for recognition and ascendancy.

Weber identified two principles which in combination constitute any mode of authority: (1) "inner justification" and (2) "external means" (1946, 78). In an attempt to clarify these two concepts, Parsons called them "disinterested" and "interested" motives (1973, 659). The defeat of traditional order may be attributed to the appropriation of all "external means," economic and political, by the charismatic authority. The "inner justifications," always the more persistent and deep-rooted of the two motives, however, are still operating, despite the charismatic victory, at various social and psychological levels. It is an important question whether they can ever be "totally" eradicated by the charismatic revolution. Certainly the charismatic authority, as any other, carries its own set of "inner justifications." Ultimately, only one set of internally homogeneous "inner justifications" can constitute the legitimacy of a claim to authority. Otherwise, a confusing state would emerge that could be identified as "cultural paralysis."

From the election of Abu Bakr in *Saqifah Bani Sa^cidah* (632) to the establishment of the Umayyad dynasty (661), there was a continuous flow of traditional elements finding their way into social and cultural recognition, sometimes acting directly against the precepts of the Prophet's message.

The emergence of traditional motifs in the post-Muhammadan period further complicates the process of routinization. Weber's assessment that material forces necessitate the routinization of charisma is too economically oriented. There were many traditional forces, such as the process of choosing a leader, tribal affinity, Arab hegemony, etc., that Arabs introduced into their administration of the Islamic state that had no direct, or even indirect, bearing on the economy as such. Tradition and its active forces are a reality *sui generis*. It is true that economic necessities constantly pushed the postcharismatic period towards a degree of stability and routinization. Yet these economic necessities were imbedded in a broader trend of traditional customs seeking to leave the charismatic event as a historical memory in their past and resume a more routine definition of life.

What Weber categorically brought under the rubric of the "routinization of charismatic authority" was a complicated course of events for Islam that consisted primarily of the old and new, that is the traditional and the charismatic, modes of authority interacting in their bid for supremacy. This broad categorization is related to Weber's "transitory" treatment of charismatic authority and is precisely the point that Parsons referred to in his following evaluation of the Weberian typology:

> the principal difficulty of the concept [charisma] arises from the fact that he [Weber] did not, apparently, originally conceive it in these general terms in relation to a scheme of the structure of action. It was, rather, conceived of in terms of a much more specific theory of social *change* and developed from there. (1973, 663)

Furthermore, Weber thought that upon the death of the charismatic leader, "incipient institutions" will substitute aspects of his authority (1946, 54). This emergence is due, according to Weber, to the "cooling off" of the extraordinary states of devotion and fervor (54). The early developments of Islamic history clearly show that in the case of the Muslim majority this was, in fact, the case; yet the significant Shi^{c}ite minority, as they gradually developed, pointed to the possibility of the continuity of the charismatic authority in most, if not all, of its dimensions.

The original doctrines of the charismatic figures, Weber maintained, would have to be "intellectually adjusted to the needs of that stratum which becomes the primary carrier of the leader's message" (1946, 54). The Quraysh aristocracy became the stratum that was the primary carrier of the Prophet's message. But Weber was not quite specific in this case. What forces the intellectual—as well as the spiritual, social, political, and cultural—adjustments of the leader's message is the deep-rooted attachment of that stratum to its traditional mores, temporarily in eclipse behind the presence of the charismatic authority.

Having identified (1) the superseded presence of the traditional Arab order seeking recognition in the absence of the prophetic authority, as well as (2) the legacy of Muhammadan charismatic authority and (3) the possibility of its segmentation, I will now devote the next three chapters to an examination of the three particular ways in which Muhammad's charismatic authority was institutionalized out of an interaction among these three forces. An institutionalization which is otherwise known as the major branches of the early Islam.

5

The Foundations of Sunnite Authority: The Routinization of Charisma

> *Muhammad is but a messenger, messengers (the like of whom) have passed many before him. Will it be that, when he dieth or is slain, ye will turn back on your heels?*
>
> —Qur'an III:144

The question of the "orthodoxy-heterodoxy" dichotomy creates a false distinction in the case of Islamic doctrinal developments. More facts are concealed than revealed by applying such dichotomies. As Watt has pointed out:

> The word "orthodox" is out of place in an Islamic context. . . . Indeed, Islam has had no machinery comparable to the Ecumenical Councils of the Christian Church which could say authoritatively what constitutes "right doctrine." (1973, 5-6)

The complexity of doctrinal developments, even within the Sunnite branch of Islam itself, prevents a monolithic categorization of "orthodoxy." More-over, at least two centuries prior to 1000, the year Watt supplied as the consolidation date of Sunnite doctrines, the Shi^{c}ite *fiqh* was fairly well es-tablished by the time of Ja^{c}far al-Sadiq (700-765), the sixth Shi^{c}ite imam. As adherents to *al fiqh al-Ja^{c}fari* (the Ja^{c}farite law), the Shi^{c}ites of this time would not have recognized themselves as "heterodox" Muslims. "Orthodox" and "heterodox" are polemical, not hermeneutic terms; they conceal a web of intricate relationships—social and doctrinal. A theoretical penetration into the foundation of the Sunnite, as well as the Shi^{c}ite and Kharijite, theories of authority is an unpacking of these terms. The extended battleground of doc-trinal oppositions in Islam clearly verifies that "orthodoxy . . . is successful heresy" (Rieff 1959, ix). It is the political success of a given interpretative reading that renders a religious position "orthodox." "Heresies" and "het-erodoxies" are partially defeated "orthodoxies"; and all these are concealing terms.

Muslim heresiographers were largely responsible for the creation of the "orthodoxy/heterodoxy" dichotomy, however indirectly. Writing their heresiographical accounts, these Muslim writers necessarily evaluated each particular formulation of the doctrinal, institutional, and devotional dimensions of Islam from their own vantage points. Their particular perspectives, to a large degree, determined the characterization of their doctrinal opponents. Watt has pointed out that

> Through my own work in this field and that of other scholars I have become convinced that, before any attempt is made to describe the development of Islamic thought, there has to be a radical critique of the sources. The standard Muslim writers see theological doctrines as already given in the revelation and as unchanging; as Henri Laoust has put it, they are concerned not with "the history of the sects" but with "a normative classification of these sects" in respect of their greater or lesser distance from Sunnism. (1968, v)

What constitutes the fundamental character of different branches of Islam is not whether they are "orthodox" or "heterodox" but the particular position that they maintain vis-à-vis Muhammad's charismatic legacy. As the initiator of a new religious culture, Muhammad had expressed Islam against an ancient traditional order. The dialectical relationship between the various particularities of these normative systems constituted the fundamental character of different Islamic branches; and it is in such terms that the various branches of Islam must be understood. To answer the most universal question, by what authority? Sunnite Islam, as did the other two branches, formulated a particular response, stemming from the aforementioned dialectical relationship, that ultimately and essentially constituted its religious character.

Weber saw the particularities of providing an answer to the question of by what authority? or, as he formulated it, "when and why do men obey?" culminating in the period of succession.

> The way in which this problem [of succession] is met, if it is met at all and the charismatic community continues to exist or now begins to emerge, is of crucial importance for the character of the subsequent social relationship. (1978a, 246)

The subsequent social relationship is determined by the particular way that the question of succession is addressed. Yet, as I will argue in this and in the next two chapters, in Islam there were a number of positions vis-à-vis this question; and, moreover, the problems surfacing at the moment of Muhammad's death were much more complex, as indicated in the last two chapters, than just finding a successor to the charismatic figure and the routinization of social relationships.

The Sunnite branch of Islam may be identified with the following three characteristics: (1) the immediate and rapid routinization of Muhammad's charismatic authority and a great propensity to the resumption of an "ordinary" life, (2) the extended influence of the pre-Islamic traditional Arab mode of authority, and (3) the fundamental segmentation of Muhammad's charisma into various spheres. As the most obvious expression of these trends on a societal level, the continued significance of the Quraysh aristocracy as the chief political elite should be noted.

The "resumption" of an ordinary daily life coincides with the Weberian notion of a "routinized" charisma, that is, social actions based on a fixed normative order. Two modifications must be made here. First, to the degree that the dialectical interaction between the two competing modes of authority has not been resolved fully, the moral demand system within which social actions are defined and oriented is still in a state of flux. The traditional Arab culture was, to a considerable degree, present, yet the intense spiritual experience of Muhammad's charismatic authority animated the Islamic normative order and fundamentally challenged the superseded moral demand system. This flexibility, however, was effectively terminated in a short period of time and through the institutionalization of Muhammad's authority. Second, the rapid military expansion of the nascent Islam, particularly during the reigns of ᶜUmar (634-644) and ᶜUthman (644-656), constantly engaged the young Muslim community in warfare. The "ordinary daily life" was thus subsumed under a general state of war.

As Weber observed, "In its pure form charismatic authority has a character specifically foreign to everyday routine structure" (1978a, 246). This generally characterizes the charismatic period of the nascent Islam. Despite the fact that, after the conquest of Mecca in 630 and before the death of the Prophet in 632, there was a resemblance of routine life in Medina, Mecca, and their vicinities, in which Muhammad presided over the Muslim community, the daily life of the believers was very much determined by the Qur'an and the prophetic Sunnah. It is important to realize that, somewhat contrary to the Weberian characterization, the social relationship pertaining to the charismatic authority of Muhammad was not totally "transitory" and "arbitrary." He personally was the ultimate source of authority, as the messenger of Allah; yet the Qur'an carefully establishes the major foundations of the Islamic moral demand system, sometimes in the minutest details. The early Muslim community lived according to these rules and under Muhammad's authority. There are verses in the Qur'an that abrogate previous ones (*nasikh* verses); but, on the whole, the Qur'an in its original form, that is, without the subsequent commentaries and exegesis gradually giving rise, along with the prophetic traditions, to *shariᶜah*, does represent a consistent and homogeneous moral demand system.

But since the structure of the communal society was ultimately centered on the Prophet's personal charisma, inevitable change and transformation of this mode of authority were to ensue. The particular social relationship established in Medina after the first year of Hijra, 622, as specially formulated in the Medinan Constitution (Watt 1968a, 130-34), inevitably necessitated the physical presence of charismatic personal qualities (Weber 1978a, 246). The most striking manifestations of such personal qualities were the Qur'anic revelations, through the authority of which Muhammad resolved innumerable problems that arose during the period of his active preaching, from 612 to 632. An example of such employment of the Qur'anic revelation, the sole prerogative of the Prophet, occurred when Muhammad decided to change the direction of *qiblah* from Jerusalem to Mecca, thereby creating confusion and disagreement among the Muslims. In resolving this problem, the Qur'anic verse II:142 is revealed, according to which:

> The foolish of the people will say: what hath turned them from the *qiblah* which they formerly observed? Say: Unto Allah belongs the East and the West. He guideth whom He will unto a straight path.

There are many such examples in the Qur'an thus giving rise to a particular tradition in Islamic sciences known as *asbab al-nuzul* (the occasions of revelation) that sought to identify the exact historical situation in which particular verses were revealed.

Weber maintained that if the charismatic movement

> is not to remain a purely transitory phenomenon, but to take on the character of a permanent relationship . . . it is necessary for the character of charismatic authority to become radically changed. (1978a, 246)

The forceful impression of Muhammadan charismatic authority, in a period of twenty-three years, upon the Arabian traditional culture, particularly animated by Islamic metaphysical sophistication, was too powerful to be easily discarded by the reemergence of traditional Arab authority in the post-Muhammadan period. Islam as the legacy of Muhammad and as extensively constituted in the Qur'an and prophetic traditions could not be experienced as "a purely transitory phenomenon" in Arabia. Institutionalization of Islam, in whatever form, was the extensive process of securing its permanence, symbolized by its formulating and prescribing a very particular form of "permanent relationships."

For the Muslim majority the most fundamental form of the "routinization" of Muhammad's charisma is observed—if by this term we refer to what Weber considered as the necessity of "charismatic authority to become radically changed" and institutionalized. This institutionalization period is inevitable for the gradual formation of permanent social relationships. On this process, Parsons maintained that institutionalization itself is in the nature of the case an evaluative phenomenon, a mode of the organization of the system of action. Therefore, the patterns which are institutionalized in the nature of the case involved an element of value-orientation on the social system level. (1951, 51)

In the postcharismatic period this "organization of the system of action" was ultimately the end result of the dialectical interactions between the constituent elements of charisma and the superceded traditional order. This process is gradual, and "value-orientation," explicit in the mode of institutionalization, is in a state of flux. Given the universality of the emerging order, if the ensuing moral demand system, that is, the emerging religious culture, is to survive, ultimately the "social-integrative" must be greater, both quantitatively and qualitatively, than the "ego-integrative."

Although the political constitution of the Muslim majority remained basically hierocratic, it considerably altered the nature of Muhammad's charismatic authority. It is reported (Ibn Hisham 1955, 682-83) that when Muhammad died, a group of Muslims gathered in the mosque of Medina. ʿUmar, totally distracted by the event, proclaimed it a sin to consider the Prophet dead, that he was alive and had never died. Abu Bakr was credited with having intervened at this point by maintaining that "Lo! as for him who worshipped Muhammad, Muhammad is dead, but as for him who worshippeth Allah, Allah is alive and dieth not." Then he recited the Qur'anic verse III:144:

> Muhammad is but a messenger (the like of whom) have passed away before him. Will it be that, when he dieth or is slain, ye will turn back on your heels? He who turneth back on his heels doth no hurt to Allah, and Allah will reward the thankful.

This episode exemplifies the attitude adopted by the majority of the Muslims, according to which the Prophet had died, Islam was his chief legacy, and life had to go back to a state of "normality."

This does not imply that other Muslims refused to accept the death of the Prophet. But their attitudes toward his death and its significance were quite different and thus consequential to their view of post-Muhammadan authority.

Perhaps the most remarkable aspect of the pre-Islamic traditional influence on the post-Muhammadan period was the direction of "traditionalization," in the Weberian sense, that Muhammad's charismatic authority assumed for the Muslim majority. The relationship between these two modes at this crucial period was best formulated by Parsons:

> in this case [the prophetic mission defining new norms] it takes the form of a traditional system of norms (a sacred law) which carries the same quality of sanctity, of charisma, as the person of the ruler. . . . By this process, from being the specifically revolutionary force charisma becomes, on the contrary, the specific sanction of immobile traditionalism. (1973, 664)

Weber identified two "principal motives underlying" the transformation of charismatic authority into its routinizing forms. The first he called "the ideal and also the material interests of the followers in the continuation and the continual reactivation of the Community," and the second "the still stronger ideal and also stronger material interests of the members of the administrative staff, the disciples, the party workers, or others in continuing their relationship" (1978a, 246). Having sided with Muhammad in his initial fight against the Meccan establishment and having fully participated in the tumultuous vicissitudes of early Islam, not to mention their genuine devotion to the faith, the Prophet's companions had both ideal and material interests in the continuation of Islam as the legacy of Muhammadan charismatic authority. Here the distinction between ideal and material interests becomes rather out of place in Islam, in whose particular formulation of religious and worldly affairs the two were practically inseparable. By following a religious injunction of *zakat* (almsgiving), one was necessarily performing an economic (material) act; and conversely, by engaging in trade, the Prophet's profession, one was simultaneously performing a religious (ideal) act. *Hajj* (pilgrimage to Mecca) was not incumbent upon Muslims unless they reached a certain degree of economic (material) prosperity; thus wealth becomes a predicate of a religious act.

The establishment of *ummah* as the Islamic community was the most significant expression of Islamic solidarity against the traditional tribal structure. It had sought to nullify and supersede its predecessor. As a "collectivity," the pre-Islamic Arab society could not be considered, as it was by Hitti, to have "developed no ancient culture of its own" (1970, 87). If by "culture" we mean a "common symbolic" or a "moral demand system" (in Rieff's theory of culture), no human collectivity, however "primitive," is without a culture. Any particular combination of interdictory, remissive, and transgressive motifs constitutes a culture. The identification of Arabs other than those of al-Hijaz and Najd, that is the Arabs of Nabataeans, Palmyrenes, Ghassanids, or Lakhmids, with the higher Aramaic, Syro-Byzantine, or Persian cultures does not render the Najdites "cultureless." To the degree that man conforms to a moral demand system, he is cultured. As Rieff has pointed out:

> To be cultivated is to know, at least by indirection, through the artfulness of our recognitions, what it is to be obedient, and what is not, in those stipulations of sacred order that constitute authority in every culture. (1981, 229)

As the exemplifier of the new cultural order, the *ummah* had to be presented and maintained against all odds. Symbolically, the Islamic community, *ummah*, was Islam externalized. Despite its metaphysical universality, Islam was nothing if not a social reality.

Despite the predominance of the *ummah* as the general and most significant form of the Islamic social structure, tribal affinities continued to be operative against the doctrinal universality of Islam. The Quraysh, for example, as the tribe from which the Prophet had emerged, continued to be prominent for a long time in the course of Islamic history. The continuation of tribal hostilities in the post-Muhammadan period was yet another expression of tribal solidarity against "the continuation and the continual reactivation of the community." Another expression of tribal affinity was expressed in the form of the self-proclaimed superiority of the Arab conquerors over the non-Arab Muslims (*mawali*), who were forced to become clients of particular Arab tribes on an inferior basis. In evaluating the causes of the fall of the Umayyads (661-750), Watt has asserted that:

> the most important of these factors was probably the discontent of the large numbers of non-Arabs who had become Muslims, especially in Iraq and the eastern provinces. . . . This was not a principle of the religion of Islam, but . . . was something implicit in the nature of Arab political thinking. (1974, 27-28)

Al-Tabari reports an incident involving the question of *mawali*; and since it occurred in Tiflis, Georgia (in southern Russia) in the year 642-643, it illuminates the extent and dimension of influence that the pre- and non-Islamic practice of tribal affinity had in post-Islamic practices.

> This is a letter from Habib ibn Maslamah for the inhabitants of Tiflis of the Georgians . . . giving you safe-conduct for yourselves, your property, your convents, your churches, and your prayers, on the condition that you submit to the humiliation of the *jizyah* at the rate of a full dinar per household. . . . If you become Muslims and perform the prayer and pay the *zakat*, then you are our brothers in religion and our *mawali*. (1879-1901, 2675)

Mawali, the non-Arab Muslims who secured a client relationship with an established and powerful Arab tribe, demonstrated a specifically pre-Islamic practice, operative long before the rise of Muhammad. The Maslamah's letter revealed three points: (1) the economic significance of *jizayah* as an integral element of the state bureaucracy, (2) the persistence of old Arab practices, such as *mawali* relationship, and (3) the continuing validity of specifically Islamic notions established by Muhammad, such as "brothers in religion."

The idea of "full-blooded" Arabs was clearly a pre-Islamic notion, embedded in the network of tribal affinities that persisted against the universality of the Islamic community. The "full-blooded" Arab hegemony is expressed against the specific commands of the Qur'an that

> The believers are naught else than brothers.
>
> O mankind! We have created you male and female, and have made you nations

and tribes (*qabilah*) that ye may know one another. Lo! the noblest of you, in the sight of Allah, is the best in conduct. Lo! Allah is knower, aware. (XLIX:10, 13)

Qabilah is the technical term used for Arab tribes, as opposed to *ummah* for the Islamic community.

In disrupting the old traditional order, the new charismatic order had created its own administrative staff, their sole qualification being companionship with the Prophet. This administrative staff was considered universally to be "blessed" with proximity to Muhammad. This proximity later became the source of authority for these companions. In whatever direction the charismatic authority of Muhammad was routinized, the successors' authority always sought legitimacy through these initial associations or proximities. The superseded source of legitimacy, that is, tradition, was also still functioning as a distinct "authorizing" force. No moral demand system, and thus no motif of social action, even in a state of flux and transition, can function and sustain itself without such an anchoring force. Among the problems that Parsons identified in the various concepts of "power" was

> its conceptual diffuseness, the tendency, in the tradition of Hobbes, to treat power as simply the generalized capacity to attain ends or goals in social relations, independently of the media employed or of the status of "authorization" to make decisions or to impose obligations. (1969, 353)

The media employed and the source of authorization are both essential components of particular modes of authority which, in turn, determine, to a large degree, the course of men's social actions within any given moral demand system.

The ten most distinguished companions of the Prophet, to whom he had promised paradise (*al-ᶜasharah al-Mubashsharah*), were Abu Bakr, ᶜUmar, ᶜUthman, ᶜAli, ᶜAbd ar-Rahman ibn ᶜAwf, Abu ᶜUbaydah, Talhah, Zubayr, Saᶜd of Zuhrah, and Saᶜid, the son of Zayd the Hanif (Lings 1983, 329). To these one might add Salman the Persian and ᶜAmmar, of whom a prophetic hadith says "for three doth Paradise long, for ᶜAli, ᶜAmmar, and Salman" (ibid.), and Bilal the Abyssinian, the slave whom Muhammad bought and released and who then became famous for his beautiful voice to which the Prophet loved to listen when reciting *adhán* (the Muslim call to prayer). Salman and Bilal were particularly important, being non-Arabs, for symbolically signifying the supratribal solidarity of the Islamic community.

Weber further believed that the new administrative staff needed to change radically the character of the charisma, because "they have an interest in continuing it in such a way that both from an ideal and a material point of view their own position is put on a stable, everyday basis" (1978a, 246). Among the chief companions of the Prophet, four, Abu Bakr, ᶜUmar, ᶜUthman, and

^cAli, became the first four caliphs of the Islamic community. In the assumption of power by the elite members of the new order, there is an element of inevitability. If the newly expressed order of authority is to supersede the older and if it is to be institutionalized, those associated with the highest figure of that order must assume the most distinguished positions for social expression of the order, and consequently for the order itself to be legitimated. Moreover, as the faithful believers of the new sacred order, the companions represent and personify the faith at its best, and if Islam was to be taken seriously, they must rule over its community. This new order, whose elite must rule it to render it legitimate, is what Parsons called a *"system* of norms":

> perhaps the most general function of a society community is to articulate a *system* of norms with a collective organization that has unity and cohesiveness. . . . Societal order requires definiteness and clarity of integration in the sense, on the one hand, of normative coherence, on the other hand, of societal "harmony" and "coordination." (1969, 40-41)

In a state of transition, however, these aspects of "definiteness," "clarity," "harmony," and "coordination" in the normative system are temporarily in a state of flux. The process is from the traditional to the charismatic to the institutional dialectics of the two.

Weber identified six "principal possible types of solution" to the question of succession, following the death of a charismatic figure. Of these, only one addresses some particularities of the Muslim majority:

> Designation of a successor by the charismatically qualified administrative staff and his recognition by the community. . . . In such a case it is easy for legitimacy to take on the character of an acquired right which is justified by standards of the correctness of the process by which the position was acquired, for the most part, by its having been acquired in accordance with certain formalities. (1978a, 247-48)

The supratribal and universal claims of Islam, embedded in the Muhammadan message, prevented the possibility of considering the nature of authority in the post-Muhammadan period as a mere continuation of the pre-Muhammadan patrimonial order with a new cultural content. Although in many ways this was apparently the case for the Muslim majority, as fundamental a charismatic revolution as the Muhammadan experience cannot be considered as merely giving a new cultural content to an otherwise persistent and continuous mode of traditional authority.

Gibb, recognizing the tension between these two modes of authority, maintained that

> the establishment of the Umayyad Caliphate of Damascus (661) was thus the outcome of a coalition or compromise between those who represented the

> Islamic ideal of a religious community, united by common allegiance to the
> heritage of the Prophet, and the Meccan secular interpretation of unity, against
> the threat of anarchy implicit in tribalism. (1962,8)

The Meccan ideas of "unity" and tribal "anarchy," however, are both among
the political implications of Arab traditionalism.

During the process of routinization, Weber also referred to the major "types
of the charismatic staff" who are present in both the political as well as
economic domains. For the majority of Muslims, who will later be identified
as the Sunnites, the first Weberian typification identified some of the major
issues involved.

> The original basis of recruitment is personal charisma. However, with routin-
> ization, the followers or disciples may set up norms for recruitment, in partic-
> ular involving training or tests of eligibility. . . . . A genuine charismatic leader
> is in a position to oppose this type of prerequisite for membership; his successor
> is not free to do so, at least if he is chosen by the administrative staff. (1978a,I:249)

The particular "norm for recruitment" established by the "rightly guided"
caliphs, as well as the Umayyads, was for the individual to be an Arab, most
preferably from the same tribe as the caliph or from a tribe which he might be
forced to recruit from because of some intertribal obligations. Membership in
the tribe became so important that in many ways and instances they went
specifically against the injunction of either the Qur'an or the Prophet or both.
This again illustrates a remarkable example of the reemergence of traditional
Arab customs and mores against the specific demands of both Muhammadan
and Qur'anic injunctions.

"Norms for recruitment" and "tests of eligibility" had to be derived normally from the precepts of Islamic injunctions. Piety and righteousness, judged
on the evaluative scale of the Qur'an, had to function as proper criteria. Yet,
during the reign of ʿUthman (644-656), some remarkable manifestations of
tribal affiliations were demonstrated through an appropriation of political and
economic power by the members of his clan and tribe, sometimes despite
obvious hostilities between these figures and Muhammad.

Cases of ʿUthman's nepotism and expressions of his tribal loyalty are
abundant (al-Baladhuri 1959, 5). ʿUthman had a cousin named Marwan ibn
Hikam whom the Prophet had ostracized and who, in fact, was known as *tarid
rasul Allah* (one whom the Prophet of God has ostracized). ʿUthman recalled
Marwan from exile, gave him his daughter, along with a high-ranking administrative position, and one-fifth of the booty from an African expedition
which was reported to have amounted to two hundred thousand dinars. It was
also reported that a certain ʿAbdullah ibn Saʿd ibn Abi Sarah, whom the
Prophet had resented bitterly and ordered to be killed, a sentence from which
he escaped, was protected by ʿUthman and later appointed as the governor of

Egypt. ᶜAbdullah was a brother of ᶜUthman through milk (*ridaᶜi*, foster brother), that is, as infants they were both breast-fed by the same mother without their having the same father.

Likewise, ᶜUthman resented some of the close companions of the Prophet. On the instigation of Muᶜawiyah ibn Abu Sufyan, a fellow-tribesman, ᶜUthman exiled Abu Dharr al-Ghifari, one of Muhammad's closest companions, to a small town, *Rabadhah*, near Medina, where he remained in ᶜUthman's disfavor until his death in 652. The means of "closing the administrative staff" was essentially dictated by tribal affinities and considerations rather than by essentially Islamic criteria. As Von Grunebaum reports:

> ᶜUthman was a member of the family from which had come the last and most obstinate leaders of the Meccan heathens against the Prophet. He has been repeatedly accused of placing family interests before those of the Muslim commonwealth, since he conferred all the key posts of government to his relatives. Many of these men quite cynically and openly exploited these appointments to their own advantage. (1970, 59)

The pre-Islamic traditional Arab mode of authority was manifested in more than one respect in the form of routinization of Muhammad's charismatic authority for the Muslim majority. As a cultural complexity, the Arab tradition had many constituencies in which to seek a reemergence. The totality of this cultural complexity is now being realized gradually. Reflecting on the major scholarship concerning the pre-Islamic Arabs, Shaban maintained that

> a picture is now emerging of highly complex relationships in Arabia prior to the rise of Islam. These relationships linked the inhabitants of Makka with the inhabitants of most of the rest of Arabia, both nomad and settled, in expanding trade. This was international trade on a large scale which involved the two great powers of the time, the Sassanid and Byzantine empires. (1971, 2)

As the commercial and religious center of pre-Islamic Arabia, Mecca seemed to have had a cultural hegemony over the rest of Arabia. At the most fundamental level, political, Watt summarized the traditional Arab perspective:

> succession to the leadership of a nomadic Arab tribe had to take account of the fact that the continuing existence of a tribe might depend on its having effective leadership. When a chief died, therefore, he was normally succeeded by the best qualified person in a certain family. The decision was made by a meeting of the adult males of the family or tribe. It was a common idea among the Arabs that noble qualities were inherent in certain stocks and were genetically transmitted. (1968a, 35)

There was a remarkable resemblance between traditional pre-Muhammadan practice and the particular way in which the Rightly Guided Caliphs, especially Abu Bakr, were elected and their authority legitimated. Just as "the continued existence of a [pre-Islamic Arab] tribe might depend on its having effective leadership," so the Islamic community after Muhammad was considered by traditionally oriented Arabs, whether they belonged to the Quraysh, Áws, or Khazraj, as a tribe on a larger scale whose preservation and continuity depended on effective leadership which they thought should naturally come from the Quraysh, to which Muhammad belonged. Muhammad's self-understanding as a prophet, a messenger sent by Allah, was not as significant as his being a member of the Quraysh tribe. It was primarily to Muhammad as a tribal chief that the question of succession to his authority was addressed by the majority of Muslims. This was demonstrated further by the caliphs having primarily political and administrative, as opposed to religious or spiritual, significance.

On the differentiation of authority in pre-Islamic Arabia, a model against which Muhammad's charisma was broken, Watt has reported that

> The power of the *sayyid* [in pre-Islamic Arabia] was also limited by powers and functions given to other persons. Leadership in war was usually given by a special decision, and might be for a fixed period only. Mostly, it would seem, it was not the *sayyid* who was appointed as war leader. In some tribes, again, before adopting some new plan the soothsayer (*kahin*) would be consulted, and this would give some power to the soothsayer at the expense of the *sayyid*. Finally, there were disputes to be settled involving traditional law or custom. If the *sayyid*'s wisdom was respected, disputes between parties within his tribe would be brought to him. In other cases, however, and where he was not sufficiently respected, recourse could be had to those men of wisdom and integrity who were widely accepted as arbiters (sing. *hakam*). (1968a, 40-41)

A similar differentiation governed the routinization of Muhammad's authority for the Muslim majority.

Of the traditionalization of authority for the Muslim majority it should be noted that this was not a case of charisma becoming traditionalized in its own right, as Weber indicated. The event most consequential was a reemergence of pre-Islamic Arab traditional elements, by definition different from Muhammad's charismatic authority or its institutionalized forms, in the course of post-Muhammadan developments.

What historically grew to be recognized as the Sunnite branch of Islam is a historical case of the routinization of charisma in which the successor to the charismatic figure is not considered to be "endowed with charisma." Weber warned against the consideration of the process through which the successor is chosen by "election" or "nomination." But in light of historical facts surrounding the leadership of Abu Bakr, he could not but be considered as being nominated by ᶜUmar and elected by the tribal leaders in *Saqifah Bani-Saᶜidah*. To be sure, it was not a "free selection" of a leader but a selection essentially determined and governed by tribal precedence and customs.

The selection of Abu Bakr was not bound to any particular stipulation of Muhammad's authority, the Qur'an, or the *Hadith* but was a designation framed primarily within tribal rivalries as well as affiliations. The intricate relationships among the Áws, Khazraj, and Quraysh fundamentally shaped the outcome of the tribal council in *Saqifah Bani Saᶜidah*, as discussed in previous chapters.

That Abu Bakr was not considered by the Muslims to be "endowed with charisma" was reflected in the limited range of his authorities. Shaban has expressed this view, as well as the traditional tribal character of Abu Bakr's authority, pointing out that:

> one must be careful not to exaggerate the powers of Abu Bakr as *Khalifah Rasul Allah*, Successor of the Prophet of God. . . . Abu Bakr had no religious authority and, *in true Arab tradition*, his secular authority as a leader was kept to a minimum. (1971, 19: emphasis added)

The "true Arab tradition" as the main characterizer of the first "Rightly Guided Caliph," and the chief standard bearer of Muhammad, "the messenger of Allah," indicates the degree of penetration of the traditional Arab culture on post-Muhammadan developments.

Von Grunebaum also maintained that

> it was as a "representative" of the emissary of God, *Khalifah rasul Allah* . . . that Abu Bakr saw himself in his office. In the view of the gradually developing Islamic law, the succession of Abu Bakr had been established by election and made legitimate by *baiᶜa*, homage through shaking hands, at which those present also pledged the absent. (1970, 50)

Bayᶜah was the traditional mode of recognizing the authority of a tribal chief.

The speech given by Abu Bakr, on the occasion of his accession to the leadership of the Islamic community, was equally illuminative:

> Abu Bakr said . . . "I have been given authority over you but I am not the best of you. If I do well, help me, and if I do ill, then put me right. . . . Obey me as long as I obey God and His apostle, and if I disobey them you owe me no obedience." (Ibn Hisham 1955, 687)

As with the traditional Arab tribes in which "when a chief died . . . he was normally succeeded by the best qualified person in a certain family," so upon the death of Muhammad, the majority of Muslims, at that time mainly Arabs with strong tribal affiliations and attachments, acknowledged the authority of Abu Bakr, who undoubtedly was among the most "qualified persons" in the

Islamic community. Yet the criteria of his "qualifications" were essentially traditional measures honored by Arab customs. This is not to suggest that he lacked qualifications as a proper Muslim. On the contrary, he had been considered universally as a close companion of the Prophet, one of the first who, despite his high economic and political status and also despite his old age, accepted Islam wholeheartedly. The distinguishing factors, however, were the mode of legitimation and the procedure of his election, the two being inevitably inseparable, that established his authority. This consideration ultimately indicates that Abu Bakr's authority was essentially legitimated through tribal customs rather than through Islamic precepts.

In understanding the circumstances surrounding the nature of Abu Bakr's authority, it is important to realize the element of "crisis" usually associated with the initial charismatic experience. As Bendix has pointed out,

> charismatic leadership is a uniquely personal response to a crisis in human experience; those who succeed the charismatic leader therefore face the problem of preserving a personal charisma after the leader and the crisis have passed away and everyday demands have again come to the fore. (1960, 301)

Commerce was a crucial institution in the traditional Arab culture. Economic necessities forced the Muslim establishment, particularly those who were associated with the Meccan merchants, to resume a more normal and stable social order congenial to commercial activities. Those Muslims who thought the "crisis" was not yet over sought, simultaneously, to perpetuate the charismatic mode of authority. From within the Muhammadan charismatic experience and the legacy that is left behind, no "Islamic" perspective was derived according to which Abu Bakr's authority could be legitimated. Consequently, Abu Bakr became the de facto ruler of a religious community without being its inherently de jure authority. Abu Bakr's authority was, of course, universally recognized by all Muslims, with the exception of a small minority who supported ᶜAli. Yet this authority and its legitimation were essentially on traditional grounds and only as such de jure.

Watt has maintained that Abu Bakr's assumption of the title of *Khalifah rasūl Allah*, "the Caliph of the Messenger of God," had no particular religious significance. Reviewing the Qur'anic sources of the term, along with its commentaries, he has concluded that "it is thus unlikely that the Qur'an was the source from which Abu Bakr derived this title. It must come rather from the ordinary secular [by which Watt meant non-Islamic and thus necessarily traditional Arab] use of the word" (1968a, 32). He has also said that

> since Abu Bakr was not appointed by Muhammad except to deputize for him in leading the public prayers, the phrase "*Kahlifah* of the Messenger of God"

cannot have meant "deputy." The primary meaning must have been merely "successor," except that there would be a suggestion of "one succeeding in the exercises of authority." (1968a, 33)

Functionally there is no significant difference between a "deputy" and "one succeeding in the exercise of authority." As the caliph succeeding the political aspect of the Prophet's authority, Abu Bakr became the de facto leader of the Islamic community and, while not exercising that sweeping authority of Muhammad, for all practical purposes ruled over the *ummah*. But whereas the definition of his position as a caliph was, as Watt has put it, "vague" (1968a, 33), the procedure of his election was quite obvious. It was clear manifestation of traditional Arab customs reemerging in the most crucial decision of the early Islamic community.

Among the three reasons Watt has enumerated as the basic justifications of Abu Bakr's election, only one is somehow related to Muhammad's message and mission. The other two are indications of traditional Arab customs.

Abu Bakr was the most experienced person available. . . . He had a specially good knowledge of the genealogies—including the intrigues—of the nomadic tribes. His daughter ᶜAisha was Muhammad's chief wife. . . . In addition, Muhammad had appointed Abu Bakr to lead the public worship when his last illness prevented him from doing this himself. (1968a, 32)

Abu Bakr's knowledge of the genealogies of the nomadic tribes referred to his ability to establish viable credentials for himself as a traditional Arab leader, defined and legitimated essentially outside of the Islamic context. His being the Prophet's father-in-law "cemented the relationship between the two men" (Watt, 1968a, 32) strictly on criteria established by the patrimonial Arab society. It is only in reference to Abu Bakr's leading the public prayers that there is a reference to Islam and to the Muhammadan message.

The election and acceptance of Abu Bakr, who was a prominent Quraysh figure, as the first caliph to succeed the Prophet, was not an isolated phenomenon. From Abu Bakr, the first ruler of the Islamic community (632-634), to ᶜAli, the fourth "Rightly Guided Caliph" (656-661); from Muᶜawiyah ibn Abi Sufyan, the first Umayyad caliph (661-680), to Marwan al-Himar, the last Umayyad caliph (774-750); and from al-Saffah, the first ᶜAbbasid caliph (749-754), to al-Mustaᶜsam, the last ᶜAbbasid caliph (1242-1258), all were from the Quraysh tribe. In this particular respect, too, Muhammad was functionally recognized as a tribal chief whose tribal affiliates were entitled to his succession. This is particularly revealing in light of the fact that, at least since the time of Qusayy ibn Kilab, the great-great-great-grandfather of Muhammad, the Quraysh tribe was in control of Mecca and its sacred precinct around "Kaᶜbah." All of the political successors

of the Prophet continued to lead the Islamic community, now an enlargement
of the Quraysh, as their forefathers used to do, and this despite a fundamental
and drastic charismatic revolution that sought essentially to alter the cultural
identity of its adherents.

Abu Bakr simply nominated ᶜUmar as his successor. The succession of
ᶜUmar, too, assumed a basically traditional posture. His close association to
Muhammad notwithstanding, he came to power primarily because Abu Bakr
had secured *bayᶜah* for him. He was a member of the Quraysh tribe. The same
tribal configurations of the Quraysh in Mecca and the Áws and Khazraj in
Medina persisted at the time of ᶜUmar's succession to power.

Before his death (al-Masᶜudi 1977, 1:661) or on his deathbed (Levi della
Vida 1953), ᶜUmar nominated a council of six members to choose the next
caliph of the Muslim community: ᶜAli ibn Abi Talib, ᶜUthman ibn ᶜAffan,
Zubayr ibn al-ᶜAwwam, Talhah ibn ᶜAbdullah, Saᶜd ibn Abi Waqqas, and
ᶜAbd al-Rahman ibn ᶜAwf. ᶜUmar had stipulated that this council had to find
a caliph within three days; and if there were a split decision, the group to
which ᶜAbd al-Rahman ibn ᶜAwf (the only member who was not himself a
candidate for the caliphate) belonged would have its nominee as the caliph.
ᶜAbd Al-Rahman was a member of ᶜUthman's clan and favored his candidacy.
He finally convinced the others to let him decide between ᶜUthman and ᶜAli,
the former from the Banu Umayyah, the latter from Banu Hashim. It is
reported (Ibn al-ᶜAthir 1851-76, iii, 74) that to ᶜAbd al-Rahman's question
"would you be faithful to God's Book (Qur'an), the prophetic tradition, and
the conduct of Abu Bakr and ᶜUmar?" ᶜAli responded, "Only the Qur'an and
prophetic tradition," while ᶜUthman said, "Yes, I will." ᶜAbd al-Rahman
voted for ᶜUthman who became the next caliph. On this council and its task
Hitti remarked:

> The constitution of this board, called al-Shura (Consultation), including the
> oldest and most distinguished companions surviving, showed that the ancient
> Arabian idea of a tribal chief had triumphed over that of the hereditary monarch.
> (1970, 178-79)

ᶜUmar had excluded his son as a candidate.

On yet another aspect of post-Muhammadan developments, when ᶜAli
became the fourth "Rightly Guided Caliph" in 656, three prominent members
of the Muslim community openly defied his rule: Marwan ibn Hikam, Saᶜd
ibn al-ᶜAs, and Walid ibn ᶜAqabah (al-Masᶜudi 1977, 1:710). The reason
given for their defiance was most revealing insofar as the persistence of
traditional customs and mores in the post-Muhammadan period is concerned.
They argued that ᶜAli had killed their fathers in the Battle of Badr, and thus
they could not pledge their allegiance to him. The Battle of Badr was a major
victory for Muslims over the Meccans in the year 624. It was among a series

of battles that gradually established Islam as the universal religion of the Arabian peninsula. As the Muslim caliph, ᶜAli's authority must have been yielded to within the context of the new religious order. Yet based on a precharismatic criterion, ᶜAli was reproached and defied because of his role in establishing the charismatic supremacy.

The murder of ᶜUthman (656) provided yet another opportunity to observe the persistence of traditional Arab mores and customs in the post-Muhammadan period. As a member of the Umayyad family, one of the staunchest enemies of the Prophet, ᶜUthman favored the members of his clan in both political and economic ways. In the words of Goldziher:

> ᶜUthman, . . . a member of the Umayyad family, succeeded at the head of the Muslim community. This was the very family whose chief and whose members had offered stubborn resistance to nascent Islam, even if in Muhammad's lifetime they had yielded to success and joined the faith. While a member of it reigned, this family gained a preponderant influence in government, and thus a preponderant share in the material benefits yielded by the state. (1981, 169)

These policies led to the disenchantment of some groups in the Muslim community and the subsequent murder of ᶜUthman. The Umayyads, the murdered caliph's clan, "*in Arab fashion* . . . now claimed the role of avengers of the blood of ᶜUthman, and recognized the Umayyad Muᶜawiyah, the governor of Syria, as their pretender to the throne" (ibid. emphasis added).

While considering the causes of the Umayyad downfall, Watt has maintained that their religious laxity had been exaggerated by the Abbasids.

> A third adverse factor [contributing to the downfall of the Umayyads] was the disaffection of many men of genuine religious concern. Most Muslims, both Arabs and others, accepted the world-view presented in the Qur'an, and indeed could think in no other terms, but only a small proportion had a deep concern about religious matters. . . . In discussions of the Umayyad period they are sometimes called the "pious opposition"; but they were not all opposed to the Umayyads. . . . The Umayyad dynasty was far from being as irreligious as the 'Abbasids alleged it was and had the support of scholars who could give a religious defense of its position. Nevertheless, many, perhaps a majority, of the members of the general religious movement came to be out of sympathy with the Umayyads and ready to support the 'Abassids. (1974, 29-30)

Not at issue, however, was the personal religious devotion of particular Umayyad caliphs, which undoubtedly could be individually verified (Goldziher 1981, 70). It was rather the overall mode of authority, the conflict between traditional Arab and charismatic Muhammadan, that shaped the specific structure of the emerging religious culture. Gibb recognized this tension when, commenting on the tribal nature of conflicts arising from the death of ᶜUthman, he maintained that

> the tribal interpretation of Islam carried with it a threat to the whole principle
> of religious authority and to the system of mutual rights and obligations upon
> which rested the unity and stability of the community. The conflict turned out
> to be one, not between the religious basis and the secular basis of unity but
> between unity on modified Meccan terms which at least respected the religious
> foundations of the community, and the disruptive forces of tribalism. (1962,
> 7-8)

The forces of tribalism finally led to the confrontation of ᶜAli and Muᶜawiyah and ultimately to the establishment of the Umayyads as the first Islamic
dynasty (658-661). As a major mark of the partial victory of traditional Arab
motifs against the Muhammadan charismatic legacy, no longer than twenty-
nine years after the death of the Prophet, the clan from which his staunchest
enemies came assumed the political leadership of the *ummah* for a period of
close to ninety years (661-750). Islam as a new religio-cultural force was, of
course, too powerful to be totally eradicated; yet the caliphate state established by the Umayyads was modeled primarily on pre-Islamic Arab motifs.

The Umayyads, of course, were recognized as a Muslim dynasty. Islam as
the charismatic legacy of Muhammad gradually permeated the entire fabric of
the Arab social structure. Yet in many significant ways, symbolized by the
exclusive right of the Umayyad clan to political authority, Islamic precepts
yielded to Arab traditionalism. Traditional Arab culture that since time immemorial had shaped the social and psychological constitution of the Bedouins resisted total eradication by the Muhammadan charismatic legacy in
each and every precinct where they both had a claim. The ensuing result, in
every case, predicted the normative behavior of its constituent members.
Gibb captures the essence of this tension between the two modes of authority
when he refers to

> the violent reaction and reassertion of the old tribal groupings and political
> tendencies which shortly afterwards challenged the Islamic organization of
> government with the same rapidity and suddenness with which it had been built
> up in the first place. This was the critical moment for the survival of the whole
> organized Islamic movement; the issue at stake in the First Civil War was none
> other than whether the new social factor and its political embodiment in the
> caliphate were to succeed in holding out or to be swept away. There can be little
> doubt that the inner impulse to the Civil War was the reassertion of tribal
> autonomy. . . . So far as can be glimpsed through the distortions of the later
> sources, Ali did not merely stand for a negation . . . but had also a positive
> vision of a structure of government which should embody the social and ethical
> values of the Islamic ideology. (1962, 40)

In its communal representation of the majority of Muslims, Sunnite Islam
crystalized the post-Muhammadan charismatic legacy. Within the Muslim
majority, the supreme authority of the caliphate became concentrated in the
Quraysh tribe, subject to recognition by the community. The recognition by

the community is what Weber called the "inner justification and . . . external means" (1946, 78) upon which a relation of authority rests. It is significant to realize that it was the practice of *bay*ᶜ*ah* through which such acceptance of authority, or obedience, was secured. "The aged and pious Abu-Bakr," reports Hitti, ". . . received the oath of allegiance (*bay*ᶜ*ah*) from the assembled chiefs, probably in accordance with a previously arranged scheme between himself, ᶜUmar ibn al-Khattab and Abu-ᶜUbaydah ibn al-Jarrah . . ." (1970, 140). Al-Tabari also reported that in the *Saqifah Bani Sa*ᶜ*adah* ᶜUmar and Abu ᶜUbaydah addressed Abu Bakr saying,

> you are the worthiest of the Emigrants . . . and the deputy [*khalifah*] of the Prophet of God in prayer . . . [so] stretch out your hand so that we may swear allegiance to you. And when they went forward to swear allegiance to him, Bashir ibn Saᶜd went ahead of them and swore allegiance to him [too] . . . [and] [p]eople came from every side to swear allegiance to Abu Bakr. (1879-1901, 1844)

The acceptance of Abu Bakr's authority and swearing allegiance to him were essentially on a traditional Arab basis. The practice of *bay*ᶜ*ah* was not limited to Abu Bakr. The authority of three other "Rightly Guided Caliphs," too, was legitimated through the same process. Abu-Bakr designated ᶜUmar as his successor and secured this prominent Muslim's *bay*ᶜ*ah* for him. ᶜUmar designated a council (al-*Shura*) to decide who was to succeed him, again legitimated by *bay*ᶜ*ah*. ᶜUthman was murdered before he could make any provisions for his successor. During the Umayyads (661-750), not only did *bay*ᶜ*ah* survive but the caliphate became entirely restricted to the clan of Banu Umayyah. Before his death, Muᶜawiyah secured the leadership of his son Yazid by arranging that the prominent Muslim's *bay*ᶜ*ah* be pledged to him. The acceptance of the caliph by the community did not represent, or exemplify, any particular procedure designated by the Prophet.

The Weberian criteria of the "correctness of the process" and "accordance with certain formalities" for the Muslim majority were expressed in the ceremony of *bay*ᶜ*ah*, in which the authority of Abu Bakr was acknowledged and legitimated, as well as in the *Khutbah* in which Abu Bakr accepted his responsibility as the leader of the Muslim community. Both the "process" and "formality" were in accordance with traditional tribal customs through which it became possible "for legitimacy to take on the character of an acquired right."

The position of the caliphate was considered as an essentially political and administrative authority. Barthold has noted that "to the caliph (vicegerent) of the Prophet only the social authority was delegated and not the religious" (1979, 9). Thus began a long process of segmentation and differentiation through which the legacy of Muhammad's charismatic authority was divided into various domains. The vast empire, being gradually established, needed a much more complicated bureaucratic apparatus than a charismatically quali- fied elite could provide. The adoption of Persian bureaucratic practices during the ᶜAbbasyds further advanced this process. The formation of various spheres of authority within the Muslim society became the expression of organic differentiation of a growing social body.

Goldziher has characterized the caliph as one who

> represents the state's judicial, administrative, and military power. As ruler he is nothing but the successor of the one who preceded him . . . and not entitled by the qualities inherent in his personality. Most importantly, the caliph of the Sunnis has no authority to dispense spiritual instruction. (1981, 182-83)

What would develop to become the Sunnite view of the caliph began taking shape from the moment the tribal council convened in *Saqifah Bani-Saᶜidah*; yet the practices of Abu Bakr, ᶜUmar, ᶜUthman, and ᶜAli (as recognized by the Sunnites) epitomized this position. In particular, ᶜUmar, who had been recognized as "the true founder of the Islamic state" (ibid., 32), provided a mode of leadership that functioned as an ideal type for subsequent Sunnite theorists.

"Not entitled by the qualities inherent in his personality" is a clear refer- ence to the lack of any recognition of charisma in the command/obedience nexus between the succeeding leader and the Islamic community. The We- berian stipulation, in its typification of a possible solution to the question of succession (Weber 1978a, 247), best corresponding to Sunnite Islam, that the successor must be recognized as "charismatically qualified," is not applica- ble here, unless by "qualification" mere association, affiliation, or compan- ionship is intended. Not being so qualified, the range of responsibilities/ authorities of the caliph was confined within the political and administrative domains, thus reflecting yet another manifestation of traditional Arab customs according to which the chief of a tribe had but limited worldly authority, with no ostensible metaphysical significance attached to it.

The political nature of the caliphate was further indicated in the self- assessment of the Umayyad rulers. Goldziher has pointed out that:

> no doubt the Umayyads' rise to power inaugurated a new system. Their idea of Islam, honestly held, was political: "Islam had united the Arabs and led them to rule a world empire." . . . The satisfaction that religion afforded them was in no small measure due to the fact that Islam "had brought glory and high rank, and had taken possession of the heritage of nations." (1981, 71)

Historically exposed to the great empires of the Sasanids and the Byzantines, the Umayyad rulers incorporated Arab tribal identity with their understanding of Persian Khosros and Roman Caesars.

The limited political nature of the caliphate authority was essentially a reflection of lingering tribal mores. Commenting on the early rapid expansion of the Islamic empire, Watt has indicated that "despite the size of this empire . . . the office of caliph was still conceived in terms appropriate to the chief of a nomadic tribe" (1968a, 40). He then analyzes the nature of authority that a pre-Islamic tribal chief, *sayyid*, exercised, and he maintains that "the *sayyid* at any level had limited powers, and was little more than a *primus inter pares*" (ibid., 40).

The authority of the caliph was not as limited and confined as that of the *sayyid*; the very complex nature of the political organization developed in the post-Muhammadan period and the expansion of the Islamic empire precluded such a limitation. Yet compared with the elaborate range of Muhammadan authority, later to be claimed, on a lower scale, by the Shi^{c}ite Imams, the caliphs essentially remained political administrators on the model of a tribal *sayyid*, yet projected into a vast empire.

Here the distinction that Bendix (1960) has made between leadership and authority sheds some light on the nature of the post-Muhammadan authority of the Sunnite caliphs:

> leadership depends upon the personal qualities of the leader in the situation in which he leads. In the case of authority, however, the relationship ceases to be personal and, if the legitimacy of the authority is recognized, the subordinate must obey the command even when he is unacquainted with the person who issues it. In a leadership relation the person is basic; in an authority relation the person is merely a symbol. (1960, 298-99)

The authority of the caliphs was acquired by virtue of their occupying the position of *Khalīfah rasūl Allah* (the vicegerent to the messenger of God); the process of their election and legitimacy was essentially pre-Islamic traditional. Muhammad's case was that of "authoritative leaders" that is, a personal relationship that commands authority and demands obedience.

One of the major offices that gradually developed in the Muslim world, due to the essentially political nature of the caliphate—leaving the other aspects vacant for future realization and institutionalization—was that of the *qadi*. This office was initially established under the Umayyads and grew into the judicial institution of Islam. But the origin of the office perhaps went back to ^{c}Umar's time. A letter attributed to ^{c}Umar addressed Abu Musa al-Ash^{c}ari on the duties of a *qadi* (Williams 1971, 141-42). Based on this letter, the development of this position may be traced back much earlier than the Umayyad dynasty. Al-Baladhuri also reported ^{c}Umar's appointing *qadis* for Damascus, Jordan, Hims, and Qumasrin (1959). Moreover, there was a report by al-Kindi, in his *Kitab al-walāh*, that as early as 643 ^{c}Umar had appointed a *qadi* for Egypt (Hitti 1970, 225). Based primarily on the Qur'anic revelations and prophetic traditions, the *qadis* constituted a distinct source of authority in legal matters. Although in many instances the caliph had the power to appoint the *qadis*, in a strict legal sense he (the caliph) did not have the authority to pass judgment in matters pertaining to *Shariʿah*, Islamic law.

It is important to note that even in the realization of these vacant sources of authority in the Muslim society, the pre-Islamic traits can be detected. Watt has maintained that

> the conception of the *qadi* may have owed something to the pre-Islamic office of the *hakam* or "arbiter." The *hakam* was a man respected for his wisdom and knowledge of tribal custom to whom cases might be submitted. (1974, 53)

Occupying a distinct position of authority, the *qadis* were designated as deputies (*nāʿibs*) of the Prophet. They gradually developed into a powerful class that could use their office for the legitimation, or illegitimation, of a ruler, as, for example, in the case of the Molaga and Granada *qadis* sanctioning the Almorvid ruler Yusuf ibn Tashfin's bid to invade Algeciras (1086) by proclaiming a number of the local princes unfit to rule (Von Grunebaum 1970, 178).

The process having started in this direction, other offices subsequently developed that further compartmentalized the legacy of Muhammad's charismatic authority in Islamic society. The offices of *wazir* (vizier) and *amir* (general) were added to that of the *qadi* during the ʿAbbasyds. The adoption of the Persian administrative apparatus by the ʿAbbasyds (750-1258) further extended this bureaucratization of charisma.

Another major office which gradually developed in the Islamic state apparatus, again due to the exclusively political and administrative limitation of the caliphal authority, was that of the *ʿulama'* (religious scholars). A firm and extensive knowledge of the religious sciences—the *Qur'an* and *Hadith* in particular—provided the *ʿulama'* with a crucial area of expertise and thus authority. As the custodians of institutionalized Islam, this class of religious scholars and their religious authority had to be recognized.

In discussing al-Ghazzali's theory of government, Lambton has indicated that

> their [the *'ulama's*] principal political function was the interpretation of the *shariʿah* in terms of the problems facing the community, and by their approval of the sultan's choice of *imam* in the *bayʿa* . . . and their *fatwas*, they expressed the functional authority of the *shariʿah*. In short, in al-Ghazzali's theory the imamate still stood for the whole of Islamic government, but it had been separated into three main elements, the *imam*, the sultan and the *ʿulama'*, each corresponding to some aspect of the authority behind Islamic government and each performing a function by that authority. (1981, 115)

Thus, in a general, gradual, and systematic process, the comprehensive and charismatic authority of Muhammad was divided into a number of different constituencies, with one class assuming authority for each of these domains. Initially, the office of the caliphate appropriated the political authority. Gradually, the judicial power was institutionalized in the office of the *qadis*. The military power was assigned to the *amirs*, administrative responsibilities to the *wazirs*, religious to the *ᶜulama'*, and finally, with the gradual development of Sufism, the spiritual authority was appropriated by the Sufi saints. These figures of authority constituted independent spheres of authority that at each particular period of Islamic history could impede or facilitate the respective claims and objectives of each other.

As this simultaneous process of routinization and segmentation of Muhammad's charismatic authority was under way for the Muslim majority, two other modes of extending this charisma into the future were operative as well. I shall turn to these two modes in the next two chapters.

6

The Foundations of Shi^cite Authority:
The Perpetuation of Charisma

*"O sons of ^cAbd al-Muttalib," he said, "I know
of no Arab who hath come to his people with a
nobler message than mine. I bring you the best
of this world and the next. God hath commanded me to call you unto Him. Which of
you, then, will help me in this, and be my
brother, mine executor and my successor among
you?" There was silence throughout the clan.
. . . But when the silence remained unbroken,
the thirteen-year-old ^cAli felt impelled to speak
and said: "O Prophet of God, I will be thy
helper in this." The Prophet laid his hand on
the back of ^cAli's neck and said: "This is my
brother, mine executor and my successor
amongst you. Hearken unto him and obey him."
The men rose to their feet, laughing and saying to Abu Talib: "He hath ordered thee to
hearken unto thy son and to obey him."*

—Muhammad ibn Jarir al-Tabari

Upon the death of Muhammad on Monday, June 8, 632, ^cAli considered
himself the legitimate successor to his authority (al-Shahrastani 1979, 1:213).
According to traditional sources (al-Mas^cudi 1977, 1:632-33), ^cAli was among
the first male Arabs to accept Islam. He was the Prophet's cousin and his
son-in-law. Muhammad was raised in the household of ^cAli's father, Abu
Talib. After the death of his father, ^cAbd al-Muttalib, Abu Talib was the chief
of the Banu Hashim clan of the Quraysh tribe. When ^cAli was born in 600,
Muhammad was already a thirty-year-old merchant who had married Khadijah five years earlier. When Muhammad received his first revelation in 610,
^cAli was ten years old; and when the Prophet began to preach in 613, ^cAli
accepted Islam at the age of thirteen. It is believed (Ibn Hisham 1955, 224)
that when Muhammad migrated to Medina in 622, the twenty-two-year-old

^cAli remained in Mecca to disguise his flight and thus protect Muhammad against a plot to assassinate him (ibid., 221). As a young man, ^cAli fought in the battles of Badr and Uhud, was present at the siege of Khandaq, and fought in almost all of the other battles the Prophet conducted. When Muhammad died in 632, ^cAli was thirty-two years old.

According to historical sources (al-Shahrastani 1979, 1:213-14; al-Ya^cqubi 1883, 2.103), a group of prominent Muslims supported ^cAli's claim as the legitimate successor to the Prophet: ^cAbbas ibn ^cAbd al-Muttalib (the Prophet's uncle), Fadl ibn ^cAbbas, Zubayr ibn ^cAwam, Khalid ibn Sa^cid, Miqdad ibn ^cAmr, Salman the Persian, Abu Dharr al-Ghifari, ^cUmmar ibn Yasir, Bira' ibn ^cAzib, and ^cAbi ibn Ka^cb. The initial supporters of ^cAli and his claim were called the "Shi^cah [Shi^cites, or supporters of] of ^cAli." Exactly when this term was used is a matter of dispute, but the Shi^cites believe that already during the Prophet's lifetime the supporters of ^cAli, particularly Miqdad ibn al-Aswad, Salman the Persian, Abu Dharr al-Ghifari, and ^cUmmar ibn Yasir, were known as the "Shi^cites of ^cAli" (Tabataba'i 1975, 39, 68). According to Muslim historical anthropologist al-Jahiz (d. 868-69), in early Islam only those Muslims who preferred ^cAli to ^cUthman were called the Shi^cites. Ibn Khaldun (1332-1406), in his *Muqaddimah*, reports that "Shi^cah" etymologically meant "the followers and supporters" and that in the vocabulary of Muslim theologians and legists meant the followers of ^cAli and his male descendants. The Andalusian historian Ibn Hazm (994-1064) maintained that only after 655, that is, after the death of ^cUthman, the third rightly guided caliph, did the supporters of ^cAli come to be recognized as "the Shi^cites of ^cAli." Muhammad ibn al-Nadim (d. 995), in his *al-Fihrist*, maintained that the expression "Shi^cah" was used after "the battle of the Camel" (December 9, 656) between ^cAli and the coalition of his two major rivals, Talhah and Zubayr, along with the Prophet's wife, ^cAishah. Others have maintained that it was after the battle of Siffin (July 28, 657) between ^cAli and Mu^cawiyah that this term was used (Mashkur n.d., 39-40). There are, furthermore, Qur'anic references to the word "Shi^cah," for example, XIX:69, XXVIII:15, XXXVII:83, that mostly denote "group," "people," "followers," etc.

The origins of the Shi^cites have been attributed to

> (1) the subversive thoughts of a certain Ibn Saba; (2) the Persian scheme to revenge the defeat of Sassanids by creating division within Islam; (3) a Zoroastrian invention with a similar purpose; (4) an invention of the Shi^cite *Imams* to claim religious authority; or to (5) a Safavid invention to legitimize their dynasty. (Tabataba'i 1969, 9-10)

Among the Western Islamicists, Goldziher maintains that

> from the very beginning there was a party of highly respected Muslims who were dissatisfied with the manner in which, in disregard of degrees of kinship

to the Prophet's family, the caliphate had been bestowed on Abu Bakr, ^cUmar, and ^cUthman, the first three men to hold it. Accordingly, they would have preferred to elevate ^cAli to the caliphate. (1981, 169)

Goldziher indicates that the Shi^cites first expressed their views openly during the caliphate of ^cUthman (644-56) (ibid)., but their view was present throughout the period of the four rightly guided caliphs 632-61 (ibid., 174-75). Barthold also believes that "we have no reason to doubt that the contemporary Shi^cite and Kharijite view is similar to those who in the seventh century fought for or against ^cAli ibn abi Talib" (1979, 11).

The persecution of the Shi^cites under the Umayyads (661-750), however exaggerated it might be in the later sources, further testifies to the strong presence of this particular view of succession to Muhammad's authority in early Islamic history. Ibn al-Athir (1851-76,3:422-23, 441, 445, 447, 450) and al-Mas^cudi (1977, vol. 2 et. passim.) provide detailed accounts of the Shi^cite persecution under the Umayyads. Barthold, however, has considered the degree of this persecution to be largely exaggerated (1979, 8-14). The negative reputation of the Umayyads, according to Barthold, is largely an ^cAbbasyd invention. Barthold's pro-Umayyads position can be balanced perhaps with Goldziher's assessment which considers their government "a scandal to pietists" (1981, 177). The severity of the persecution under the Umayyads, however, did not alter the religious and political presence of the Shi^cites in early Islamic history. Mu^cawiyah's brother, Ziyad, was reported to have persecuted the Shi^cites severely. Mu^cawiyah himself excluded the Shi^cites from receiving any benefit from the early Islamic expansions. When ^cUmar ibn ^cAbd al-Azia (reigned 717-20) banned the cursing of ^cAli of the minbars, many objected that "a prayer that does not include the cursing of ^cAli is not performed correctly" (Mashkur n.d., 33-34). During this period in particular the Shi^cite doctrine of *taqiyyah* (a religious obligation to conceal one's true religious identity in the face of danger) was developed.

^cAli's opposition to the leadership of Abu Bakr, ^cUmar, and ^cUthman and the process of their election constituted, along with ^cAli's argument for the legitimacy of his succession, the major religious and political cornerstone upon which the Shi^cite theory of authority was gradually constructed. An examination of the Shi^cite theory of authority after Muhammad points to three distinct and fundamental characteristics: (1) the perpetuation of the Muhammadan charismatic authority (on a lower scale) in the process of its institutionalization, (2) a minimal influence of pre-Islamic traditional Arab forces in the post-Muhammadan theoretical and practical development of authority, and (3) the preservation of the all-inclusive Muhammadan charismatic authority (on a lower scale), preventing its being segmented into different spheres.

The nature of authority in Shi^cite Islam is composed of ingredients similar to those that had originally shaped the initial Muhammadan charisma. The transitory mechanism of one to the other, Muhammad to ^cAli, was centered around the question of succession.

Among the principal types of solutions to the question of succession that Weber identified is the possibility of the designation of a successor by the charismatic figure himself: "designation on the part of the original charismatic leader of his own successor and his recognition on the part of the followers. . . . In this case legitimacy is *acquired* through the act of designation" (1978a, 247). Among the Shi^cites, chief arguments for the legitimacy of ^cAli's claim is that he was selected by the Prophet himself as his successor:

> for the Shi^cites, the central evidence of ^cAli's legitimacy as successor to the Prophet is the event of *Ghadir Khum*, when the Prophet chose ^cAli to the "general guardianship" (*walayat-i ^cammah*) of the people and made ^cAli, like himself, their "guardian." (Tabataba'i 1975, 40)

Ghadir Khum, according to the Shi^cites, is the residing place where Muhammad, returning from his last pilgrimage to Mecca on March 10, 632, designated ^cAli as his successor. Tabataba'i refers to Islamic sources that have reported this incident and quotes Abu Sa^cid Khudari as having said

> the Prophet in *Ghadir Khum* invited people toward ^cAli and took his arm and lifted it . . . high. . . . Then this verse was revealed: "This day have I perfected your religion for you and completed My favor unto you, and have chosen for you as religion Al-ISLAM." Then the Prophet said, "God is great (*Allahu akbar*) that religion has become perfected and that God's bounty has been completed, His satisfaction attained and the *walayat* of ^cAli achieved." Then he added, "For whomever I am the authority and guide. ^cAli is also his guide and authority." (1975, 179)

There are extensive reports by both the Sunnite and Shi^cite authorities concerning this episode (ibid. 179-82). Although with a different interpretation, most of the Sunnite authorities verify the authenticity of this hadith. According to Jafri,

> as far as the authenticity of the event itself is concerned, it has hardly ever been denied or questioned even by the most conservative Sunnite authorities who have themselves recorded it. Most noteworthy among them are *Imam* Ahmad b. Hanbal in his *Musnad*, Tirmidi, Nasa^ci, Ibn Maja, Abu Daud and almost all other *Sunan* writers, Ibn al-Athir in his *Usd al-Ghaba*, Ibn ^cAbd al-Barr in his *Isti^cab*, followed by all other writers of biographical works and even Ibn ^cAbd Rabbih in his *^cIqd al-Farid* and Jahiz in his *^cUthmaniyya*. . . . Ibn Kathir, a most staunch supporter of the Sunni viewpoint, has devoted seven pages to this subject and has collected a great number of different *isnads* from which the tradition is narrated. It is also Ibn Kathir who informs us that the famous

historian al-Tabari, in a two-volume unfinished work entitled *Kitab al-Fada'il* (mentioned also by Yaqut in his *Irshad*, VI, p. 452), wrote in full details the Prophet's discourse in favour of °Ali at Ghadir Khum. A modern scholar, Husayn °Ali Mahfuz, in his penetrating researches on the subject of Ghadir Khum, has recorded with documentation that this tradition has been narrated by at least 110 Companions, 84 *tabi°un*, 355 °*ulama*, 25 historians, 27 tradition-alists, 11 exegetes, 18 theologians, and 5 philologists. Most of them were later counted by the Sunnis as among their own number. (1979b, 19-20)

Many Islamicists, however, have challenged the validity of the *Ghadir Khum* incident. A representative view is that of Shaban who has maintained that Muhammad

> made no pronouncement on the question of how the *ummah* should continue after him. The famous Shi°ite tradition that he designated his cousin °Ali as his successor at Ghadir Khum should not be taken seriously. Such an event is inherently improbable considering the *Arab traditional* reluctance to entrust young and untried young men with great responsibility. . . . One can only conclude that Muhammad intended that his followers should settle, on their own, the problem of succession, if indeed there was to be any successor at all. This fits in very well with his deep understanding of *his times* and it was the only practical course for him to take. (1971, 16; emphasis added)

The remarkable aspect of Shaban's argument is his insistence that Muhammad would not have transcended "the Arab-traditional" norm by designating a successor. It is, yet, in precisely transcending the political culture of his time that Muhammad is an Arab prophet.

The designation of °Ali by the Prophet, authentic at least in the Shi°ite collective self-understanding, carried unsurpassed importance for the Shi°-ites, who maintain that this is incontrovertable evidence that both divine will and wisdom, as well as the self-conscious prophetic decision were set on keeping the leadership of the Islamic community in the household of Mu-hammad and designating °Ali and his male descendants as successors to the prophetic authority. According to al-Baghdadi (d. 1037), the Shi°ites attribute the legitimacy of °Ali's authority to divine wisdom: "If you ask: does (divine) wisdom require and necessitate that an Imam is designated and established, I would answer: Yes, [divine] wisdom necessitates and requires the establish-ment of an Imam" (1954, 246).

In his examination of the routinization of charisma, Toth has pointed out that in many historical cases charismatic figures appeared in pairs, such as Christ and Peter. The first figure, Toth has identified as "the charisma of the outer call," the second as "charisma of an inner consolidation" (1972, 93-98). Muhammad and °Ali may be considered in such a category as well. Yet this application will remain limited to the Shi^cite minority of early Islamic history. For the larger Sunnite world the Muhammad/Abu Bakr pair cannot be considered in such a category for the reasons that I examined in the last chapter.

The particular nature of ^cAli's designation necessitated a significant clause in the Weberian stipulation of the "routinization" of charismatic authority. If "routinization" refers to "the charismatic authority to become radically changed" (Weber 1978a, 246), then the continuation of authority from Muhammad to ^cAli and the subsequent institutionalization of the Imamate (the legitimate leadership of ^cAli and his male descendants) cannot be considered as the "routinization" of charisma, a situation in which the social relationships are *not* "strictly personal, based on the validity and practice of charismatic personal qualities" (246). The qualification which can be applied in this particular case is a "perpetuation" of charisma through which the original source that was believed to have legitimated Muhammad's authority now, through him, established and legitimated ^cAli's authority.

Among modern Islamicists, Watt recognized specifically the charismatic nature of ^cAli's authority as well as that of his successors:

> The distinctive Shi^cite belief was in the existence of supernatural powers in the clan of Muhammad, the Hashimites—powers which had been manifested in him, and which were transmitted or bequeathed to succeeding generations. In modern sociological terms this might be described as a belief in the charismatic leader. The actual charismatic leaders—first ^cAli, then his sons al-Hasan and al-Husayn—were far from successful in their political activities. (1968a, 119)

While "acquiring" legitimacy through the act of designation, the successor also receives the quality and nature of authority thus delegated. In the larger metaphysical context, the death of Muhammad is considered as an inevitable phase, inevitable because of the natural laws established by the source of the Prophet's charismatic authority, which does not alter, qualitatively, the nature of authority to be transferred to his successor.

The sweeping authority claimed by ^cAli and recognized by his followers went directly against the pre-Islamic notion of authority which, in the Arab spirit of freedom, was traditionally circumscribed. In fact, as Shaban has pointed out, the roots of Talhah's and Zubayr's animosity toward, and their final battle with, ^cAli may be in their rejection of any antitraditional and comprehensive authority after Muhammad. Talhah and Zubayr, Shaban has maintained,

> were looking back to the severely limited powers of the *Amir al-Mu'minin*, under Abu Bakr and ^cUmar. Although they had backed ^cUthman in the *Shura*,

he had disappointed them and had therefore lost their support. They must have been aware that 'Ali would be even more likely to make radical changes in the organization of the empire and the position of the *Amir al-Mu'minin*. (1971, 71).

Obviously any continuation of the charismatic mode of authority disrupts resumption of normal economic life. As representatives of the Meccan merchant establishment, Talhah and Zubayr exemplified the forces of routinization that sought to terminate the charismatic experience. But for 'Ali and his followers, that experience, crystallized in its definitions of charismatic authority, could not be terminated. To be sure, as the last prophet, Muhammad was considered to have sealed the prophetic line; thus 'Ali's authority was not considered to be equal to Muhammad's, since he could not receive revelations. Yet, insofar as the sociological nature of his authority was concerned, he was a charismatic leader, exercising "the authority of the extraordinary and personal *gift of grace* (charisma), the absolutely personal devotion and personal confidence in revelation, heroism, or other qualities of individual leadership" (Weber 1946, 79). Although it is believed that 'Ali received no revelations, his charismatic authority was considered to be legitimated by the Qur'anic revelations. Defining the word "Imam," al-Baghdadi has said an "Imam is a person who in worldly and other-worldly affairs is the successor to the Prophet, and is the leader of people" (1954, 280). "Successor to the Prophet" here means a persistent continuation of his charismatic authority.

This transition from one charismatic leadership to another may have a particular stipulation within Weberian sociology if the crisis of leadership, caused by the death of the first charismatic leader, is considered carefully. Bendix has pointed out that

> charismatic leadership is a uniquely personal response to a crisis in human experience; those who succeed the charismatic leader therefore face the problem of preserving a personal charisma after the leader and the crisis have passed away and everyday demands have again come to the fore. (1960, 301)

The crisis created by the charismatic movement was ultimately resolved by the successful establishment of Islam, in one form or another, as the core element of Arab cultural identity. This cultural identity, to whatever degree it has been influenced by both the charismatic "message" and precharismatic traditional motifs, constitutes the oral demand system within which Muslims have regulated their lives. In this context Abu Bakr, 'Umar, and 'Uthman did not face "the problem of preserving a personal charisma" simply because they had no such claims. 'Ali, on the other hand, whether as the Imam of the Shi'ites or as the caliph of all Muslims, had charismatic claims. For him "the crisis" was not resolved. He and his supporters always had a precarious relationship with Abu Bakr, 'Umar, and particularly 'Uthman. In fact, the history of the early Shi^{c}ite developments is far more tumultuous than can be considered as a resumption of routine daily life. Indeed, this situation has been present throughout Shi^{c}ite history, a direct result of an attempt to institutionalize charisma in its pure form.

In another possible solution to the question of succession, Weber has formulated

> the conception that charisma is a quality transmitted by heredity; thus that it is participated in by the kinsmen of its bearer, particularly by his closest relatives. This is the case of hereditary charisma. . . . In the case of hereditary charisma, recognition is no longer paid to the charismatic qualities of the individual, but to the legitimacy of the position he has acquired by hereditary succession. This may lead in the direction of either traditionalization or legalization. The concept of divine right is fundamentally altered and now comes to mean authority by virtue of a personal right which is not dependent on the recognition of those subject to authority. Personal charisma may be totally absent. (1978a, 248)

Muhammad was not survived by a son. If "heredity" refers exclusively to a son following his father, the case was not applicable to Muhammad. However, if this concept refers to the more general application of "the kinsmen" and particularly "closest relatives," then Muhammad can be considered ^{c}Ali's father-figure. ^{c}Ali was Muhammad's cousin. Muhammad grew up in Abu Talib's (^{c}Ali's father) house. After the death of his grandfather, Muhammad, then eight years old, was raised by his uncle, Abu Talib. Abu Talib was particularly instrumental, as chief of the Banu Hashim clan, in protecting Muhammad during the early stages of his preaching. ^{c}Ali was born ten years (600) before Muhammad began his mission. When he was six years old, he left his own house to heed the Prophet's request to live with him. He was then raised under Muhammad's guardianship (Tabataba'i 1975, 190-91). ^{c}Ali was also Muhammad's son-in-law, the husband of his only surviving child, Fatima. Traditionally, ^{c}Ali is considered as a member of the Prophet's "household" (*ahl al-bayt*) and, as such, having been in constant proximity to Muhammad, the recipient of the divine gift of grace through the Prophet. According to the Shi^{c}ites, *ahl al-bayt* refers to the following five persons: Muhammad, ^{c}Ali, Fatima, and al-Hasan and al-Husayn (the two sons of ^{c}Ali and Fatima, grandsons of the Prophet). For the Shi^{c}ites, this constitutes the holy family from which the leadership of ^{c}Ali, al-Hasan, al-Husayn, and their subsequent male descendants are legitimated. This legitimacy stemmed from their proximity to the Prophet which sanctified their leadership. There is a Qur'anic reference to *ahl al-bayt* that the Shi^{c}ites consider the divine source of both the legitimacy and infallibility of ^{c}Ali and his descendants. Allah commands the *ahl al-bayt* to stay in your houses. Bedizen not yourselves with the bedizenment of the Time of Ignorance. Be regular in prayer, and pay the poor-dues, and obey Allah and His messenger. Allah's wish is but to remove uncleanness far from you, O Folk of the Household, and cleanse you with a thorough cleansing. (Qur'an XXXIII:33)

This "divine sanctity and blessing" is taken as the ultimate sign of His favor to the Prophet's household, through which the authority of ᶜAli and his male descendants is legitimated. This infallibility is, in fact, considered the symbolic sign of the hierarchical continuity of authority from Allah to Muhammad and, through him, to ᶜAli and his descendants.

For Weber this category constituted the "hereditary charisma" by which he referred to some form of traditionalization or legalization of the charisma. His emphasis on the particular form of the appropriation of rights and the selection and establishment of one mode of designation are indications of his concern with the specific form of "routinization" that charisma assumes under this category. This concern is emphasized explicitly in the second part of his typification when he stresses that "in the case of hereditary charisma, recognition is no longer paid to the charismatic qualities of the individual, but to the legitimacy of the position he has acquired by hereditary succession."

The Shi‘ite case, however, discloses a possibility distinctively different from Weber's stipulation. In the Shi‘ite view, ᶜAli was deemed to have charisma, the *divine gift of grace*. Although he was not considered a prophet, the source of his authority, which defined and constituted its nature as charismatic, was Allah, through the medium of His Prophet. The distinction between Muhammad and ᶜAli, in terms of their respective charismatic authorities, was also emphasized by the latter's introducing no new religion. In Shi‘ite Islam, as in Sunnite Islam, Muhammad is considered the last "messenger" of God. It is by virtue of this position that he brought a new Book, or Law, and superseded the previous order of authority. He set the framework, as well as the essential interdictory, remissive, and transgressive motifs, of the new political culture. It was within this new framework, as interpreted by the Shi‘ites, that ᶜAli's charismatic authority was defined and legitimated.

In their examination of the Mahdi movement in the Sudan, Dekmejian and Wyszomirski have identified a number of social and psychological factors that surround a charismatic revolution. Among them are the existence of a situation of social crisis, the appearance of an exemplary personality, and what they called a "value transformation" (1972, 193-214). In the Shi‘ite position towards ᶜAli, there is no "value transformation" similar to that among the Islamized Arabs. But there is an obvious social crisis, exemplified by the *mawali* problem, that demands a charismatic mode of solution. There are internal forces, however, within the Muhammadan charismatic revolution that seek its permanence independent of any external factor. In the very careful wording of Watt, fundamental to the appearance of Shiᶜism was the belief—[initially] vague at the intellectual level, but held with vehemence—that security and prosperity were to be attained by following and obeying a leader with the charisma of "the family," whether this was interpreted as the clan of Hashim or as the descendants of ᶜAli and Fatima or in some other way. (1968a, 110)

In the Shiᶜite theory of authority—which began to develop immediately after the death of Muhammad—because of the charismatic nature of the Imam, considered to be a continuation of Muhammad's charismatic authority, there was no (as in the Sunnite case) fundamental disintegration of the Prophet's authority into different domains. On the whole, the Shiᶜite Imams were believed to possess the same mode of personal and comprehensive authority— maintained more de jure than de facto—as Muhammad's.

The Shiᶜite Imams represent for the Shiᶜites the embodiment of both the esoteric and exoteric dimensions of Islam, the two having been separated, and separately institutionalized, in Sunnite Islam. As S.H. Nasr has noted,

inasmuch as there were exoteric and esoteric interpretations from the very beginning, from which developed the schools (madhhab) of Shariᶜah and Sufism in the Sunni world, there also had to be an interpretation of Islam which would combine these elements in a single whole. This possibility was realized in Shiᶜism, for which the Imam is the person in whom these two aspects of . . . authority are united. (Tabataba'i 1975, 9)

The charismatic authority of the Shiᶜite Imams is the mechanism through which the comprehensivity of Muhammadan authority, including both this-worldly and other-worldly affairs, was preserved and continued. ᶜAli's personal charisma, as the continuation of Muhammad's, is also attested to by this assessment by Huart, commenting on Caetani's appraisal of ᶜAli,

Caetani observed that the half-divine aureole which soon encircled the figure of ᶜAli was derived not only from his relationship with the Prophet, but also from the personal impression which he left on his contemporaries, but he did not indicate the qualities which gave rise to the legend. If it is recognized that his was a profoundly religious spirit, and that he supported by his authority a programme of social and economic reforms, at the same time placing them on a religious basis, this question also may find its solution. (1979, 30-32)

For the Shiᶜites the question of succession to Muhammad "was not so much who should be the successor . . . as what the function and qualifications of such a person would be" (Tabataba'i 1975, 191). One of the most significant doctrines underlying the possibility of the Imams' comprehensive authority is their infallibility (ᶜismah). Al-Shahrastani has pointed out that the "Shiᶜites all believe . . . that it is necessary for prophets and Imams to be infallible to any sin" (1979, 191). It is through this doctrine that the sweeping authority of the Imams assumes its de facto validity. If the Imams were considered to be subject to sin and error, an element of noncharismatic "rationality" would have been introduced into the command/obedience nexus between the leader and the led that would effectively paralyze the operative function of charismatic domination. As shall become evident in the case of the Kharijites, this factor was precisely the cause of their failure to institutionalize a viable mode of authority after Muhammad.

The comprehensive, personal, and unspecified nature of charismatic authority is evident from the following passage:

> In contrast to any kind of bureaucratic organization of office, the charismatic structure knows nothing of a form or of an ordered procedure of appointment or dismissal. It knows no regulated "career," "advancement," "salary," or regulated and expert training of the holder of charisma or of his aides. It knows no agency of control or appeal, no local bailiwicks or exclusive functional jurisdictions; nor does it embrace permanent institutions like our bureaucratic "departments," which are independent of persons and of purely personal charisma. (Weber 1946, 246)

Within the context of Shiʿite Islam, this personal and informal nature of recruitment, as well as both the appropriation and delegation of power, was kept intact. The only recognized criterion of the followers was their faith, piety, and devotion to their charismatic leader and, through him, to the "ultimate authority" that he represented. This "representation" constitutes the legitimacy of the Imams' "personal" authority.

Following Weber, Wach has made the distinction between "personal" and "official" charisma:

> Charisma of personal character appeals more to the emotions; official charisma is more "rational." Whereas the former claims complete loyalty, even personal surrender, the latter usually demands a circumscribed or "tempered" obedience. (1944, 337)

The Shiʿite link of Allah/Muhammad/ʿAli, with the particular stipulation that there is a hierarchical continuity that legitimates their authority in that order, renders ʿAli's charismatic authority personal. Imams are living embodiments of charismatic authority.

The comprehensive and indispensable nature of the Imams' authority is also represented in the doctrine of *walayah*, the esoteric function of constantly providing the Muslim community with legitimate authority. This function has not become officialized or canonized. *Walayah* derives its source of legitimacy from the Imams' exclusive knowledge of the hidden meaning of the Qur'an. The oral tradition, which is believed to have existed among the succeeding Imams, legitimates, on an external level, this exclusive function of the Imams. A corollary doctrine to *walayah* is *^{c}ismah*, or the infallibility of the Imams. If they are to rule the Muslim community with justice and if they are to provide continuous authoritative interpretation of the Qur'an, then they have to be free from any possible sin or error. On *^{c}ismah*, al-Baghdadi wrote: "With the same token that in the Prophet infallibility (*^{c}Ismah*) is necessary, so it is a condition for the Imam" (1954, 280). All these qualifications necessarily require the designation of the Imams, according to the Shi^{c}ites, by God Himself and through His Prophet. No human intervention, this perspective maintains, could arrange for these charismatic qualities; and thus Shi^{c}ism is considered as a divine dispensation, independent of any human recognition. Weber recognized this when he pointed out that the charismatic leader "does not derive his 'right' from [the followers'] will." (1946, 246).

As a charismatic leader, ^{c}Ali's range of authority knew no specific limitation. The comprehensive and overwhelming charismatic authority claimed by the Shi^{c}ite Imams and attributed to them by their followers constitutes the very nature of the Shi^{c}ite belief. As Fakhry, a contemporary historian of Islamic philosophy, points out in regard to

> the nature of belief or faith (*iman*), the Shi^{c}ite position presents certain revo-lutionary features that are of considerable interest to the historian of Islamic ideas. Whereas, for instance, the Kharijites had declared the "Book of God" to be the ultimate court of appeal for the settlement of religio-political differences, the Shi^{c}ites proclaimed the *Imam* as the ultimate theologian and judicial authority in Islam and recognized him as the fount of religious instruction (*ta^{c}lim*); thus the name of *Ta^{c}limis* is sometimes applied to the extreme Shi^{c}ah, particularly the Isma'ilites. (1983, 41)

This theological necessity of the Imams is the foundation upon which their charismatic authority is sought to be institutionalized. The Qur'an and the Imams' unique "knowledge" of interpreting it, after the death of Muhammad, became an integral part of one another and together constituted the sole source of authority.

In the organization of authority in Shi^{c}ite Islam there is a persistent presence of charisma, as the chief Muhammadan legacy, that legitimates the specifics of its order. Highly charged by this charisma, the Shi^{c}ite organization of authority proved the most resistant to pre-Islamic resurgences.

Essentially a continuation of Muhammadan charismatic authority, Shi^{c}ite Islam is least influenced by the resurgence of pre-Islamic Arab traditionalism. Muhammad's charismatic authority was expressed explicitly against particularities of the Arab life. In its triumphant establishment, Islam negated, particularly in the Qur'an, the authority it had superseded. As a mode of authority that sought to perpetuate Allah's sovereignty on earth, by considering Him the ultimate legitimizer of any form of authority, Shi^{c}ite Islam remained essentially, but not totally, resistant to the contending elements of Arab traditional order. The Shi^{c}ite argument against Sunnite Islam is centered precisely on the Shi^{c}ite insistence on prolonging the Muhammadan—and necessarily antitraditional—experience. What further substantiates this position is the identification of the *mawali* (non-Arab Muslims) with Shi^{c}ite Islam. As disinherited believers, the *mawali* became the chief advocates of the Shi^{c}ites cause, thus perpetuating the charismatic condition which initially saw the emergence of Muhammad.

There are elements in Shi^{c}ite Islam, however, that are essentially pre-Islamic and Arab in nature. The supremacy of the Banu Hashim, expressed in the belief of its sole legitimacy to hold power and particularly the exclusive right of the Prophet's household (*ahl al-bayt*) to leadership of the Islamic community, was a traditional Arab practice being expressed in Islamic terms. It could be argued that the Shi^{c}ite insistence on the exclusive right of the *ahl al-bayt* to provide leaders for the *ummah* is a particularization of the ancient traditional practice of oligarchical families exercising authority over a long period of time. The Quraysh had been the leading tribe of al-Hijaz for many generations. Since the time of Hashim, the Prophet's great-grandfather, the Banu Hashim clan was the leading family in this part of Arabia, a position contested by the clan of Hashim's brother, the Banu ^{c}Abd Shams. The Shi^{c}ites' insistence on the exclusive right of the Muhammadan household, now considered a clan, is to be seen as an attempt to further particularize the oligarchy from the Qurayah tribe to the Banu Hashim clan to Muhammad's household. What would challenge this assessment, however, is the particular mode of legitimating the position of the Shi^{c}ite Imams, according to which they were considered to be *divinely* inspired, in the particular Islamic understanding of this word. Of the early Shi^{c}ites, Watt wrote: "It was a matter of principle with them that the ruler ruled by a kind of divine right and not as the nominee of the people" (1969, 104).

Contrary to this Shi^{c}ite position, the Sunnite-accepted outcome of the *saqīfah Banī Sā^{c}idah* is both formally and essentially an Arab practice of selecting a tribal chief. Thus, although in the Shi^{c}ites' insistence on the exclusive right of Muhammad's household to leadership particular manifestations of Arab traditional culture are to be detected, in the manner of justification and legitimation of this authority there is a genuinely charismatic quality.

Although hereditary succession was not part of the traditional mode of Arab authority, it is possible to attribute this practice among the Shi^{c}ite Imams to the pre-Islamic encounter of the Arabs with the Sassanids (226-651) who did exercise, in the transition of authority from one to the next ruler, hereditary succession. In fact, this particular aspect has been one of the chief reasons of attributing the development of Shi^{c}ite Islam to Iranian influences. E.G. Browne, the eminent Iranist, has indicated that

> I believe that Gobineau is right in asserting that this doctrine of the Divine Right of the House of Sassan had had an immense influence on all subsequent Persian history, more especially on the tenacity with which the Persians have clung to the doctrine of the Shi^{c}a or sect of ^{c}Ali. To them the idea of electing a Caliph, or spiritual successor to the Prophet, natural enough to the democratic Arabs, could not appear otherwise than revolting and unnatural. (1902, 130)

This practice among the Shi^{c}ite Imams is to be attributed to some particular influence by non-Islamic elements present in pre-Islamic Arabia. Yet if this is the case, the justification of the Imams authority as charismatic leaders is through their association with Muhammad as the messenger of Allah. This characterizes the Imams' authority as divinely ordained.

The Persian kings, too, were believed to be divinely gifted and sanctified. The idea of the *farrah-i iyzadi* (divine light or grace) was their chief legitimizer. Wach has suggested *kvarnah* (glory) as the Persian equivalent of charisma (1944, 229). But the ultimate recognition of this gift of grace rested on the discretion of the chief Zoroastrian priest, *Mubadhan Mubadh*, and thus kings did not have the independent authority of the Shi^{c}ite Imams which, as a reality *sui generis*, was defined solely within the particularities of Shi^{c}ite theology, prophetology, and imamology, and thus was not subject to institutional recognition by any other equally significant authority.

On yet another level, the exclusive Arab ethnicity of all the Shi^{c}ite Imams can be seen as a particular influence of Arab hegemony. This is expressed implicitly in the doctrine of *ahl al-bayt* (the Prophet's household) that, by definition, excluded any non-Arab from becoming a Shi^{c}ite Imam. The very idea of the "household," as Weber has indicated, is an anticharismatic element. In specifying the economic peculiarity of charismatic authority, Weber has maintained that

> the sharp contrast between charisma and any "patriarchal" structure that rests upon the ordered base of the "household" lies in this rejection of rational economic conduct. . . . "Pure" charisma is contrary to all patriarchal domination. (1946, 247-48)

There were non-Arab Muslims, particularly the Abyssinian Bilal and the Persian Salman, who were especially close to the Prophet. Theoretically, they could have been considered among his household on the Islamic doctrine of Muslim brotherhood. In the case of Salman, this theoretical possibility was even stronger, because, according to traditional sources, Muhammad did consider him as a member of his household. Reporting the details of the *Khandaq* siege, in which Salman was the chief military strategist who suggested digging a trench (*Khandaq*) around Medina, Lings relates the Muslim anxiety during the construction of this trench:

they continually reminded each other that the time was short. The enemy would soon be upon them, and if any man showed signs of flagging he was at once an object of mockery. Salman, on the other hand, was an object of admiration, for he was not only very strong and able-bodied but for years he had been used to digging and carrying for the Bani Qurayzah. "He doth the work of ten men," they said, and a friendly rivalry started up between them. "Salman is ours," the Emigrants claimed, in virtue of his having left many homes in search of guidance. "He is one of us," the Helpers retorted, "we have more right to him." But the Prophet said: "Salman is one of us, the people of the House." (1983, 217)

Despite the persistence of such notions of "the household" in Shi^cite Islam, the influence of pre-Islamic Arab traditions remained generally at a low and scattered level. Watt has made some revealing observations on the nature of the Shi^cite communal composition. For example, he argues that most of the initial Shi^cites came from southern Arabia where for centuries they were exposed to the idea of the divine right of the ruler:

In the South Arabian kingdoms the king had been regarded as a charismatic leader (a superhuman being); . . . and something of the aura of kingship seems to have clung to the kinglets or princes of South Arabia who still maintained themselves as local rulers especially of the settled population. . . . With such a background it is not surprising that, in the malaise caused by the transition from the pre-Islamic to the Islamic social structure, many of these people from South Arabia turned towards the conception of a superhuman or semi-divine leader. Perhaps they had been originally attracted to Islam because they unconsciously found in Muhammad a leader of this sort. The underlying idea would be that salvation or significance was to be found in membership of a community with a semi-divine leader. . . . Thus, while the Kharijites revived an Islamic form in the tradition of the nomadic tribe, the Shi^cites . . . were giving an Islamic form to the old South Arabian tradition of a kingdom with a semi-divine king. This difference in background and tradition is the chief reason why some former nomads became Kharijites and some Shi^cites. (1969, 105-6)

Watt has also referred to some possible pre-Islamic religious affiliation of the Arab tribe subscribing to the Shi^cite or Kharijite cause:

Another possible reason for the difference is the religious affiliation of the various tribes. It could be argued that in South Arabia there had been such monophysite Christian influence from Abyssinia, whereas the northern tribes had been rather under Nestorian influence from Al-Hirah. This argument could be further supported by the fact that there is a certain correspondence between Shi^cite and monophysite views and between Kharijite and Nestorian views. The monophysites placed emphasis on the "theandric (or superhuman) activity" of Christ as a divine leader, while the Nestorians insisted on the need for fulfillment of the moral law. (1969, 105)

Rahman, too, attributed some pre-Islamic tribal causes to the rise of the early Shi^cite movement, maintaining that there was no clear motive for the "curious legitimist claim" of ^cAli's supporters, except the fact that certain southern tribes, in their traditional enmity against the northerners, decided to champion the Hashimites against the ruling Umayyads. (1966, 171-72).

He has similarly attributed the momentum the Shi^{c}ites assumed after ^{c}Ali to "Persian discontent" and "old oriental beliefs about Divine light" as well as the "Christian Gnostic neoplatonic ideas" (171-72).

A significant aspect of such pre-Islamic traits is their assumption of a new meaning and significance within the context of the Shi^{c}ite theory of authority. The outcome of the *Saqifah Bani-Sa^{c}idah* and the *bay^{c}ah* with Abu Bakr was a manifestly traditional Arab act with no reference to the Muhammadan charismatic experience, while the Shi^{c}ite adaptation of pre-Islamic ideas, to the extent that it is detectable, was characterized by redefining these ideas into an essentially new metaphysical perspective. On the whole, Shi^{c}ite Islam considered itself the rightful heir to the essential doctrines of Islam, introduced through the Muhammadan charismatic revolution, and thus sought to preserve it as a distinct religious/cultural entity. This resistance was due particularly to the charismatic nature of ^{c}Ali and his male descendants, which naturally and consciously rejected any association or identification with the superseded traditional culture and its order of authority.

Within the Shi^{c}ite organization of authority, the central figure of ^{c}Ali and the specific modality of his charismatic legitimacy are of unsurpassed significance. As the prototypical figure of authority for the rest of Shi^{c}ite history, ^{c}Ali personified, in both his historical and his symbolic character, whatever is sacred to the Shi^{c}ites.

The charismatic nature of ^{c}Ali's authority is verified by the fundamental Shi^{c}ite belief that the Qur'anic verse V:67 was revealed on the occasion of *Ghadir Khum* and specifically designated ^{c}Ali as the Prophet's successor. "O Messenger! Make known that which hath been revealed unto thee from Thy Lord, for if thou do it not, thou wilt not have conveyed His message. . . ." The Shi^{c}ites also believe that the Qur'anic verse V:3 was revealed once ^{c}Ali was designated by the Prophet as his successor: "This day have I perfected your religion for you and completed my favour unto you, and have chosen for you as religion Al-ISLAM." It is also significant to note, in order to realize the Shi^{c}ites' perspective, that through this verse "Islam" as such finds its name. The Qur'an is generally considered as a symbol of divine grace by all Muslims. This, however, assumes a particular significance for the Shi^{c}ites. Nasr has indicated that

the grace (*barakah*) of the Qur'an, as conveyed to the world by the Prophet, reached the Sunni community through the companions (foremost among them were Abu Bakr, ^{c}Umar, ^{c}Uthman, ^{c}Ali, and a few others such as Anas and

Salman), and during succeeding generations through the ulama and the Sufis, each in his own world. This *barakah*, however, reached the Shi^cite community especially through ^cAli and the Household of the Prophet—in its particular Shi^cite sense. (Tabataba'i 1975, 13)

^cAli's charismatic authority is also realized in the hierarchical order of authority stipulated in Shi^cite metaphysical self-understanding. The following trilateral structure of authority is thus apparent in the Shi^cite notion of legitimacy.

1)–*Allah's authority*, which is Universal and Absolute. According to the Qur'an, "it is Allah unto Whom belongeth the Sovereignty of the heavens and the earth" (II:107); also,

> Say: O Allah! Owner of Sovereignty! Thou givest Sovereignty unto whom Thou wilt, and Thou withdrawest Sovereignty from whom Thou Wilt. Thou exaltest Whom Thou wilt, and Thou abasest Whom Thou wilt. In Thy Hands is the good. Lo! Thou art Able to do all Things. (III:26)

2)–*The Prophet's authority*, which is personal and charismatic, legitimated by the grace of Allah and His choosing Muhammad as His messenger. According to the Qur'an:

> Say (O Muhammad): O mankind! Lo! I am the Messenger of Allah to you all—(The messenger of) Him unto Whom belongeth the Sovereignty of the heavens and the earth. There is no God save Him. He quickeneth and He giveth death. So believe in Allah and His Messenger, the unlettered prophet, who believeth in Allah and in His Words,and follow him that haply ye may be led aright. (VII:158)

3)–*The authority of ^cAli*, which is by virtue of his personal qualifications, of his proximity to the Prophet, and of his being blessed by the divine grace for the leadership of the Islamic community after Muhammad. The Shi^cites believe that the authority of ^cAli, thus sanctified and established, was then preserved and transferred to his male descendants.

The charismatic nature of ^cAli's authority for the Shi^cites can be verified further by considering the particular characteristics attributed to him by his pious followers: (1) the lineage of ^cAli, who had close family ties to the Prophet; (2) the birth of ^cAli inside Ka^cbah, the holiest shrine of Islam; (3) ^cAli's childhood, spent under the protective care of Muhammad; (4) ^cAli's marriage, to the Prophet's daughter, Fatimah; (5) the Qur'anic references to ^cAli—the Shi^cites believe that verses such as II:255 refer to ^cAli; (6)^cAli's membership in *ahl al-bayt*, which, according to Qur'anic verses III:61 and XLII:23, among others, is infallible; (7) ^cAli as guide (*hadi*) to his people, from Qur'anic verse XIII:7; (8) ^cAli as the leader (Imam) of his people, from

Qur'anic verse XXXVI:12; (9) ᶜAli as the most knowledgeable Muslim, from Qur'anic verse XIII:43; (10) ᶜAli as the most virtuous person, from Qur'anic verse LXVI:4; (11) ᶜAli as the foremost amongst the truthful, from Qur'anic verse IX:119; (12) ᶜAli as a charitable Muslim, from Qur'anic verse V:55; (13) ᶜAli's bravery in the battles of Badr, Uhud, Khaybar, the siege of Khandaq, and other battles; (14) ᶜAli's merits according to many Shiᶜite-accepted prophetic traditions, among them "I and ᶜAli are from one and the same light"; "O ᶜAli your flesh is my flesh, your blood is my blood, your self is my self, and your soul is my soul"; "Verily, ᶜAli is from me and I am from him and he is the ruler of all the faithful"; "O ᶜAli, your relationship to me is similar to the one that existed between Moses and Aaron"; "I am the city of knowledge and ᶜAli is its gate" (Khan 1981, 92-129). Summarizing the Shiᶜite position, Goldziher said that the early supporters of ᶜAli "saw in ᶜAli, and only in him, the embodiment of the divine right to the institution of the caliphate" (1981, 170).

It is within this trilateral hierarchical structure that ᶜAli's charismatic authority was considered rightful and legitimate. His authority claimed no direct connection to divinity, despite the fact that later some extreme Shiᶜites did develop such ideas. Essentially, the legitimacy of his authority was considered by the mainstream Shiᶜites to be the result of his proximity to Muhammad. Bendix has pointed out that "the charismatic leader is a man who demands obedience on the basis of the mission he feels called upon to perform" (1960, 301). Whereas Muhammad claimed to have such a mission from Allah, ᶜAli's charismatic authority was legitimated by Muhammad and, through him, by Allah. Thus, ᶜAli's charismatic authority was in no way "revolutionary," as Muhammad's was. His was the continuation of Muhammadan charismatic authority, seeking to establish the same cultural order that the Prophet had introduced and consolidated.

If "traditionalization" and "legalization" refer to any fundamental changes in the social relationship that existed during the charismatic period, the continuity of authority from Muhammad to ᶜAli would not warrant such a characterization. The force of charisma, persisting in the post-Muhammadan era, seeks its perpetuation, rather than traditionalization or legalization, in the figure of ᶜAli and his posterity. While emphasizing the transient nature of charismatic authority, Weber maintained that "nevertheless charisma remains a highly important element of the social structure, although of course in a greatly changed sense" (1946, 262), which he defined as "routinization," or the gradual and systematic abandonment of the charismatic experience.

But Shiᶜite Islam manifests the successful attempt to perpetuate charisma. Functionally and socially similar, yet hierarchically inferior, ᶜAli's authority followed Muhammad's. Weber underestimated the force of charisma to perpetuate itself, despite the loss of its primary embodiment, in its original, spontaneous form. Weber's statement may be modified—particularly by emphasizing "nevertheless, charisma remains a highly important element of the social structure"—by maintaining that charisma will remain indefinitely a highly important element in the historical course of the society in which it has appeared, because that society, in each and every facet of its charismatic existence, must respond continuously to that moment despite other independent social factors, changes, and alterations in the modes of economic production that influence the course of historical progression. Shiᶜite Islam seeks to perpetuate the Muhammadan charismatic legacy, to make it permanently present in the figures of the Imams. The culture that developed this metaphysical world-view reflected this tendency. The Muslim majority, however, broke the Muhammadan spontaneous charismatic authority into specified nomadic Arab traditions—determined spheres of authority; this, too, was reflected later in the institutional development of the Sunnite world.

What animates this perpetuation of charisma is the nature of the Muhammadan message, so unique and particular in the religious consciousness of the Arabs. Al-Baghadadi (d. 1038), the Muslim historian of religion, considered the first cause of disagreement among Muslims to be the interpretation of Muhammad's death.

> Some thought that he has not died and as Jesus the Son of Maryam, God has taken him to the heavens, but once Abu Bakr recited the divine words to Muhammad: "You shall die, and so will they," and said to them, "he who worshipped Muhammad, he has indeed died, and as for those who worship the God of Muhammad, He is alive and shall not die," the disagreement stopped and they all acknowledged his death. (1954, 9)

In such circumstances the personal continuity and transference of charisma from Muhammad to ᶜAli was a viable alternative to immediate "routinization"; and this is exactly what constitutes the Shiᶜite view of authority after the Prophet. This view, however, had to be elaborated within an Islamic concept of authority, to the extent that the essential foundations of this religion were established in its sacred text.

Due in part to such circumstances, ᶜAli and his descendants were considered as charismatic leaders continuing the cultural revolution introduced by the Prophet. As S.H. Nasr has noted:

> inasmuch as the *Imams* constitute for Shiᶜism a continuation of the spiritual authority of the Prophet—although not, of course, his law-bringing function—their sayings and actions represent a supplement to the prophetic hadith and sunnah. From a purely religious and spiritual point of view, the *Imams* may be said to be for Shiᶜism an extension of the personality of the Prophet during the succeeding centuries. (Tabataba'i 1975, 12-13)

This personal continuity of charisma from one figure to another constitutes the essential characteristic of the Shiᶜite view of authority after Muhammad.

Commenting on the transient nature of charismatic authority, Bendix has observed that "the leader's disciples and the people at large want to see that power preserved for themselves and their descendants, as long as they believe in its legitimacy" (1960, 304). The Weberian understanding of this "preservation" is through one of the two courses of traditionalization or rationalization. The Shi°ite case, however, exemplifies a personal preservation or continuity, one in which a figure of authority, as opposed to an institution, embodies charismatic authority and enforces such social relationships. Thus, although inferior to Muhammad in the Shi°ite hierarchy of authority, °Ali demanded the same *type* of obedience and commanded the same *mode* of authority.

In Huart's judicious wording:

> In Muhammad's lifetime, °Ali took part in almost all expeditions, often as standard-bearer, twice only as commander. . . . He always displayed a courage which later on became legendary; at Badr he killed a large number of Kurayshites; at Khaybar he used a heavy door as a shield, and the victory of the Muslims over the Jews was due to his ardour; at Hanayu (8/630) he was one of those who stoutly defended the Prophet. (1979, 30-32)

Commenting on °Ali's religious character, while criticizing the negative and neutral assessments of Lammens and Caetani, Huart has also asserted that

> neither Lammens nor Caetani has brought out the religiosity of °Ali and its reflections in his policy. There is an abundance of notices on his austerity, his rigorous observances of religious rites, his detachment from worldly goods, his scruples in regard to booty and retaliation; and there is no reason to suppose all these details were invented or exaggerated, since all his actions were dominated by this religious spirit. (1979, 30-32)

Perhaps the best moderate commentary upon °Ali's strict religiosity is Huart's assessment that

> obedience to divine Law was the keynote of his conduct, but his ideas were governed by an excessive rigorism, and it was perhaps for this reason that his enemies described him as *mahdud*, "narrow-minded." Imprisoned in his strict conformism, he could not adapt himself to the necessities of "a situation which was very different from that of Muhammad's time," thus he lacked that political flexibility which was, on the other hand, one of the pre-eminent qualities of Mu°awiyah. (ibid.)

°Ali was also considered a judicial authority, *Nahj al-Balaqhah*, the book attributed to him, being full of judgments that he had passed on specific occasions. He was followed also as a spiritual authority, many Sufi orders traced their origins back to him. These qualities were subsequently claimed by other Shi°ite Imams and thus recognized by their followers. The charismatic nature of these Imams prevented the rapid disintegration of the prophetic authority into different domains and their subsequent institutionalization.

Thus the perpetuation of charisma from Muhammad to 'Ali prevented, simultaneously, either the "routinization," in the Weberian sense of this word, that is, economic forces altering the charismatic social relationships, of the former's charismatic authority, or an overwhelming resurgence of the pre-Islamic Arab traditional order, or the disintegration of Muhammad's charismatic authority into various institutionalized forms of domination. Instead, Shi'ite Islam is a historical experience in the perpetuation and continuity of charisma.

The question of the "continuity of charisma" was examined by Scarrilla (1974, 91-108), who has maintained that there is a paradox, if not a contradiction, in the Weberian concept of "the routinized charisma." The argument is that personal as charismatic authority is, it cannot be "routinized." She thus stipulates the continuity of charisma from "pure" to "routinized," as opposed to "charismatic" to "noncharismatic" authority. The Shi'ite case, however, is the peculiar process of the continuity from "pure charisma" to "pure charisma"; only the definition of the form of relationship between the charismatic figure and "divinity" changed from Muhammad to 'Ali.

A tension has thus been created by the "institutionalization" of a form of authority which is inherently, as Weber indicated, anti-institutional; the result has been the tumultuous history of Shi'ite Islam, attributable equally to different social and economic factors of each historical period and to the tenacious attachment of the Shi'ites to the charismatic legacy of Muhammad, 'Ali, and the other Imams. "Charisma," as Weber noted, "knows only inner determination and inner restraint" (1946, 246). Expanded out of a charismatic episode to a historical scale, "inner determination" and "inner restraint" consume any external pressure that seeks to "routinize" and "organize" the social and psychological life.

The specific doctrinal attributes of 'Ali, as the central figure of authority in the Shi'ite conception of legitimacy, gradually constituted the institutional basis of its historical survival. A number of interrelated doctrinal institutions form the dogmatic structure of the Shi'ite order of authority.

The charismatic authority of 'Ali and his descendants constitutes the Shi'ite doctrine of *imamah*: the rightful authority of 'Ali and his descendants as the legitimate leaders of the Muslim community after the Prophet. The doctrine of *imamah* is based on the two principles of *nass* (the explicit designation of a member of *ahl al-bayt* as the rightful successor to the Prophet) and *'ilm* (the esoteric knowledge of the Qur'an to be transmitted from one Imam to the other). The doctrine was particularly developed by Ja'far al-Sadiq, the sixth Shi'ite Imam (700-765).

Immah and *nubuwwah* (the prophethood of Muhammad) are two of the five fundamental pillars of Shi'ite Islam. The other three pillars are *tawhid* (the unity of God), *'adl* (the justice of God), and *ma'ad* (the resurrection on the

Day of Judgment). Within the Weberian context, *nubuwwah*—which indicates that as Muslims Shi^cites believe Muhammad was sent by God as His messenger—is the charismatic authority of the Prophet, and *imamah*—which indicates that ^cAli and his descendants are divinely ordained as the Imams of the Muslim community—is the charismatic authority of ^cAli and his descendants. *Nubuwwah* and *imamah* are both founded on the same principle, divine dispensation of leadership for the human community, but on two different levels of proximity to Allah as the organizer and "author" of their authority: *nubuwwah* is higher than *imamah*.

As Shahrastani has pointed out, the Shi^cites maintain that

> *imamate* is not a judicious matter to be left to people's choice, so that *Imams* are chosen by them; the question is rather a matter of principle, and a pillar among the pillars of the faith. And it is not right [to assume] that the Messenger— May God's greetings be upon him—disregarded this matter or left it unspecified, or to the choices of the masses. (1979, 191)

The Prophet, in his position as the "messenger of God," becomes the sole source of legitimacy for the Imam's charismatic authority.

Further verifying the charismatic nature of the Imams, considered to be divinely sanctified, the Shi^cites believe that their Imams have esoteric knowledge of the faith (*al-^cilm al-ladunni*). They believe this knowledge was first revealed to ^cAli by the Prophet, and by ^cAli to his subsequent descendants. The possession of this knowledge, especially in its esoteric dimension, is a testimony to the flow of authority down from the Prophet to each and every Imam. The Shi^cites believe that while Muhammad was the last prophet, and thus the last person to receive divine revelation (*wahy*), the Imams receive divine inspiration (*ilham*) and are, as such, in contact with the "Holy Source of all knowledge."

The question of *ilham* is very important in distinguishing the personal charisma of the Shi^cite Imams from the "charisma of office." The Imams are considered to be charismatic not because they occupy the "office of *imamah*" but because of their own personal qualities. This distinguishes the Shi^cite Imams from figures such as the Hasidic Zaddiks whose authority, according to Bosk (1979, 150-67), was not gained through "personal illumination" but by inheritance. The most important attribute of this office was that the Zaddiks derived their authority from an "erotic union" with the Shekhina (divine presence), the feminine aspect of God. The Shi^cite Imams, however, are considered the personal recipients of the gift of grace from the Omnipresent Source of all authority.

The forceful presence of the Muhammadan charismatic legacy animated Shi^cite Islam as a divine dispensation designed to perpetuate Allah's ultimate authority on earth. Corbin has categorically indicated that

I believe that Shi°ism is the only religion that has permanently preserved the relationship of divine guidance between God and humanity forever, and continuously perpetuates the *wilayah* [the authority of Shi°ite *Imams* by virtue of their esoteric knowledge of the Qur'an]. Judaism ended the prophethood, which is a true relationship between God and the human world, in Moses, and after that did not recognize the prophethood of Christ or Muhammad, and has thus disconnected the relationship; and similarly the Christians have stopped with Christ, and the Sunnite Muslims with Muhammad, and after the completion of prophethood in him they do not recognize the existence of any relationship between the creator and the created. And it is only Shi°ism that, while considering the period of prophethood ending with Muhammad, keeps the *wilayah*, which is that relationship of guidance and completion, forever alive. (tabafaba°i, 1969, 7)

Discounting Corbin's generalization about Judasism and Christianity, in Shi°ite Islam, where Imams are considered to be divinely ordained to succeed the Prophet and thus possess and exercise personal charisma, there develops neither the "traditionalization" nor the "legalization" of Muhammad's charismatic authority. Although, "in a strict sense," as Bendix has indicated, the "problem [of succession] is insoluble, for charisma is an inimitable quality that some higher power is believed to have bestowed upon one person" (1960, 305), the Shi°ite response to this crisis is the stipulation of a "leader . . . who will manifest his own charismatic qualification" (305).

But Muhammad, according to the Qur'an, was the last prophet; and, as Bendix has pointed out, "a new incarnation of charisma may be ruled out by dogmatic consideration, as in the case of Christ or in the original conception of Buddha" (1960, 305). The charisma of °Ali is thus not independent of Muhammad; for the Shi°ites it is its "logical" continuity. Consequently, in the postprophetic period, there is a continuation of the same set of social relationships among the small but influential Shi°ite minority that had existed during Muhammad's time, yet now maintained through the charismatic quality of °Ali, a condition to be continued with other Shi°ite Imams. These Imams are, in a strict Weberian sense, "natural" leaders who appear

in times of psychic, physical, economic, ethical, religious, political distress . . . holders of specific gifts of the body and spirit; and these gifts have been believed to be supernatural, not accessible to everybody. (Weber 1946, 245)

The Shi°ite organization of authority is further complemented by a system of sacred symbolics that collectively lend legitimacy to its derivative continuity with both the Qur'anic revelation and the Muhammadan legacy. In the Qur'anic references to the particular characteristics of a legitimate leader, two divine attributes, knowledge (*°ilm*) and power (*qudrah*), are emphasized as the indication of a rightful authority. In the story of the Israelites, the Qur'anic verse II:247 reads

> Their prophet said unto them: Lo! Allah has raised up Saul to be king for you.
> They said how can he have kingdom over us when we are more deserving of the
> kingdom that he is, since he has not been given wealth enough? He said: Lo!
> Allah hath chosen him above you and hath increased him abundantly in wisdom
> and stature. Allah bestoweth His sovereignty on whom He will. Allah is All-
> Embracing, All-Knowing.

Such passages for the Shi^{c}ites indicate the divine origins of any form of
earthly power. Furthermore, the legitimating leadership qualities, such as
knowledge (^{c}ilm) and power (qudrah), are considered as the earthly manifestations of divine attributes. "Knowledge" (^{c}ilm) becomes an essential
attribute of the Shi^{c}ite Imams and is manifested in qualities, such as the
knowledge of the hidden meaning of the Qur'an, that the Shi^{c}ites maintain
their Imams possess. Allah's favoring those who possess knowledge (for
example, verse LVIII:11, "Allah will exalt those who believe among you and
those who have knowledge, to high ranks . . .") then becomes an added
justification for the legitimacy of the Shi^{c}ite Imams. This knowledge of the
hidden meaning of the Qur'an ultimately gives rise to the esoteric aspect of
Shi^{c}ite Islam, of which S.H. Nasr has maintained that:

> Shi^{c}ism and the general esoteric teaching of Islam which are usually identified
> with the essential teachings of Sufism have a very complex and intricate rela-
> tionship. Shi^{c}ism must not be equated simply with Islamic esotericism as such.
> In the Sunni world Islamic esotericism manifests itself almost exclusively as
> Sufism, whereas in the Shi^{c}ite world, in addition to a Sufism similar to that
> found in the Sunni world, there is an esoteric element based upon love (ma-
> habbah) which colors the whole structure of the religion. (Tabataba'i 1975, 14)

Physical power, bodily stature, and courage, too, will become essential
attributes of the Shi^{c}ite Imam that, particularly in the case of the first and the
third Imam, will function as the archetype of such qualities to be emulated by
the multitude of the Shi^{c}ites. The believer in such attributes perpetuates the
charismatic relationship and prevents the "routinization" of the message. In
a typical routinization process, "the charismatic message," as Bendix has
pointed out, "becomes variously a dogma, theory, legal regulation, or the
content of an oral or written tradition" (1960, 304). In ^{c}Ali's case, however,
a continuous interpretation of the Qur'an is believed to be related to his
"personal knowledge."

The dogmatic doctrines of the Shi^{c}ites are, perhaps inevitably, gradually
established, but ^{c}Ali, as well as other Shi^{c}ite Imams, are believed to be the
necessary sources of their interpretation and application. Furthermore, for the
Shi^{c}ites the prophetic traditions are supplemented by traditions about the
Imams; that is, as exemplary figures of authority they function as Muhammad
did. Such qualifications of the Imams establish the foundation of their authority in divine sanctity and justification.

Thus, insofar as the Shi°ites express a particular mode of the continuity of authority after the charismatic figure, the Weberian position that in the case of a successor "the concept of divine right is fundamentally altered and now comes to mean authority by nature of a personal right . . ." is not valid; and, based on this historical case, probably a new mode of continuity, after a charismatic event, can be recognized, that is, the perpetuation of charismatic authority, considered to be justified by divine right, due primarily to the persistence of the similar social conditions that gave rise to the initial charismatic event.

The Shi°ites consider °Ali's charismatic authority—due to his divine right—to be yet another form of justification. They maintain that it is a divine dispensation to designate not only prophets but their "deputies" as well. They refer, for example, to the Qur'anic verse XX:25-36, according to which the following exchange occurs between Moses and God:

> (Moses) said: My Lord! Relieve my mind, And ease my task for me; And loose a knot from my tongue, That they may understand my saying. Appoint for me a henchman from my folk, Aaron, my brother. Confirm my strength with him And let him share my task, That we may glorify Thee much And much remember Thee. Lo! Thou art ever Seeing us. He said: Thou art granted thy request, O Moses.

There are other such Qur'anic verses that the Shi°ites refer to: "We verily gave Moses the Scripture and placed with him his brother as henchman (*wazir*)" (XXV:35). The Shi°ites read these verses as the indications of the divine right of the "deputies" of the prophets (among them °Ali) and the close proximity of these "deputies" to the prophets. What intensifies this justification for the Shi°ites is the prophetic tradition in which Muhammad says to °Ali: "Your relation to me is as Aaron to Moses . . ." (Khan 1981, 79). This argument is used further by the Shi°ites to nullify the outcome of the *Saqifah Bani-Sa°idah* (the election of Abu Bakr as the caliph).

Within the Weberian framework, it may be argued that the same set of social conditions within which the Muhammadan charismatic revolution emerged necessitates the persistence of a charismatic form of social relationships. Weber's argument for the necessity of the immediate routinization of charisma rests on purely economic grounds. He believed that charisma

> is the opposite of all ordered economy. It is the very force that disregards economy. . . . Charisma can do this because by its very nature it is not an "institutional" and permanent structure, but rather, where its "pure" type is at work, it is the very opposite of the institutionally permanent. (1946, 248)

In a very peculiar way, however, Shi°ite Islam is an institutionalized form of charismatic authority. The tension thus created by the institutionalization of an uninstitutionalizable mode of authority accounts for the tumultuous history of Shi^{c}ite Islam up to the present time.

An example of such a social condition, without intending to reduce the complex development of Shi^{c}ite Islam to only one cause, would be the disinherited *mawali* who were particularly attracted to the Shi^{c}ite cause. Thus, whereas the occupational basis of the Sunnite majority was essentially Meccan merchants, anxious to resume a routine economic life, that of the Shi^{c}ite minority was disinherited *mawali* who were still to realize the social and economic equality they had been promised. As Jafri has reported, "the Shi^{c}ites in Kufa, especially the *mawali* among them, wanted an active movement which could relieve them from the oppressive rule of the Syrians [the Umayyads]" (1979b, 239-40). Hitti has also pointed out that

> reduced to the position of clients (*mawali*), these neophyte Moslems formed the lowest stratum of Moslem society, a status which they bitterly resented. This explains our finding them in many cases espousing such causes as the Shi^{c}ite in al-Iraq or the Kharijite in Persia. (1970, 232)

The Muhammadan charismatic movement engendered a vital religious consciousness in the Arab collective experience that not only energized the period of his life so forcefully as to give rise to a new moral demand system but also refused to be immediately and totally "routinized" in established institutions. Despite specific economic conditions that may have anticipated the Muhammadan movement, the charismatic event thus engendered superseded apparently insurmountable material difficulties, which ranged from a deeply rooted and pervasive traditional mode of authority to commercial networks of ancient origin. With almost the same metaphysical stamina that the Muhammadan charismatic authority overcame its material obstacles, the Shi^{c}ite continuity of the Muhammadan legacy surpassed immediate material forces to routinize a pervasive charismatic experience. Throughout the trajectory of the personal authority of the Shi^{c}ite Imams, however restricted to their small community of followers it may have been, the same charismatic force that had animated Muhammad's time perpetuated itself in the course of Islamic history. This continuity was ultimately guaranteed through the doctrinal agency of the "Hidden Imam," according to which the charismatic energy engendered during Muhammad's time became permanently present and active for the rest of Islamic history. The absence of the "Hidden Imam" is, in fact, the permanent presence of the active Muhammadan legacy.

Whereas the Muhammadan charismatic legacy was thus perpetuated in the Shi^{c}ite Imams, the Kharijites dispensed with this legacy in an entirely different manner, to which I shall turn in the next chapter.

7

The Foundations of Kharijite Authority: The Dissemination of Charisma

> *The Messenger of God . . . said, "Whoever obeys me obeys God, and whoever disobeys me disobeys God. Whoever obeys the Commander obeys me, and he who disobeys him disobeys me. The Imam* is simply the shield behind whom the fighting takes place, from which one seeks protection. So when he orders fear of God and is just, he shall receive his reward, but if he holds otherwise, it will bring guilt upon him." The Messenger . . . said, "Even if a mutilated slave is made your commander, and he leads you in accord with the Book of God, hear him and obey." The Messenger of God . . . said, "Hear and obey, though an Abyssinian slave with a head like a raisin be placed over you."
>
> —Hadith on the Ruler, from al-Khatib al-Tibrizi's *Niches of Lamps* (1336)

In the thirty-sixth year of Hijra (656) ⁽Uthman was murdered, ostensibly by malcontent Muslims disillusioned with his partiality towards the members of his own family. Yet tribal conflicts, as opposed to merely political factionalism, could not have been totally absent. Watt has maintained that

> there is no obvious economic or social difference between those who were dissatisfied with ⁽Uthman and those who were prepared to tolerate him. Most of these men were from nomadic tribes, and it may be that tribal rivalries played a part in deciding which sections supported ⁽Uthman and which took an active part in the movement against him. Distinct from the former nomads were the Quraysh of Mecca, and among them it appears that members of clans formerly in alliance with ⁽Uthman's clan (Umayya) tended to support him, while men from the rival group associated with the clan of Makhzam tended to oppose him. (1973, 9)

ᶜUthman was from the clan of Banu Umayyah. Compelled by their traditional web of affiliation, this tribe, headed by Muᶜawiyah, set out to avenge the murder of their fellow clan member. Muᶜawiyah and his fellow Banu Umayyads considered ᶜAli, now the fourth caliph of the Muslim community by general consent, chiefly responsible for ᶜUthman's murder. In July 657, ᶜAli and Muᶜawiyah engaged in their historical battle at Siffin. ᶜAli's army was on the verge of a decisive victory when Muᶜawiyah shrewdly proposed that he and ᶜAli each nominate a *hakam* ("arbiter," a traditional, pre-Islamic position occupied by recognizably wise men) who would argue the case of their respective leaders based on Qur'anic doctrines. A majority of ᶜAli's supporters accepted this arbitration; yet a strong minority objected by proclaiming the principle of *La hukma illa li-Llahi* ("no judgment other than God's"), maintaining that the obvious victory of ᶜAli over Muᶜawiyah was divine judgment on the former's righteous cause, and thus ᶜAli should not yield to any human arbitration. This group "seceded"—and thus their name *Khawarij,* "those who seceded"—to a village near Kufah, Harura, and elected a certain ᶜAbdullah b. Wahb al-Rasibi as their leader.

The most important primary sources of the Kharijites include al-Baghdadi (1954), al-Masᶜudi (1977), al-Shahrastani (1971), and al-Tabari (1879-1901). On the reliability of these sources, Levi della Vida has warned that "it should be noted that the narratives of Arab historians on the origin of the Khariji movement are very confused and contradictory" (1953, 246-49), while admitting that "this is probably the most obscure and controversial period in the whole of Islamic history" (ibid.). Watt, however, has concluded that "nevertheless it becomes possible to discern the political groupings and alignments from which there emerged the 'religio-political' parties with which we are here concerned" (1973, 9).

The Kharijites are also known as *al-Haruriyah, al-Muhakkimah* ("those who recite the motto: '*La hukma illa li-Llahi*'"), and *al-Shurat* ("the vendors," those who have sold their souls for the cause of God). Watt has examined extensively the various meanings the word "Kharijite" might have conveyed (1973, 15-19). The most generally accepted understanding of this word is "those who withdrew their support from ᶜAli." The Muslim historian of religion, al-Shahrastani (d. 1153), provided the following definition of the *Khawarij* (Kharijites):

> Whoever disobeys (*kharaja*) the rightful Imam who has been accepted by the majority of Muslims, he is called a *khariji,* whether this disobedience is in the time of the four rightly guided caliphs or during the time of *tabiᶜin.* (1979, 144).

According to al-Baghdadi, the initial Kharijites were mostly from the tribe of *Tamim,* and they elected two leaders: ᶜAbdulla ibn Whab al-Rasibi and Harqus ibn Zahir al-Bajli (1954, 43).

The arbitration resulted in the nominal victory of Mu°awiyah over °Ali, an outcome which caused further dissension within °Ali's camp and thus strengthened the Kharijites position. °Ali diverted his attention from Mu°awiyah and attacked the Kharijites in a battle known as al-Nahrawan on 17 July 658. Ibn Wahb, leader of the Kharijites, and a significant number of his followers were killed in this battle. The Kharijite rebellion was not suppressed by this battle and continued throughout the tenure of °Ali's caliphate (656-661) and subsequently during the tenure of the Umayyads (661-750) and even the °Abbasyds (750-1258). °Ali himself was murdered on 24 January 661, by a Kharijite avenging the al-Nahrawan defeat.

Historical sources on the Kharijites are confusing and sometimes contradictory. Modern historians are not unanimous in their views either. The standard reading of the emergence of the Kharijites was provided by, among others, Levi della Vida, whose account differed from Welhausen's, Lammen's, and Caetani's who dissociated the "arbitration" episode from the beginnings of the Kharijite movement (1953, 246-49).

What can be safely assumed is that the Kharijite movement was essentially an embodiment of the aspirations of a multitude of disillusioned and disinherited Muslims who, while in their acceptance of the new faith, were released from the stabilizing bonds of their traditional order, and yet did not come totally under the cohesive command of a new political culture, stemming from the predicates of Islam as the new moral demand system. Most of the Kharijites, whether tribal Arab or *mawali*, were primarily from the lower social and economic strata of their respective societies. However, the intellectual leadership of the Kharijites did not come necessarily from these lower strata. There were many scholars and men of letters among the later adherents of this movement (Levi della Vida 1979).

On the economic exploitation of the *mawali* and their social status, von Grunebaum wrote

> Conversion brought the *maula* (plural *mawali*) neither social nor economic equality although the "democracy" of the Prophet's message had seemed to give them this right. The *mawali* troops received maintenance pay and a share of booty, but no pension; they often served on foot, while the Arabs were mounted; neither did Islam free them of land tax, *Kharaj*, or if it did it imposed a tithe, *°ushr*, on the harvest instead. The relatively numerous middle class of *mawali* of good education and considerable wealth enjoyed high respect in the circles of the pious. . . . This, together with the circumstance that their social position in no way corresponded to their contribution, sharpened the explosive potential of their grievance, (1970, 73).

Hitti has also verified this point:

> Reduced to the position of clients (*mawali*), those neophyte Moslems, formed

the lowest stratum of Moslem society, a status which they bitterly resented. This explains our finding them in many cases espousing such causes as the Shiᶜite in al-ᶜIraq or the Kharijite in Persia. (1970, 232)

Brought into the new collectivity—the Islamic community (*ummah*)—the Kharijites believed their aspirations had been betrayed by both the Umayyad aristocracy of the Quraysh tribe and the Shiᶜite oligarchy of the Prophet's household. Disillusioned with both, the Kharijites vowed to establish a form of Muslim "democracy" in which anyone, "even a black slave," could become the leader of *ummah* through popular "election" and consent.

For the Kharijites, the fate of authority in the post-Muhammadan period may be characterized as the dissemination of charisma. They equally rejected the routinization that the Prophet's charismatic authority had assumed under the Muslim majority and its perpetuation strived for among the partisans of ᶜAli. One of their major doctrines, according to which the multitude of Muslims have the prerogative right to proclaim the authority of their leader illegitimate, indicates the precarious state of leadership in their community. In reporting the origin of the Kharijite movement, al-Baghdadi has pointed out that

it is said that in the Battle of Siffin, once the agreement of the two armies was set on the arbitration between ᶜAli and Muᶜawiyah, a certain Rabiᶜi from Banu-Yashkat, who was a supporter of ᶜAli in this battle, mounted his horse and attacked the Muᶜawiyah's army and killed a number of them; then he turned toward ᶜAli's supporters and killed one of them, shouting: "Lo and behold that I have deposed [both] ᶜAli and Muᶜawiyah from caliphate, and I rebel against their authority." (1954, 42-43)

Here, neither the traditional Arab practice of selecting and paying tribute (*bayᶜah*) to a leader, through which the Muslim majority chose their caliph, nor the divine right of the leader, according to which the partisans of ᶜAli considered his authority legitimated, constituted any institutional and established mode of authority, so vitally crucial for the survival of any doctrinally based community.

Their lack of any institutional form of authority, an external mechanism which could guarantee the continuity of their brand of Islam, resulted in a radical puritanism as the only means of securing some measure of membership in the community. One of the major doctrinal characteristics of the Kharijites was their strict moral austerity, their total rejection of the doctrine of justification by faith as opposed to justification by act. They considered anyone committing a sin as a *murtadd* (apostate) and, as such, subject to irrevocable expulsion from the Muslim community. An extremist wing of the Kharijites, the Azraqites, considered such apostates to be disbelievers and subsequently directed their terroristic activities towards them and their women and children. To these "apostates" the Kharijites applied the doctrine of isti^{c}rad (religious murder). On the moral puritanism of the Kharijites, Levi della Vida has asserted that

> it demands purity of conscience as an indispensable complement to bodily purity for the validity of acts of worship; one of their sects goes so far as to remove Sura XII from the Kur^{c}an (Surat Yusuf) because its contents are worldly and frivolous and make it unworthy to be the Word of God. (1953, 246-49)

Von Grunebaum recognized the ramifications of these puritanical positions, in terms of the lack of any institutional order, when he observed that

> the equation of moral absolutism with the right to rule made it a duty to depose a caliph who had fallen into grave sin and did not publicly repent; this of course provided a foundation in dogma for internal dissent and divisions into sects, in short for the impossibility of building a state. (1970, 62)

Von Grunebaum has expressed this same lack of institutionalization of authority when he refers to the Kharijites as "religious individualists" (71). "Religious individualism," in light of the social and universal claims of Islam, becomes extremely volatile and self-contradictory.

Among the Azraqites, as the representation of the original Kharijite position, no excusing reason was stipulated for any sin, no matter how insignificant. As a result, no viable cultural pattern could develop from the Kharijite doctrinal positions. As Rieff points out,

> Every culture has two main functions: (1) to organize the moral demands men make upon themselves into a system of symbols that make men intelligible and trustworthy to each other, thus rendering also the world intelligible and trustworthy; and (2) to organize the expressive remissions by which men release themselves, in some degree, from the strain of conforming to the controlling symbolic. . . . (1966, 232-33)

The most important reason for the failure of the Kharijites to formulate a workable cultural paradigm, develop an acceptable basis of legitimacy for the positions of authority, and ultimately survive historically was the lack of Rieff's second stipulation, recognition of some excusing reasons because of which some measures of tolerance, and thus persistency, would have been introduced into their otherwise totally interdictory system.

Both the Sunnite and Shi^{c}ite theories of authority, in their gradual and historial formation, were either immediately or subsequently translated into a particular form of what Weber would call a political association. Routinization of charisma in the case of the Muslim majority resulted in the immediate institutionalization of the caliphate as the political expression of the Muslim community; also, despite the tension resulting from the perpetuation of charisma in the Shi^cite case, the figure of the Imam and the position of the Imamate constituted a focal center around which the Shi^cite form of political structure could be established. The Kharijites, however, did not establish any form of continuity with the Muhammadan charismatic authority and its legacy and, at the same time, categorically rejected the pre-Muhammadan mode of traditional authority, particularly in its political and administrative aspects. As a result, the Kharijites remained "perpetual revolutionaries," as von Grunebaum noted:

> Incapable and perhaps unwilling to build a worldwide community, they were ready to "sell" their lives to gain paradise. They provided a rallying point for all those who felt it more important to destroy political and social injustice by breaking through the narrow mesh of reality in the name of a never fully thought-out divine law, than to preserve the all-embracing *ummah*, whose universality they yet confirmed with their concept of the equality of all believers. (1970, 62)

Reflecting both the pre-Islamic and traditional tendencies of the early caliphs and the anarchical nature of the Kharijites, von Grunebaum has also pointed out that

> the Kharijites as the champions of anarchy served as a focus of resentment of all those who harboured social grievances or who objected to the "un-Islamic" behaviour of the authorities, and it was impossible to eradicate them. (1970, 69)

The precarious position of leadership among the Kharijites was also recognized by Lambton:

> The legitimacy of the *imam* thus depended on his moral and religious probity (*^cadl*). He lost his legitimacy by any infraction of the divine law and was then to be removed, if necessary by force. No means, however, were laid down for when an *imam* ceased to be legitimate. (1981, 24).

Hitti called them "ever the deadly enemy of established order" (1970, 284) or "the most dangerous to Moslem unity" (208). On their puritanism, he remarked: "in endeavouring to maintain the primitive, democratic principles of Islam, the puritanical Kharijites caused rivers of blood to flow in the first three Moslem centuries" (247).

The dissemination of Muhammadan charismatic authority in the Kharijite case is demonstrated not only in the lack of any particular form of institutionalized political authority that could endure their puritanism and "democracy" but also in their essential opposition to the formation of any other spheres of authority, such as, religious (the *^culama'*), spiritual (the Sufis), military (the *amirs*), etc. As Hitti has pointed out, "in the course of time they forbade the cult of saints with the attendant local pilgrimages and prohibited

Sufi fraternities" (1970, 247). Of course, it has to be noted that the Kharijites lacked, for all intents and purposes, a territorial boundary within which they could develop such institutions over a long period of time because, as Weber indicated, "territory" is an essential part of any form of political association (1946, 78). Yet the intrinsic nature of the Kharijites, as a community, by definition precluded such institutional developments. What verifies this argument is that the Shiᶜites did not have territorial security for many centuries (until the establishment of the Egyptian Fatimids early in the tenth century) either, and yet their doctrinal position warranted the institutional development of the Imamate as the established, although not routinized, form of continuity of Muhammadan charismatic authority.

There were occasions, however, when the Kharijites did control considerable territory, and by abandoning some of their essential doctrinal positions they could secure some measure of stability. Watt has reported on the Najdite branch of the Kharijites, who ruled over Arabia for a period, that they "soon realized that exclusion from the community (leading to death or exile) was not a punishment that could be inflicted for every crime" (1973, 18-19). Najdah, the leader of the Najdite Kharajites, did not survive his conciliatory reforms and was deposed and murdered in 692. Watt provides a careful description of both the doctrinal modifications of the Najdites and their relations to the territorial necessities of organizing a state:

> the doctrinal views of Najda and his followers were conditioned by the fact that they accepted the responsibility for maintaining order over a large area, and were not simply concerned for a small body of people in a "camp." In these circumstances it was impossible to make death or exile (which were implied by exclusion from the community) the punishment for every instance of theft or adultery. This matter led Najda to make a distinction between fundamentals and nonfundamentals in religion. The fundamentals for Najda were the knowledge of God and of His messengers, acceptance of the revealed scriptures, and acknowledgment that the life and property of every Muslim was sacrosanct; in these respects ignorance was not condoned. In all other points, however, ignorance was excused, especially when it referred to some action about which there was no clear prescription in the Qur'an. (1973, 23)

Without this indispensable distinction between "fundamentals" and "nonfundamentals," which is functionally present in both Sunnite and Shiᶜite Islam, the Najdites would not have been able to last beyond their initial stage. Some particular remissive occasions had to be stipulated in the interdictory Kharijite system for it to become culturally viable. As a whole, the Kharijite movement lacked this built-in, self-perpetuating mechanism and, as a result, failed to survive. Najdah's formulation of an excusing reason for "a sinful act" won his group the title ᶜAdhiriyyah, "excusers" (24).

The Kharijite movement can be considered as a theological catalyst that generated doctrinal disputations among the Muslim community. They posed fundamental questions of "who is a Muslim," "what is a Muslim community," "who is a rightful leader of the Muslim community and how should his authority be justified," and "what should be the reaction of the Muslim community to a sinful act?" Any major split within the Kharijite subgroups was always in relation to the definition of a "sinful act." For example, the Safrites, one of the major subgroups of the Kharijites, were divided into three distinct divisions:

> one of their groups similar to Azraqites considered every sinner to be an infidel; another group said that an infidel is he who does not receive a legal punishment for his sin, and if he receives such a punishment he is unfaithful and not infidel; the third group said he who the qadi punishes according to the law is infidel. (al-Baghdadi 1954, 54)

All of these became crucial religious/political questions for which not only the Kharijite but also the Sunnite and the Shi^{c}ite theoreticians were compelled to formulate answers. But while the latter two positions stipulated their answers on a particular mode of continuity with the Muhammadan charismatic authority, the former remained an essentially precarious and impromptu dialectic between the contemporary political events and the Kharijite theological spontaneity. Thus, despite its obvious exaggeration, there is an element of truth in Watt's statement that "it seems likely that without the actions of the Kharijites they [i.e., non-Kharijite Muslims] might well have allowed the caliphate to become a secular Arab state" (1973, 35).

Al-Baghdadi reported al-Ash^{c}ari's definition of the Kharijites as those

> who consider ^{c}Ali, ^{c}Uthman, the leaders of the Battle of Camel [i.e., Talhah, Zubayr, and ^{c}A'ishah], and those who arbitrated [between ^{c}Ali and Mu^{c}awiyah], and those who yielded to this arbitration, or acknowledge the judgment of one or both of the arbitrators, as infidels; and who also consider it obligatory to rise and fight against a tyrannous ruler. (1954, 42)

This antiauthoritarian attitude became the most characteristic attribute of the Kharijites. Their radical "democracy," along with the lack of any institutional order of authority to regulate it, rendered any position of authority precarious and unstable. As Weber pointed out, "The introduction of elected officials always involves a radical alteration in the position of the charismatic leader. He becomes the 'servant' of those under his authority" (1968, 64).

The Kharijites' lack of any state organization, which would be derived from their doctrinal position vis-à-vis the question of succession to Muhammad, is linked directly to their use of violence as the legitimated form of expressing their religious views. Throughout the first Islamic century, the Kharijites continued to use extreme violence. They so influenced Muslim society with terroristic activities that they left their mark on architectural developments. In the interior of the mosque, around the *mihrab* (where the Imam leads the prayer), a fenced-off space (*maqsurah*) was gradually developed to protect the caliph from assassination. The construction of this device was attributed to Mu°awiyah (ruled 661-680) after an attempted assassination by the Kharijites (Hitti 1970, 261-62).

Isti°rad (religious murder) became one of the major terroristic devices through which the Kharijites sought to destabilize any power that confronted them. Lambton has remarked that the Kharijites "permitted assassination for religious reasons and also considered it lawful to kill the wives and children of the heterodox" (1981, 24).

The extreme puritanism of the Kharijites, as a functional substitute for an institutional form of authority, ultimately did not work to the benefit of the Kharijites and contributed to their final defeat, both doctrinally and politically. As Lambton has pointed out:

> the weakness of the Khariji movement lay in its attempt to push principles to extreme limits. Except in its more moderate form as followed by the Ibadiyyah, who in practice differed little from the Hanbali school of Sunnism, their doctrine proved unworkable and eventually died out. (1981, 27)

The Kharijite doctrine remained unworkable essentially due to its lack of any institutional continuity with Muhammadan charismatic authority. The question of leadership in their doctrine was so precarious that the legacy of Muhammadan authority began to diffuse and evaporate in the absence of either its routinization (for the Muslim majority) or perpetuation in a charismatic figure (Shi°ite Islam). For the Kharijites, the Muhammadan charismatic movement became a "transitory" event, in a Weberian sense, giving way to more immediate forces of institutional authority. But uses of violence among the Kharijites went so far that they considered *jihad* (religious war) as the sixth pillar of Islamic faith. This made any form of an institutionally legitimate and operative mode of authority virtually impossible.

The doctrinal "anti-establishment" of the Kharijites continued throughout their activities in different parts of Islamic lands. As late as the early eighth century (734-42), the Kharijite Berbers fought against the Umayyads in North Africa and Spain. In 741, caliph Hisham sent an army of 27,000 Syrians to fight the Kharijites (Hitti 1970, 502). The Zanj movement of the late ninth century (870-83) was also attributed to the remnants of the Kharijites. This Mesopotamian slave movement paralyzed al-Mu°tamid's reign (870-92); an army dispatched to fight the slaves was severely crushed and "the negroes overcame them all and, in accordance with a Kharijite doctrine now adopted by their leader, mercilessly put all prisoners and non-combatants to the sword" (Hitti 1970, 468). In the eastern part of the Muslim lands more horrific stories of Kharijite terror were reported by Muslim historians.

> Khawarij in cities and villages did not spare any one, and even put school
> children to the sword, and government officials harshly revenged these acts.
> Sometimes they [the Kharijites] surrounded children and their teacher in a
> mosque and demolished the mosque upon them; in some other places they
> burned the houses, or tied a man to two trees that had been forced to bend over,
> then releasing them, so that each part of the man is on one tree. (Zarrinkub
> 1951, 216)

The increasingly complicated development of the Muslim community, particularly through the rapid routinization process of the Muslim majority, was
bitterly resented by the Kharijites who lacked any viable alternative which
could survive their own relentless moral austerity, itself an impediment to
formal political and social structures. Watt believes that "the Kharijites were
protesting against the vastness of the organization structure in which they
were now caught up" (1973, 20). Their democratic spirit equally rejected the
alternative of the Shi^{c}ite charismatic continuity with Muhammad which in-
vested too much authority in their infallible *Imams*.

We must note, however, that in their self-understanding the Kharijites were
genuine Muslims and true believers. In fact, they considered themselves the
only Muslims and the rest as infidels. Their break with ^{c}Ali, particularly in
emphasizing their famous slogan *La hukma illa Li-Llahi* ("no judgment but
God's"), which has its Qur'anic origin in VI:57 and XII:40, was fundamentally on Islamic grounds; so was their moral austerity as well as their insistence that body politics should be founded on the Qur'an. The Muslim historian al-Dinawari (d. 895), in his *al-Akhbar al-Tiwal,* quotes the Kharijite
leader ^{c}Abdullah ibn-Wahb al-Rasibi as having said, "now I profess that our
enemies . . . have followed their whimsical desires and did not act upon the
Qur'anic command, and became tyranneous, indeed *jihad* against them is a
righteous act" (1967, 225). They indeed intended to establish Islam as the
new religious foundation upon which all Muslims, and not only Arabs, could
organize their lives. Yet despite their intentions, Muhammadan charismatic
authority was so diffused and disseminated in the Kharijite response to the
question of succession that no institutional form of authority was, or could be,
formed to secure its continuity. Watt's assessment of the Azraqites, a radical
group of the Kharijites, captured the essence of this dilemma:

> They may have thought of themselves as creating a new community of "be-
> lievers" in much the same way as Muhammad had done at Medina; at least they
> spoke of making the Hijra to their camp. Muhammad's community at Medina,
> however, had the advantage of having Muhammad to guide it with his personal
> wisdom and authority and with the fresh revelations which he received appro-
> priate to novel circumstances which had arisen. The Azraqites, on the other
> hand, based their community on a fixed set of rigidly defined principles, which
> gave little flexibility for adaptation to changing circumstances. (1973, 22)

The difficulty the Kharijites had in translating their doctrinal principles into operative communities was also evident in the rapid multiplication of their hostile sects. Al-Baghdadi enumerates twenty different Kharajite subgroups (1954, 41). The three major groups of the Kharijites in early Islamic history, the Azraqites, the Najdites, and the Waqifites, demonstrated, each in its particular way, the difficulties that this doctrinal position faced due to its lack of any specific mode of continuity with Muhammadan charismatic authority. The Azraqites, so named because of their leader, Nafiaᶜ ibn al-Azraq, were the most radical and revolutionary wing of the Kharijites. Particularly from 684 to 691 they paralyzed the Umayyad rule in Basra. This group, more than any other, developed the doctrinal formulation of strict moral austerity, a single sin excommunicated a Muslim. This group also held the position that the leader was particularly precarious and subject to the constant moral scrutiny of his followers. Not only did they not establish any particular mode of institutional authority but they also bitterly fought any such development in the main Sunnite establishment. They considered anyone who was not an Azraqite a *murtadd* (apostate) and called themselves "the people of heaven," as opposed to others who were "the people of hell." They considered their small community "the realm of Islam" (*dar al-Islam*) and the rest of the world "the house of war" (*dar al-harb*). Those who "sat still," as opposed to those who had made the "migration" (*hijrah*) to *dar al-Islam*, were all considered unbelievers and, as such, subject to terroristic attacks. As Watt has noted, "this puritanical theology became a justification for terrorism, and the Azraqites became noted and feared for their widespread massacres" (1962, 12). Within such a context no institution of authority could develop. Nor could the Kharijites' doctrinal positions in general establish the foundations of a cultural paradigm. "Cultures," as Rieff has pointed out, "achieve their measure of duration in the degree that they build releasing devices into the major control" (1966, 233). The Kharijites' extreme moral austerity and "democratic" spirit in practice were translated into sheer anarchy.

One of the peculiar aspects of the Azraqite movement was the considerable participation of women in their military campaigns, a remarkable instance that cannot be attributed readily either to pre-Islamic influences or to any particular Islamic doctrine. Petroshevsky has pointed out that

> one of the peculiarities of the armed struggle of the Kharijites was the participation of women. Particularly Um al-Hakim, the Azraqite woman hero (c. 71-79 A.H.), achieved many honors and became famous. During the campaigns, she was seeking martyrdom herself, shouting: "I am tired of washing my head and applying oil to it, is no one here to release me from this arduous task?" (1976, 60)

Shabibiyah, a Kharijite subgroup, accepted the leadership of women as well as men (Mashkur n.d., 38).

At the same time, the Kharijites extended their violent animosity to their enemies, and their women too. Al-Masᶜudi reports that after the Siffin incident,

> four thousand Kharijites got together and accepted the leadership of ᶜAbdullah ibn Wahb al-Rasibi and went to al-Madaᶜin; there they killed ᶜAbdullah ibn Khabab who was ᶜAli's governor in that province, cut off his head, slashed his wife's stomach who was pregnant, and killed other women, too. (1977, 763).

Al-Baghdadi, too, reports similar horrifying stories (1954, 43), including one about a particular group of Kharijites, the Sufrites, who had a special hatred of children and thought they should be avoided until they were mature and had consciously accepted Islam (52).

Insofar as the grip of their previous traditional order confined them within a mode of authority, the Kharijites broke away from their past; and insofar as the establishment of some form of continuity with Muhammadan authority could give them a measure of permanence, they failed to formulate it. For the Kharijites the transition of the moral demand system from pre-Islamic traditional to Muhammadan charismatic and from this to post-Muhammadan was particularly confusing. In the post-Muhammadan period, other Muslims accused them of many a *bidᶜah* (innovation into Islamic sacred law). Al-Baghdadi reports that "the Azraqites rejected the stoning, considered the betrayal of a trust as permissible, . . . they would cut the hand of a thief regardless of the degree of theft . . ." (1954, 48-49). All these injunctions were, of course, against either the specific Qur'anic precepts or the major schools (*madhahib*) of the Sunnite *shariah*. The particularities of the Kharijite religious laws were more in tune with their revolutionary and radically anti-authoritarian spirit than consistent within a body of an institutionalized moral demand system.

They believed that the Muslim community should be founded on the Qur'an, and yet they failed to stipulate within what particular institutional order that foundation should be formulated. Neither the traditional Arab authority, with which they consciously broke, nor the Muhammadan charismatic authority, to which they were devotionally and yet not organizationally attached, in the Kharijite (Azraqite) formulation provided their community with a workable institution of authority.

The Najdites were a more moderate Kharijite group of central Arabia. Having established a community for an extended period of time, as opposed to the Azraqites who were constantly on the run, the Najdites had some fundamental problems in their doctrinal positions when it came to institutionalizing their authority. From 686 to 692, they ruled autonomously over Bahrayn, ᶜUman, Yemen, and Hadramawt. This was a period when the Umayyad authority was being challenged by a certain Ibn al-Zubayr, giving the Kharijite Najdites an opportunity for a rather long period of stabilization. Even in this moderate group of Kharijites the question of authority was not resolved definitely. Watt has pointed out that among the Najdites "there were many quarrels about the leadership, and after the death of Najda in 692 the sect split up, and the parts either disappeared or were suppressed by the Umayyad generals" (1962, 13).

Yet the Najdites were faced with a number of harsh realties that led to some major modifications of their views. "Their responsibility for governing a large territory," Watt has remarked, "made them less rigorous in their interpretation." Watt has also noted that "for the Azraqites living in a camp, the man guilty of theft or adultery could easily be excluded from the camp; but it was not easy for the Najdites to banish every thief and adulterer from the entire region which they ruled" (14). "Less rigorous," in the Kharijite case, meant the introduction of some remissive occasions into their strict interdictory motifs. Thus they divided the Muslim obligations into fundamentals and nonfundamentals and consequently did not excommunicate a member from their community for any "nonfundamental" transgression, as the original Azraqite formulation would have done. Al-Baghdadi reports that the "Nadjdites, who are among the Kharijites, do not consider those of their fellow-believers who deserve legal punishment among the unbelievers" (1954, 42). The Azraqites did, of course, consider such a person among the unbelievers and executed the punishment. The Nadjdites' "revision" of the original Kharijite positions stipulated that an adulterer would be recognized and punished only as such and not as an unbeliever; so would a robber, a drunkard, etc. (42). They also modified their views of those who "sat still" and did not consider them "apostates"; they were now called the al-munafiqun, "hypocrites." The Nadjdites greatly toned down their violent radicalism and even recommended taqiyyah ("dissimulation" or "prudent fear") to their followers in the face of danger. Provisions were also stipulated for less vigorous punishments than excommunication in cases of theft and adultery. These changes and emendations, however, were to be considered as practical policies, however religiously justified, that remained isolated events without altering the character of the Kharijite doctrine as essentially prone to anarchism and a diffused dissemination of Muhammad's charismatic authority.

Towards the end of the seventh century, almost simultaneously with the Azraqites and Najdites (680s), a group of Kharijites lived in Basrah who could have been considered apolitical. Watt has called them a "body of pious men, with little direct interest in politics" (1962, 15). While they supported Ibn al-Zubayr's anti-Umayyad campaign, they also yielded to the Umayyad governor in Basrah (15). They were engaged primarily in the theological elaboration of the Kharijite positions. Those theological arguments, however, were influenced heavily by their political sterility and did not alter essentially the Kharijite doctrinal position vis-à-vis the question of succession.

No major reformulation, from which could be derived a lasting doctrine of institutional order, came out of these theological disputations and justifications. The most crucial inconsistency that they had to justify religiously was the question of living as Kharijites in a non-Kharijite community. They could not identify this community as either *dar-al-harb* ("the war zone") or *dar al-Islam* ("the Islamic zone"); neither could they identify non-Kharijite Muslims as *Kafir* ("unbeliever") or *mushrik* ("polytheist"). Some of them thought to consider themselves as living in the "zone of monotheists," others as "mixing"; still others maintained that they were in a state of "indefiniteness" or "indecision," that "things cannot be precisely stated" (Watt 1962, 15-16).

These dubious and precarious groupings finally led to the creation of one particular subgroup called the Waqifites. Their designating name means "those who suspend judgment." The formation of this position was the logical conclusion of the doctrinal uncertainty that ultimately characterized the Kharijites and prevented their historical endurance. In a remarkable departure from the initial Kharijite position, the Waqifites maintained that there could be no distinction between "the people of Paradise" and the "people of Hell" (Watt 1962, 17). All of this indicates a complete lack of systematic formulation in regard to the question of succession. The Basrah Kharijies, the intellectual crust of the movement, epitomized this whole position in their doctrinal diffusion and ad hoc theological improvisation that failed to give a sustainable and enduring response to the destabilizing death of the Prophet.

The occupational basis of the Kharijites seemed to have been essentially among the lower social/economic strata. Petroshevsky has pointed out that "the Kharijite movement was always based on the masses, the farmers, the poorest bedouins, the city artisans, and Muslim slaves and *dhimmi* people (non-Muslim monotheists)" (1971, 54). He has also maintained that

> the Kharijites were the staunchest enemies of great Muslim feudals, and opposed private properties. They essentially opposed social inequality in the Islamic society. Some Kharijites maintained that as soon as a slave accepted Islam he had to be freed, and a Muslim cannot be a slave. Thus, the Kharijite movement from the seventh to the ninth century (first to third Islamic century) was a movement supported by the masses. (59)

These social and economic conditions were congenial to the continuity of the charismatic movement. But in the absence of the initial charismatic leader, Muhammad, and also in the absence of a new charismatic figure that the Kharijites would recognize, such as the Imams for the Shiʿites, this popular discontent resulted in nothing more than the anarchic nature of the Kharijite movement, in the radical Azraqite wing, or the raising of some essential theological issues, in the more tepid Waqifite wing of the Basrah.

None of the six Weberian possibilities that may characterize the charismatic movement in the process of its "routinization" can be applied properly to the Kharijite case (1978a, 246-49). Watt's conceptualization of the Kharijites as a "charismatic community," in the absence of any particular charismatic figure, seems to be misconceived. The Kharijite "community" did, indeed, appear to be the ultimate arbiter of authority in this case. But this authority, theoretically confused and doctrinally impromptu, did not, in any recognizable way, derive its legitimacy and continuity from Muhammad as a charismatic leader. Moreover, this "communal authority" did not in any way become institutionalized in the course of the Kharijites' political and religious activities. Thus, the original Muhammadan charismatic authority, neither routinized, as in the case of the Muslim majority, nor perpetuated, as among the partisans of ᶜAli, disseminated, in the Kharijite case, into either dispersed violent revolts or constant theological disputations, completely failing to institutionalize a permanent mode of authority.

Weber has indicated, however, that "a charismatic principle which originally was primarily directed to the legitimization of authority may be subject to interpretation or development in an antiauthoritarian direction" (1968, 61). In their lack of any particular institution of authority, as well as in the precarious status of their leaders, the Kharijites demonstrated the realization of such a possibility. Weber points out that

> when the organization of the corporate group undergoes a process of progressive rationalization, it is readily possible that, instead of recognition being treated as a consequence of legitimacy, it is treated as the basis of legitimacy. (ibid.)

Here the Kharijites presented a particularly interesting case. They, of course, may not have been considered as having gone through any process of "rationalization." In fact, none of the three major responses to the legacy of Muhammad's charismatic authority could be identified as rationalization/legalization in the specific Weberian sense. What historically grew to be recognized as Sunnite Islam is a clear example of "traditionalization," both the assimilation of traditional Arab order and the traditionalization of Muhammad's charismatic authority itself; Shiᶜite Islam, as argued, has been an attempt towards the "perpetuation" of charisma. The Kharijites, however, seemed to consider their "recognition" of any form of post-Muhammadan authority as the "basis," and not the "consequence," of their leaders' legitimacy. The Kharijite leaders could not commit any "sin"; otherwise, they would have been deposed. The ultimate arbiter of this "sin" was, of course, the Kharijite community. This was thus an inversion of any form of authority; it was delegated from "below" and constantly under the supervision of ad hoc standards. The "democratization" of legitimacy, in the absence of any permanent form of institutional "democracy," rendered it always potentially illegitimate. There was a direct link between this lack of institutional authority, that holds the structure of a community together, and the impractical moral austerity of the Kharijites. In the absence of a thread of compelling authority to hold the community together, so loose and unstable were the individual components that the slightest moral laxity threatened the whole communal structure.

On this category, Weber has further maintained that

> once the elective principle has been applied to the chief by a process of reinterpretation of charisma, it may be extended to the administrative staff. Elective officials, whose legitimacy is derived from the confidence of those subject to their authority and to recall if confidence ceases to exist, are typical of certain types of democracies. (1968, 62)

Insofar as this "recalling" is not stipulated within the framework of an institutionalized form of authority, for each particular act of leadership, the figure of authority must have, explicitly or implicitly, the approval of the led; and this is an inversion of authority, or authority from below. A Kharijite leader was subject to the constant moral scrutiny of his followers, without this morality being specified in a particular moral demand system stemming from Muhammad's charismatic authority. In the immediate aftermath of Muhammad's death, the authority of the caliphs was "sanctified" through a combination of traditional Arab customs and companionship with "the messenger of Allah"; the Shiʿite *Imams'* authority was equally, if not more, sanctified through a belief in the divine right of the Prophet's Household to leadership of the Islamic community. No such sanctification, not even popular "election," provided the Kharijite leadership with a measure of institutional, as opposed to precarious and momentary, legitimacy. Since it is the doctrinal belief in a mode of sanctity that renders an authority legitimate and animates the moral demand system encompassing it, the lack of such institutional obedience destabilizes the order and makes its historical continuity highly problematic.

Pointing out this inversion of authority, Weber maintained that because such modes of charismatic continuity

> have an independent source of legitimacy, they are not strongly integrated in a hierarchical order. To a large extent their "promotion" is not influenced by their superiors and, correspondingly, their functions are not controlled. (1968, 62)

The source of legitimacy of any form of authority cannot be independent and lower, it is always independent and higher—as "Allah" to Muhammad, "tradition" to a tribal chief, or, in modern terms, a "constitution" to a president. And once promotion is not influenced by superiors and actions are not controlled, the community is on the verge of anarchy. Thus, there is something problematic in the Weberian stipulation about the nature of this form of "authority":

> in its fundamental significance it is a type of charismatic authority in which the authoritarian element is concealed, because the traditional position of the leader is held to be dependent on the will of those over whom he exercises authority and to be legitimized only by this will. (1968, 63)

Once a leader's authority is "dependent on the will of those over whom he exercises authority," there is no "concealment" of authority but its total absence. Even in a popular election of a president, it is the constitution according to which this election has been carried out that constitutes his source of legitimacy, and based on the particular stipulation of this constitution, the president may order his "electors" to act against their own wishes. In the Kharijite case, no such institutional form of legitimacy existed. At any particular moment the followers of a Kharijite leader could question his authority and violently depose him.

The Kharijite doctrinal position, according to which the multitude of Muslims themselves have the prerogative right of selecting their leader, is a unique example of their essential resistance to the emergence of the pre-Islamic Arab traditional mode of authority, according to which a tribal council decided the fate of leadership for the whole tribe and subsequently obedience to the chief, however limited in range, would be incumbent upon all the members. On this, the most crucial element of the Islamic community, they opposed a reemergence of the traditional order. By rejecting the infallibility of the Imams, as well as their divine right to leadership, they equally opposed the particular brand of Islamic response to the question of authority formulated by the Shiʿites. Yet in stipulating the sole criterion of the leadership of the Muslim community as religious (i.e., Islamic) piety, they demonstrated a particular position vis-à-vis the question of post-Muhammadan authority, which was clearly derived from inherently Islamic precepts. None of their leaders, consequently, were from the *Quraysh* tribe, and none was believed to have been divinely ordained to lead the Muslims; all were popularly elected on the basis of their religious piety and physical strength.

The same resistance was demonstrated in the Kharijites' view of the *mawali* (non-Arab Muslims). As an indication of traditional Arab influences, the Umayyad caliphs either encouraged, accepted, or condoned the inferior position of the *mawali* in relation to the Arab Muslims. In yet another demonstration of their resistance to Arab traditionalism, the Kharijites took the Islamic injunction of Muslim brotherhood seriously, sometimes to exaggerated extents. As Levi della Vida has pointed out, the tendency to the leveling of the Arabs and the *mawali* . . . was pushed so far by one of the theorists of Kharijite doctrine, Yazid b. Abi Anisa (founder of the Yazidiya), that he says that God will reveal a new Kor'an to a prophet among the Persians and that he will found a new religion for them, divine in the same sense as Judaism, Christianity and Islam, which will be no other than that of Sabi^{c}un mentioned in the Kor'an. (1953, 246-49)

The opposition of the Kharijites to Arab hegemony has led a number of Islamicists, among them Goldziher and Gibb, to conclude that they were, in fact, the forerunners of the *Shu^{c}ubiyyah,* a nationalistic movement, particularly predominant among the Persians, who expounded the idea of the inferiority of Arab conquerors to their non-Arab subjects (Gibb 1962, 66-67). On the relationship between the Kharijites and *Shu^{c}ubiyyah,* Hitti has also remarked, "whilst among the Kharijites and the Shi^{c}ites it took dynamic and political aspects, . . . yet the form which al-Shu^{c}ubiyah assumed in general was that of literary" (1970, 402).

This egalitarian tendency on the part of the Kharijites regarding the question of succession contributed, in turn, to the attraction of the disillusioned *mawali* to their camp. Lewis has taken issue with Goldziher's argument that the Kharijite position of universal acceptance of any leader, even an Abyssinian slave, was an indication of their essential egalitarianism. He believes that this reference to a prophetic tradition indicates not "equality but obedience." He believes this to be a reference to "the quietist doctrine of submission to authority in whatever form it comes" (Goldziher 1981, 171, footnote e). Whatever the original intention of this prophetic tradition, it is quite obvious that the Kharijites used it against the Arab aristocracy of the *Quraysh* for the Muslim majority and the oligarchy of the Prophet's household for the partisans of ^{c}Ali. This principle of equality, in fact, constituted the foundation of the Kharijite popularity among the *mawali.* Moreover, if the Kharijites were known for anything in Islamic history, it was for their violent anti-authoritarianism and not for their "submission to authority in whatever form it comes." The Kharijite leaders were under the constant and close moral scrutiny of their followers, a fact that denied them any measure of prolonged and stable ruling while impeding the continuity of the Kharijite doctrines on an institutional basis.

In their communal organization and structure, the Kharijites demonstrated some particular traits of their traditional Arab background. Watt has observed that

all the leaders [of the Kharijites] were former nomads and not townsmen. It is therefore all the more significant that in their rising they might be said to be restoring the life in small groups with which they had been familiar in the desert. . . . [J]ust as the members of a nomadic tribe regarded as potential enemies members of all other tribes, except where there was an alliance, so the

Kharijite bodies tended to regard all outsiders, even Muslims of differing views, as enemies whose blood might be shed. . . . The Kharijites appear to have had a pride in their group analogous to that of a nomad in his tribe; and, again like some of the desert tribes, they became noted for their mastery of the Arabic language in both poetry and oratory. (1973, 20)

Yet Watt has also reported a particular Kharijite practice that was essentially antitraditional—the initiating rites for joining the Azraqites:

> before joining the Azraqites, . . . a test (*mihna*) was made; and this is said to have consisted in giving the candidate a prisoner to kill. If the man complied, he would be more closely bound to the Azraqite body, since, especially if the man killed was of his own tribe, he would have broken existing ties, and would be dependent on Azraqites for "protection." This test, however, may have been an occasion rather than a regular practice. (1973, 22)

Killing a fellow tribesman, however occasionally, could be considered as the most striking indication of a total break with the traditional order and a simultaneous acceptance of a particular interpretation of the new order. However, there was something traditional in the Kharijite expectation to be protected by his community, that is, the functional equivalent of a "tribe."

As tribesmen, the early Kharijites were attached to some particular aspect of the pre-Islamic Arab traditional order. This aspect was characterized essentailly by a free spirit and a simple life. The grandeur of the Islamic state, as a particular expression of the routinization of Muhammadan authority for the Muslim majority, not only did not appeal to them but it was against their religious asceticism, if not tribal simplicity. Muhammad had attracted these simple nomads by his message of Muslim brotherhood. Both the Sunnite aristocracy of the Quraysh and the Shiᶜite oligarchy of the Prophet's household alienated them from the core of the Islamic community. They justified their social rebellion religiously; yet in expressing it they revealed their traditional attachment to the pre-Islamic Arab order of life.

Watt further believes that the Kharijite/Shiᶜite hostility might have had tribal roots:

> From 675 to 684 the governor of Basrah, ᶜUbayd-Allah ibn Ziyad, maintained order on the whole, despite the presence of turbulent Kharijite and Shiᶜite factions, whose animosity against one another may have been intensified by tribal rivalries. (1973, 21)

He also detects some particular nomadic traits among the Najdites:

> In some respects Najda himself and his followers exhibit attitudes typical of the nomadic Arabs. On the question of appropriating captive women, Najda himself is said to have made the decision, but his followers may have been unwilling to

> concede to him any special right in this matter. . . . This suggests the egali-
> tarianism of nomads. . . . It is perhaps also worth considering whether the
> Najdite toleration of occasional theft, adultery and wine-drinking may in part
> spring from the toleration of these, at least in certain circumstances, by the
> pre-Islamic nomads. . . . (24-25)

These resorts to pre-Islamic elements of cultural order are esentially what
gave the Najdites the opportunity to seek permanence and endurance for their
religious community. Thus, it is important to note that it was primarily some
vestiges of the pre-Islamic traditional order that stabilized, for a short time, a
Kharijite state. Otherwise, based on their sole interpretation of Islamic leadership, no such opportunity would have been created. To the extent that they
adopted pre-Islamic measures, the Najdites abandoned characteristic Kharijite
attributes.

In their persistent formulation of fundamental religious questions that ultimately defined the nature of Islamic community, its members, and its leader,
the Kharijites maintained their essential and doctrinal attachment to Islam and
particularly to the Qur'an. It was the Kharijites who for the first time made a
specific theological point of establishing the Islamic community on the Qur'an.
This same resistance to pre-Islamic tendencies was observed in their opposition to the "arbitration" procedure in the ᶜAli-Muᶜawiyah conflict, on which
Watt has remarked:

> If everyone had acquiesced in ᶜUthman's failure to inflict Qur'anic penalties,
> and the apparent return to pre-Islamic principles in the dispute between ᶜAli and
> Muᶜawiya and the appointment of arbiters, there might never have been any
> genuinely Islamic empire. (1973, 35)

In fact, as Watt himself has observed,

> the Kharijites, in their zeal for a community based on the Qur'an, went too far
> in some directions, as when they asserted that the grave sinner was excluded
> from the community. (35)

They were pious Muslims, insofar as this description is defined in terms of
adherence to the Qur'an and its implications for an ethical life; yet their
devotion to Islam was not translated into a viable institutional order within
which some measures of cultural homogeneity and political continuity could
be preserved.

Watt has attributed the "communalistic" tendencies of the Kharijites to
pre-Islamic influences. "The distinctive Kharijite views belong to a communalistic and not individualistic way of thinking" (1973, 35). Watt has also
maintained that

> this communal thinking about the Islamic community found among the Khar-
> ijites is closely paralleled by the thinking of the pre-Islamic Arabs about the

> tribe. . . . This parallelism of the communalistic thinking in Islam and that among the pre-Islamic Arabs further suggests . . . that the early Kharijites may be regarded as attempting to reconstitute in new circumstances and on an Islamic basis the small groups they have been familiar with in the desert. (36)

Watt even extended this generalization to the entire Islamic community (36-37). The problem with such an assessment is that Islam, as a reality unto itself, is "communalistic." The *ummah* (Islamic community) is strictly a Qur'anic term. Examples are abundant: II:128, II:134, III:104, IV:41, V:48, VI:108, among others. The so-called "five pillars of Islam" are all essentially communal: the profession of faith (*shahadah*), prayer (*salat*), almsgiving (*zakat*), fasting (*sawm*), and pilgrimage (*hajj*). *Jihad,* considered by the Kharijites as the sixth pillar, is also communal in nature. There is practically nothing totally individualistic in Islam. Monkhood, for example, is strictly forbidden in Islam by no less an authority than a prophetic tradition. It could be argued that in its conception, Islam assumed the pre-Islamic communalistic tendencies of the tribal Arabs, but in its distinctive characteristic, the *ummah*, the Islamically defined community, was expressed deliberately and consciously against the tribal affinities of the early Muslims, as is clearly obvious from the first article of the constitution of Medina which asserts that Muslims "are a single community distinct from (other) people" (Watt 1968a, 130).

Based on this "communalistic" tendency which existed, however, among the Kharijite Muslims, although not as a pre-Islamic influence but due to intrinsically Islamic stipulations, Watt has identified the Kharijites as a "charismatic community" which is equally problematic, if this term refers to its sociological typification by Weber. Watt made specific reference to Weber, but not in reference to the particularities of the "charismatic community." His two references to Weber in *Islam and the Integration of Society* (1969) were related to Weber's treatment of Hinduism and Buddhism in *Gesammelte Aufsatze zur Religionssoziologie* (1978b) and to his examination of political parties in relation to ideologies in *From Max Weber: Essays in Sociology* (1946). In his conceptualization of the "charismatic community" and the "charismatic leader," Watt did not refer specifically to Weber (or to Rudolph Sohm, for that matter); yet he used the phrase "in modern sociological terms" (1968, 119).

By a "charismatic community" Weber meant:

> an organized group subject to charismatic authority will be called a charismatic community (*Gemeinde*). It is based on an emotional form of communal relationship (*Vergemeinschaftung*). (1978b, 243; translated)

As Weber's formulation clearly shows, the existence of a "charismatic community" is subject to the physical presence of a "charismatic authority," that is to say a "charismatic leader," a "prophet," a "warlord," or a "leader," etc. In the post-Muhammadan period, when the routinization process of his authority was begun, to refer to a "charismatic community" was to confuse this conceptualization and its theoretical basis. It is possible, however, that outside the Weberian context, Watt had a particular understanding of the "charismatic community" in terms of some form of continuity with charisma. Watt formulated his conceptualization of this phrase in the following terms:

> the community as thus conceived may be called a "charismatic community." Its charisma is that it is capable of bestowing salvation on those who become members of it. It possesses this charisma because it has been divinely founded (through the revelation given by God to Muhammad) and because it is based on and follows the divinely given rule of life or Shari^{c}a. . . . The community is the bearer of the values which constitute meaningfulness, and so transmits some of this meaningfulness to the members. While the Kharijites thought that this charisma was attached to their small sect-community, one result of their striving was that the Islamic community as a whole (or at least the Sunnite part of it) came to regard itself as a charismatic community. Much of the strength and solidarity of the Islamic community today comes from the belief of Sunnite Muslims in its charismatic character. (1973, 36)

The latter association of the Sunnite community with the concept of "charismatic community" reveals the essential problem with Watt's formulation. Distanced from its charismatic founder, the increasingly routinized community discards all of its precarious, disorganized, irrational, and personal characteristics and substitutes a new formal social relationship for that of the charismatic period. Thus *Shari^{c}ah* became the *institutionalization* of Muhammad's judicial authoirty, and not a charismatic authority in itself. The Sunnite (majority) community was not a "charismatic community"; its members received salvation only to the degree that they participated in and responded to the institutions of authority in the community created during the process of the routinization of Muhammad's charisma. The same held true for the Kharijite community. It did not dispense salvation; the believer's participation in the particular dogmatic stipulations of this movement presumably "saved" the believer. The Shi^{c}ite community, too, to examine Watt's conceptualization in comparison and contrast, could be considered as a "charismatic community." Did Shi^{c}ites not receive salvation through their membership in their community? Could a Shi^{c}ite follow his *Imam* and not be in his community at the same time?

Keeping the same reservation about the identification of the Kharijites as a "charismatic community," I should refer to Watt's most perceptive passage on the pre-Islamic traditional influences on both the Shi^{c}ite and Kharijite religious ideas. After a rather detailed examination of the tribal affiliations of the Shi^{c}ites, who were mostly from the southern part of Arabia (Yemen), and those of the Kharijites, who were mostly from the northern tribes of Tamim, Hanifa, and Shayban,Watt has concluded that

> it may be suggested as a hypothesis that an important factor in the final result was a difference in the traditional culture of the two groups. The Yemenites came from South Arabia, the land of an ancient civilization, where for a thousand years kings had succeeded one another according to a dynastic principle and had been regarded as having superhuman qualities. . . . Even if the seventh-century Arabs had no personal experience of kingship, the Yemenites came from a land where civilization had been based on charismatic leaders, and they must somehow have been influenced by the tradition. The "northern" tribes, on the other hand, had come under no comparable influence. Though some had known the Lakmid rulers of al-Hira, the latter stood in the nomadic egalitarian tradition according to which all the adult males of a tribe were roughly equal and had a right to share in the business of the tribe. This nomadic tradition was dominant in the Arabian deserts at that time, and there are traces of "democratic" communities in Iraq in the distant past. . . . The hypothesis here suggested, then, is not that there was any conscious attempt to re-create a former polity, but that in a time of stress and tension men's conduct was controlled by deep-seated urges, varying according to the tradition to which they mainly belonged. In some men the unconscious urge was to rely on the charismatic leader, and they eagerly searched for such a person and, when they thought they had found him, fervently acclaimed him without giving too much thought to evidence of his unsuitability. Others looked rather to the charismatic community, and again assumed too readily that they had found it and understood how it should be constituted. (1973, 43-44)

Whatever the degree of pre-Islamic influences on the Shi^cite view might be, the continuity of Muhammadan charisma in the figure of the Imams constituted a genuinely Islamic institution in the context of which Shi^cism survived as a major formulation of the Islamic faith. These pre-Islamic influences, irresistable because deeply held by the Arab mind, might have further contributed to the confused nature of authority in the Kharijite case.

Sunnite Islam gradually formulated an optimum mixture of pre-Islamic traditional forces and the Muhammadan charismatic legacy, so that an immediate period of routinization of charisma and stabilization of the social relationships ensued. The gradual segmentation and institutionalization of Muhammadan charismatic authority secured and guaranteed a permanent cultural stability and identity within which Islam in this particular aspect found a universal expression. Shi^cite Islam, by attempting an "institutionalization" of charisma in which its character was preserved and perpetuated, had a much more tumultuous history. Yet the charismatic presence of the *Imams* guaranteed the historical survival of Shi^cism despite the tension that this branch of Islam always maintained as regards the political authority. Kharijite Islam, however, failed to formulate a workable solution to the disruptive death of the Prophet. Instigating, instead, theological disputations, the Kharijites always remained in a confused state, incapable of permanently institutionalizing a workable doctrine of authority, religious or otherwise, that would guarantee social stability and historical survival. The moderate Kharijites of the Najdites and Waqifites clearly demonstrate that whatever degree of stability they achieved was done by abandoning original Kharijite positions, for example, the Azraqite formulation, and subsequent justification of their inevitable strategical maneuvers theologically.

The Kharijites essentially tended towards the disintegration of Muhammadan authority into different domains. Since no fundamental institutionalization of the Prophet's authority materialized in the tumultuous case of the Kharijites, the elaborate development of various domains of authority, present in the Sunnite case, was precluded in this instance. Yet in the limited external expressions of their ideals of authority in the post-Muhammadan period, a basic distinction between religious and political authorities was observable. Comparing the Shi^cites and Kharijites, Lambton concludes that

> the Khawarij and the Shi^ca represent two opposite extremes. The former were the most radical of all Muslims and tended to separate the religious and the political elements of the imamate, while the latter heavily stressed the religious element. (1981, 21)

She also points out that

> the Kharijis did not regard it as an absolute duty upon the community that there should be an *imam*. Thus, they separated the religious leadership of the community from political headship. (23)

What secured for the Shi^cites the comprehensive authority of their Imams were both their divine right and their infallibility. Denying both of these attributes, the Kharijites saw no ground for granting their leaders, within the context of their democratic view of leadership, sweeping authority. Even in the case of the Najdites who did establish some mode of stabiltiy for a short period of time, this precarious nature of authority was most evident. According to al-Baghdadi, they followed Najdah "until they did not agree with some of his acts and considered them abominable; they objected to him and finally broke into three [different] groups because of this disagreement" (1954, 51). All the Kharijite subgroups had a similar attitude towards leadership.

Weber noted that "the chief and his administrative staff often appear formally as servants or agents of those they rule" (1978a, 215). This, however, he thought "naturally does nothing whatever to dispose the quality of dominance . . . a certain minimum of assured power to issue commands, thus of domination, must be provided for in nearly every conceivable case" (215). The Kharijite leaders, as an example of a radical—and thus failed—democracy, proved to be too much of "a servant of those they ruled." The

Kharijite community practically paralyzed the operative system of any meaningful measure of authority with constant supervision, manifested in a relentless moral and ethical scrutiny on the basis of a constantly shifting set of criteria. Once institutionalized, as it was not in the Kharijite case, "democracies" forfeit the individuals' right to the elected leader and render all subservient to him, within the boundaries stipulated by the constitutional foundation of that democracy. Having failed to institutionalize such a relatively permanent mode of legitimacy, the Kharijites' radical and spontaneous "democracy" could not but fail. The hierarchical structure of authority cannot stand on its head; that is impossible. The hierarchy must be triangularly stable on its base, even if the source of the legitimacy of the commanding officers is not from above, as in traditional and charismatic cases, but from below, as in democracies. Democracy is not anarchy; it is a change of direction in the source of the legitimacy of the hierarchical order.

The confusing and contradictory nature of the Kharijite's doctrines, as well as the transitory nature of their revolutionary—and in the extreme Azraqite case terroristic—community, inhibited the historical continuity of this group; and thus a factual assessment of their gradual segmentation of Muhammadan charismatic authority would be impossible. Yet insofar as it can be assessed from their doctrinal position, we can conclude that the question of authority in their community essentially remained precarious and uncertain. They certainly did not grant any sweeping authority to their leaders. The sole source of justification for the leader was the democratic consent of his followers. He was essentially a military leader, such as Nafi^c ibn al-Azraq or Najdah ibn ^{c}Amir al-Hanafi, without any particular religious authority. There were many religious scholars among the Kharijites of Basra; yet they developed no particular religious authority. Every Kharijite considered himself equally capable of dispensing theological arguments. Thus, the charismatic authority of Muhammad, having found no channel of institutional or personal continuity, disseminated into the anarchic diffusion of the Kharijite movements. A charismatic authority has to be either "routinized," in a traditional or legal manner, as Weber pointed out, or sought to be perpetuated in particular charismatic figures, as the Shi^{c}ite example shows. In the absence of these two modes of continuity, the momentous force of charisma is disseminated into history and, despite sporaradic revolts, lost forever.

8

The Charismatic Revolution as a Reconstitution of a Moral Demand System and an Originator of New Paradigmatic Patterns of Authority

> *A "revolution," then, refers to some radical and significant discontinuity in the moral demand system; what is permitted, so to say, becomes interdicted and what is interdicted is permitted. Revolutions may be defined as reversals—violent or non-violent—of significant behavioral contents. The Christian movement in Roman culture was revolutionary, although non-violent in a culture that encouraged official (state) acts of violence. . . . The established interdictory-remissive motifs of Roman culture were reversed in significant ways. In turn, the Christian motifs did not triumph without partially incorporating the defeated Roman motifs. Cultures rarely die; they merely marry.*
>
> —Philip Rieff

Culture is "to belong somehow . . . to a common symbolic" (Rieff 1972b, 90-91). The "symbolic" is "a pattern of moral demands, a range of standard self-expectations about what we may and may not do, in the face of infinite possibilities" (99). By way of example, Rieff refers to "the great Western symbolics, Jewish and Greek, which have been constituted by repressive, militant ideals opposing the destructive splendor of human possibility" (99). The "pattern" and "range" of moral demands and standards are what constitute the distinctive homogeneity of one culture as compared with another. What a people may or may not do characterize one culture in contradistinction to another. What distinguishes two cultures, two sets of common symbolics, is not necessarily and solely geographical boundaries. In fact, within one geographical setting one culture may, through some fundamental revolution-ary movement, substitute and supersede, with varying degrees of success, another. Thus "revolution," as Philip Rieff points out, "is a significant discontinuity in the moral demand system, an interchange in the relation of interdictory-remissive contents by which men may well do what they have not done before—and do not as they have done" (100). The "discontinuity" is thus a phase in which the superseded culture yields, though it resists, to the authority of the triumphant culture. In the same phase, moreover, the defeated system of symbolic salvages, to the extent possible to its defeated spirit, its most persistent motifs. Thus "cultures," in their sweeping authority over the public and private lives, "rarely die; they merely marry" (102).

A charismatic movement is a revolution that radically alters the faltering common symbolic towards the creation of a new culture. "At the breaking point," Rieff points out, "a culture can no longer maintain itself as an es-tablished span of moral demands" (1966, 234). The "breaking point" is reached by a reversal of the interdictory-remissive order and is the end result of a perpetual tension that constitutes the dialectic of these two universal motifs. Charismatic, or any other, revolution is the final indictment of the existing order, changing the balance towards the creation of a new order of life. Once the old culture cannot "maintain" itself, it yields—however reluc-tantly, and not without a final resurgence—to the rising authority of the new, stronger order. Authority, as the universal organizer of culture, always is. There is, however, a stage of flux in which one culture supersedes another. The new order reformulates and universalizes the contents of authority struc-ture. "At times of impending transition to a new moral order," Rieff points out, "symbolic forms and their institutional objectification change their rel-ative weight in that order" (1966, 234). Such symbolic forms, always uni-versal expressions of a moral and normative system, transubstantiate to con-stitute the elements and organization of the new order.

Through the gradual, yet persistent, process of the recognition of charisma the pattern of moral expectations constituting the established culture yields to that of the emerging authority. A charismatic movement is thus a destructive/ constructive process. While it challenges and discards "what is written," it "says," simultaneously, what is—and is not—to be done. Since "culture," as Rieff points out, is "our ingeniously developed limitations" (1972b, 99) in the face of infinite possibilities, a charismatic movement, as the originator of a new culture, opens up and closes down new possibilities and impossibilities, shifting the established traditional motifs. This shifting of the traditional motifs is what Weber called the revolutionary ability of the charisma which has "inverted all value hierarchies and overthrown custom, law and tradition"

(1978a, 1117). "The process by which a culture changes at its profoundest level," Rieff points out," may be traced in the shifting balance of controls and releases which constitute a system of moral demands" (1966, 233).

What is known of pre-Islamic Arabia, the *jahiliyyah* (the time of ignorance) as later Muslims called it, indicates a thriving patriarchal society. "Under patriarchal domination," Weber noted, "the norms derive from tradition: the belief in the inviolability of that which has existed from time out of mind" (1978a, 1006). This "time out of mind" is what sanctifies the norms governing the culture and animates them. What constitutes the authority of these norms and holds them within one order is a symbolic system of three interrelated motifs that Rieff calls interdictory, remissive, and transgressive. The interdictory motif embodies all acts which are not to be done, in the face of infinite possibilities to which men are inclined; the remissive motif embodies all acts that are not to be done, yet are done under what the symbolic system considers an exculpating reason; the transgressive motif embodies all lowering acts that will bring severe and immediate punishment by the operating culture (Rieff 1959, 358-97; 1966, 1-27, 232-61; 1972b; 1981, 225-55).

In the pre-Islamic Arab patriarchal society, fighting in the sacred month of *Muharram* was forbidden. If this interdictory command was broken, it would have been considered a punishable transgressive act. Or if a member of a tribe was murdered by an outsider, it was incumbent upon all of the members of the tribe to avenge his blood. Failing to do so would have been considered a grave transgression punishable by specific sentences. The metaphysical foundation upon which these and other acts were established, what has been referred to as "pre-Islamic Bedouin religion," consists of astral divinities, atmospheric divinities, ancestors and ginns, all under the all-but-practically forgotten supreme authority of a deity known to Arabs as Allah (Henninger 1981, 3-22). Within this metaphysical context, the particular interdictory, remissive, and transgressive acts were stipulated. Muhammad's charismatic authority fundamentally changed this moral demand system, along with its common symbolic, and introduced and established a new religious culture.

What is particular in a charismatic figure? Barnes (1978, 1-18) has identified four major attributes that most charismatic leaders have in common: (1) they live in periods of radical social change, (2) they are cut off from the mainstream of society, (3) they perceive religious tradition as relative, and (4) they have innovative teachings. In the case of Muhammad, the second characterization was not applicable. As a merchant, he was involved directly in the daily Arab life. He did, however, have occasional retreats to Mount *Hira*, outside of Mecca. He gradually introduced a unique monotheistic Arab religion, based on the Jewish and Christian models, into the Arabian peninsula. According to this religious movement, through the prophetic agency Allah established His sovereignty over mankind. The Qur'an says "O mankind! Worship your Lord, Who hath created you and those before you, so that ye may ward off [evil]" (II:21). He alone is the God, the Alive, the Sustainer, the Owner of the universe.

Allah's Supreme Omnipotence is the sine que non of Muhammad's message and legitimacy. It is emphasized in particular that He alone should be worshipped against all other gods, a direct and emphatic reference to pre-Islamic deities.

Allah selects and sends prophets for the guidance of mankind; Muhammad was the last of these prophets, and consequently his command must be obeyed. The "seal of the prophets" lacks any divine attribute; yet his receiving the Godly message is emphasized: "Muhammad is not the father of any man among you, but he is the messenger of Allah and the Seal of the Prophets; and Allah is ever Aware of all things" (Qur'an XXXIII:40). The hierarchy of authority, extended from Allah to common humanity, is established through a metaphysical/physical order of command and obedience. Based upon this doctrinal position, and its extensive elaboration throughout the Qur'an, a new set of "common symbolics," a new system of interdictory, remissive,and transgressive motifs, is introduced and established, essentially seeking to supersede that of the pre-Islamic Arabs. The "legitimacy" of this order was founded on the specific Qur'anic stipulation that

> those who follow the messenger, . . . He will enjoin on them that which is right and forbid them that which is wrong. He will make lawful for them all good things and prohibit for them only the foul; and he will relieve them of their burden and the fetters that they used to wear. Then those who believe in him, and honor him, and help him, and follow the light which is sent down with him, they are the successful. (Qur'an VII:157)

A new moral demand system is thus established within which what is—and what is not—to be done is stipulated. This order is expressed in contradistinction to the old traditional authority, the particularities of which are superseded by what is now defined by the charismatic leader to be right and wrong.

Muhammad established his charismatic authority, legitimated through the prophetic relationship to Allah. Gradually, a new set of moral demands was established for the daily life of the converts. By conforming to this new "common symbolic," the believers became *Muslims*. It is important to note that Muhammad's opposition to the old traditional Arab order was simultaneous with the construction and establishment of his charismatic—and through it the Islamic—authority. This authority was comprehensive and multidimensional and, as such, constituted the foundation of a new culture, that is, a system of interrelated restrictions and releases. There is a tendency to regard charismatic movements as expressions of "individual" against "society."

Meddin (1976, 382-93), for example, in his study of sociocultural changes, has argued that there is a strong element of "individual vs. society" present in such major changes. He has referred to Durkheim's "instinctual expression vs. moral or social goals," Freud's "id vs. superego," and Simmel's "spirit vs. form," as well as Weber's theory of charismatic authority, to show the theoretical foundation of this opposition.

The Weberian formulation of "charismatic authority," by definition, is a mode of "authority" and, as such, has particular stipulations of command and obedience which could occur only within the structure of a moral demand system. "A symbolic," as Rieff points out, "contains within itself that which one is encouraged to do and that which one is discouraged from doing, on pain of whatever animates the interdict" (1972b, 99). A new set of interrelated interdictory, remissive, and transgressive motifs is established against the pre-Islamic Arab order. Thus, the Qur'an asserts

> they question thee (O Muhammad) with regard to warfare in the sacred month. Say: Warfare therein is a great (transgression), but to turn (men) from the way of Allah, and to disbelieve in Him and the Inviolable Place of Worship, and to expel His people thence, is greater with Allah; for persecution is worse than killing. And they will not cease from fighting against you till they have made you renegades from your religion, if they can. And who so becometh a renegade and dieth in his disbelief: such are they whose works have fallen both in the world and the Hereafter. Such are the rightful owners of the Fire: they will abide therein. (Qur'an II:217)

Now "to turn men from the way of Allah, and to disbelieve in Him," etc., becomes transgressive, and "warfare in the sacred month" remissive. From the most universal metaphysical beliefs to the minutest acts of daily routine, life is regulated and specified within this new order (Qur'an XXXIV:35, II:222). The Qur'an issues specific commands against the order it has superseded:

> Warfare is ordained for you, though it is hateful unto you; but it may happen that ye hate a thing which is good for you, and it may happen that ye love a thing which is bad for you. Allah knoweth, ye know not. (Qur'an II:216)

The most essential attribute of any order of authority is to demand particular obedience despite the possibility of that command being "hateful" to those who are ruled. The source of what is "good" and what is "bad" is separated from the human community, and consequently a new moral demand system stipulates what is "good" — that is, to be done (interdictory motif) — and what is "bad" — that is, not to be done (transgressive). The Muhammadan charismatic movement as a cultural revolution consists of the Qur'anic stipulation that "it may happen that ye hate a thing which is good for you; and it may happen that ye love a thing which is bad for you."

After a temporary eclipse, the traditional Arab order reemerged upon the death of the Prophet, seeking recognition and reestablishment. The charismatic movement and the sacred order it established are too powerful and have penetrated too deeply into the social and psychological lives of the Arabs/ Muslims to be totally eradicated. Thus, with the emergence of the question of succession to the Prophet, the defeated Arab traditional order and the legacy of the triumphant Muhammadan charismatic authority once again bid for cultural dominance and supremacy.

From the death of the Prophet in 632 until the establishment of the Umayyad dynasty in 661, the Sunnite, Shiʿite, and Kharijite responses to the crisis of succession to Muhammad's personal authority supplied three competing stipulations of the sacred order that is Islam, which resembles all others in its hierarchical form. The interdictory motif, rendered supple by the remissive motif: both of these motifs opposed the lowest, the transgressive motif. But within the universally accepted sacred order of Islam, the observant community living within the complex authority of that order became divided, in less than thirty years, into distinct readings of that order, and its effects were based upon a competing rationale of how the highest authority survives the death of its messenger.

The appearance of Islam as a new moral demand system in the early seventh century in Arabia was an indication of some contemporary tension between the interdictory and remissive motifs of the traditional Arab order. This tension is what Weber called the social, economic, and psychic crisis that usually precedes a charismatic event. "A cultural revolution occurs," Rieff points out,

> when the releasing or remissive symbolic grows more compelling than the controlling one; then it is that the inherent tensions reach a breaking point. Roman culture may have been moving toward such a breaking point when Christianity appeared, as a new symbolic order of controls and remissions. (1966, 233-34)

Probably a similar diagnosis can be made of the pre-Islamic traditional Arab order and the rise of Islam. Throughout the Qur'an there is a hidden order against which Islam is expressed as a new order of authority, most of the time in specific terms. After Muhammad's death the two orders came into a continuous clash resulting in competing formulations of three distinct cultural paradigms.

This period of less than thirty years remains the most crucial in the historical conscience of the Muslims. In the course of later Islamic history, from implications for Islamic culture, character, and society, latent in the doctrinal struggles over the succession to Muhammad's personal authority, other issues of great consequence emerged. The particular attributes of the leadership of the Islamic community, as well as the very nature of this community, that is, in what terms it should be defined, became subject to interpretation and disputes. Moreover, the exegesis and practical application of the sacred text could not be separated from the critical matter of the succession. The very question of who is a Muslim was also subject to debate. Islamic jurisprudence was divided along doctrinal lines set by the succession controversy.

Sunnite Islam, in its immediate routinization of Muhammad's charismatic authority on essentially pre-Islamic models and in its gradual segmentation of that authority into different domains, represents the faith in its most stabilized and traditionalized form. One of the most obvious manifestations of this "stable" social life is the economic prosperity of the early Sunnite Muslims. Weber, however, erred in maintaining that

> the most pious adherents of the religion, i.e., Islam in its first generation became the wealthiest, or more correctly, enriched themselves with military booty—in the widest sense—more than did other members of the faith. (1978a, 624)

Piety and wealth were essentially two separate issues in this period. The rich Muslims were basically from the aristocratic families of the pre-Islamic period who continued to accumulate wealth under the new circumstances. ʿUthman, Muʿawiyah, and his son, Yazid, were probably the wealthiest of all the early caliphs. They were all from the Banu Umayyah clan of the Quraysh tribe, one of the wealthiest and most influential tribes of Meccans who generally joined Islam after its success. Muʿawiyyah, Yazid, and many other Umayyad caliphs were not particularly known for their piety. Moreover, many pious Muslims, such as Abu Dharr al-Ghifari, who were among the initial companions of the Prophet, led very ascetic lives. The institutionalization of Muhammadan authority into various political and religious positions and offices guaranteed the continuity of Islam as a culture and as a religion. Sunnite Islam thus represented the Muhammadan charismatic movement in its traditionalized continuity. Out of the Qur'an and the Hadith the Shariʿah (Islamic religious law) gradually developed and has regulated the various aspects of Muslim life. The offices of the caliphate, ʿulma, wazirs, and the spiritual status of the Sufis polarized various nexus of authority/obedience in Islamic life. The charismatic domination of Muhammad, regulating the actions of the nascent Muslim community, was transformed into stable and institutionalized loci of authority regulating and coordinating the public and private lives of the Muslims in specific interdictory, remissive, and transgressive motifs.

Shiʿite Islam, in its attempt to perpetuate the charismatic authority of Muhammad, stipulated the necessity of the Imamate (the need of the Muslim community to be permanently guided by the rightful leadership of a descendant of ᶜAli). A tension was thus created, both political and religious, by the "institutionalization" of a form of authority which is essentially anti-institutional. Shiᶜite Islam remained characteristically, but not totally, resistant to reemerging traditional forces. It further maintained the totality of Muhammadan authority in the figure of the Imams. For Shiᶜites, the Imams functioned as charismatic figures with sweeping and multidimensional authority. In accordance with its dynamic and tumultuous nature, particular forms of social relationships and norms of conduct developed in Shiᶜite Islam, establishing, too, a unique set of interdictory, remissive, and transgressive motifs. Life was regulated, possibilities curtailed, and impossibilities set, all in harmony with a mode of authority which was fundamentally charismatic.

Kharijite Islam, in its defeated attempt to democratize and relativize Muhammadan charismatic authority, and any other following authority, represented a distinct case of the dissemination of charisma. Here no particular form of institutionalized authority survived to regulate daily life. The authority of the Kharijite leader was so precarious and so constantly under the scrutiny of the led that no proper nexus of command/obedience could be established permanently. "Domination," as Weber noted, is a

> situation in which the manifested will (*command*) of the *ruler* or rulers is meant to influence the conduct of one or more others (*the ruled*) and actually does influence it in such a way that their conduct to a socially relevant degree occurs as if the ruled had made the content of the command the maxim of their conduct for its very own sake. Looked upon from the other end, this situation will be called obedience. (1978a, 946)

Sunnite and Shiᶜite Islam did establish, each in its own particular way, such a command/obedience relationship. As a doctrine of permanent revolution that sought to discredit any form of authority, Kharijite Islam failed to survive institutionally. In its strict and unconditional moral ascetism, the Kharijites remained in a radically and solely interedictory/transgressive modality. Except for the Najdites, a moderate Kharijite group who deviated from essential doctrinal positions of this branch, the Kharijites stipulated no remissive motif. Every sin, no matter how insignificant, resulted in the excommunication of the member. No claim to authority, in its bid to offer a superseding culture, can survive without a built-in remissive motif that gives the interdictory motif flexibility and thus authority. According to Rieff,

> There are two kinds of remissive motifs: first, those remissions which subserve— that is, support the moral demand system of which they are a part; second, those same motifs, expanding their jurisdiction in the system of action, can become subversive of that system. (1972b, 102)

Neither "subserving" nor "subverting" remissive motifs were observable in any form in the Kharijite case.

Figures and institutions of authority: no culture can survive without their legitimate agencies. The Shi᷄ites did with the former, the Sunnites with the latter, and in the absence of both the Kharijites failed.

The Muslim experience during the formative years of Islam has remained active in the Islamic collective consciousness throughout history. Despite the vicissitudes of specific historical exigencies, the cataclysmic establishment of Muhammad's prophetic authority, immortalized on the pages of the Qur'an, has been registered on the Muslim collective memory as an archetypal event of mythical proportions. Through the textual intermediary of the Qur'an, the prophetic traditions, and the historical, theological, and exegetical sources, the drama of a single man, guided and moved by an inner conviction provided by an omnipotent God, establishing a world religion, has been re-enacted in Islamic history to the point of its collective internalization by masses of Muslims. Thus what happened in the latter part of the sixth and the early part of the seventh century has been carried forward, in the Muslim collective consciousness, as the single most important set of common symbolics identifying and defining what it means to be a Muslim.

Muhammad introduced and forcefully established his charismatic authority against the staunch resistance of a traditional mode of authority, dominant and thriving in pre-Islamic Arabia. From around 610 B.C.E. when he commenced his divine mission until his death in 632 B.C.E., a period of some twenty-three years, Muhammad successfully established his charismatic authority, and with it the Islamic religion. But the traditional Arab mode of authority, temporarily superseded by the Muhammadan experience, re-emerged in a post-Muhammadan battle of succession to his authority. Out of a dialectical interaction between these two modes of authority, with the simultaneous force of Muhammad's charismatic authority being divided into various modes and modalities of command and obedience acting as a catalyst, three distinct paradigmatic patterns of authority emerged.

Externally and nominally, these three paradigms of authority have been identified with three branches of Islam: the Sunnite, Shi'ite, and Kharijite versions of the faith. Throughout history, various communities of Muslims have recognized themselves as adherents of these different readings of the Muhammadan legacy.

But equally as important, and equally as active, are the simultaneous presence of these three definitions of post-Muhammadan authority in the collective consciousness of all Muslims, regardless of their nominal identification as Sunnite, Shi'ite, or Kharijite. In the Muslim collective consciousness, these three modalities of command and obedience supersede the nominal identification of a Muslim as a Sunnite, a Shi'ite, or a Kharijite. The collective participation of all Muslims in their common history, actual or mythical, has rendered them all receptive to symbolic signals that these different readings of Islam have orchestrated.

Through historical and theological disputations, members of these branches of Islam have at once constituted and consolidated their respective self-understanding of post-Muhammadan authority and yet, by virtue of the interpenetrative impulse of opposing forces, adopted and assimilated, however negationally, each other's discourse. The ultimate result of this has been the simultaneous and juxtapositional presence of all three modes of authority, Sunnite, Shi'ite, and Kharijite, in the Muslim collective memory.

The independant and collective validity of these paradigmatic patterns of authority receive their credence and legitimacy by having been meticulously founded on the theological verification of their truth. The verification, as always, is based on a thorough and exclusionary reading of the Qur'an, the prophetic traditions, and, through them, the whole prophetic experience during the time of Muhammad. Once thus independantly and collectively legitimated, and even sanctified, in the Muslim collective consciousness, these paradigmatic patterns of authority shape and direct, consciously or unconsciously, the course of social actions assumed by a given Muslim or a given community of Muslims.

Thus understood, the Sunnite branch of Islam is the generic identity of those internal forces within the Islamic political culture that necessitate routinized, stable, and rationally founded institutions of authority. Here, the Muhammadan charismatic experience is a blessed memory that has to be cherished and remembered but only as the sacred legitimizer of established institutions that collectively render the social structure operative and trustworthy. For the Sunnite understanding of Islam, the Muslim community is, after the textual authority of the Qur'an, the most sacred Muhammadan legacy. Its territorial integrity, its communal identity, and its indubitable foundation on the Islamic sacred law are the chief factors that safeguard its salvation. When Muslims are in the Sunnite state of their mind, history is the blessed path that God almighty has designated for them and for all mankind, should they know better and join them, to traverse, in their way to their final reckoning with their creator.

Thus understood, the Shi'ite reading of Islam is the generic identity of those forces within the faith that seek to perpetuate that momentous experience of charismatic community felt and lived during the life of the Prophet. So ecstatic, glorious, and divine was that historical moment when the heavens had opened their gates, as it were, and when through the Muhammadan charismatic agency, God Himself spoke to mankind, that when in the Shi'ite state of their mind, Muslims yearn to freeze the course of history in that magnificent moment. This is the most logical conclusion of extending the charismatic presence of the Prophet through the agency of his flesh and blood into the course of history. And the equally logical conclusion is that in the figure and frame of the Hidden Imam, that charismatic presence ought to be perpetuated for ages to come. Figures, not institutions, of authority are the loci of charismatic experience in which the Shi'ite reading of the post-Muhammadan Islamic destiny rests its case. The Muslim community is nothing but the aggregate of consent and obedience to the figure and glory of the Imam of the Age. Central is the figure of the Imam; and at the periphery is the collective extension of his charismatic presence and personality into the shape of the Muslim community. The Imam is there, at the center of the community. If the community recognizes him, it is saved; if not, not. Thus the Muslim community does not have a reality sui generis. It is merely an extension of the charismatic presence of the Imam. Put more simply, if the Islamic community does not recognize the Imam of the Age, it is not an Islamic community anymore. History, for those Muslims who are occasionally or permanently in the Shi'ite state of their mind, is the path that God almighty, through the agency of his last prophet *and* those of the Imams, has designated for them and whoever else knows enough to join them. Traversing this most blessed path, guided by the Imam of the Age, they move toward their final reckoning with their creator.

And thus understood, the Kharijite branch of Islam is the generic term for those forces equally present in the Muslim collective consciousness that seek to hold the Muhammadan divine message of the brotherhood and sisterhood of humankind to its original promise. Neither figures nor institutions, but the truth of the Muhammadan message is at the heart of the Kharijite reading of the post-Muhammadan definition of authority. When devoid of the truth that was promised them in the equality of the humankind, neither the figures nor the institutions of authority carry any inherent legitimacy for Muslims, permanently or occasionally, in the Kharijite state of their mind. A promise was made to them, that all men, "even an Abyssinian slave," are created equal. After the blessed experience of the charismatic rule of the Prophet, neither aristocracy nor oligarchy but the true and original message of the Qur'an, the actual and practical equality of all Muslims, was the form of government they considered legitimate. The Muslim community, the aggregate composition of individual Muslims with rights and responsibilities, is the sole source of authority and legitimacy for Muslims in the Kharijite frame of their collective mind. And history is that blessed path that God almighty has designated for them, and whoever knows enough to join them, to traverse, if they have lived up to His commands of following a just ruler whose pious virtuosity is predicated, more than anything else, on the actual and doctrinal equality of all Muslims.

These three frames of reference, states of mind, modalities of power, modes of authority, or readings of the Muhammadan charismatic experience, form the collective paradigms of social action upon which the Islamic history has been articulated. As to how these overlapping states of mind and modes of authority interact in a given historical period, or in a given historical figure, these are episodes of a longer story that I should probably tell at some other time.

Bibliography

Abel, A. 1970. "Le Chapitre sur l'imamat dans le Tamhid d'al-Baqillani." In *Le Shi^{c}isme imamite*, 55-67. Paris.

Ahmad, H. 1972. "Infallibility in Islam." *Islamic Studies* 11:1-11.

^{c}Ali, Jawad. 1971. *Al-Mufassal fi Tarikh al-^{c}Arab qabla al-Islam*. Beirut.

Andrae, T. 1936. *Mohammed: The Man and His Faith*. London: George Allen and Unwin.

Arberry, A. J. 1955. *The Koran Interpreted*. New York: Macmillan Publishing.

al-Azraqi, Abu al-Walid M. ibn Ahmad. 1857. *Akhbar Makkah*. Edited by F. Wustenfeld. Leipzig. (Reprinted as vol. I of *Akhbar Makkah al-Musharrafah*. Beirut, 1969.)

al-Baghdadi, Abu Mansur. 1954. *al-Farq bayn al-Firaq*. Tehran: Ishraqi.

_____. 1965. *Kitab al-Munammaq fi Akhbar Quraysh*. Edited by Khorshid Ahmad Fariq. Heyderabad.

al-Baladhuri, Ahmad ibn Yahya. 1916. *The Origins of the Islamic State*. Translated by Philip Hitti. New York.

_____. 1959. *Ansab al-Ashraf*. Edited by M. Hamidullah. Cairo.

Barnes, D. F. 1978. "Charisma and Religious Leadership: An Historical Analysis." *Journal for the Scientific Study of Religion* 18 (March): 1-18.

Barthold, W. 1979. *Khalifah wa Sultan (The Caliph and the Sultan)*. Tehran: Amir Kabir.

Becker, C. H. 1915-16. "Bartholds Studien Uber Kalif und Saltan." *Der Islam* 6:350-412.

Bendix, R. 1960. *Max Weber: An Intellectual Portrait*. Berkeley: University of California Press.

Berger, P. 1973. *The Social Reality of Religion*. London.

Blachere Regis. 1952. *Le probleme de Mahomet*. Paris: P. V. F.

Bosk, C. 1979. "The Routinization of Charisma: The Case of the Zaddik." *Sociological Inquiry* 49:150-67.

Brockelmann, Carl, ed. 1948. *History of the Islamic People*. London: Routledge and Kegan Paul.

Browne, E.G. 1902. *A Literary History of Persia*. 4 vols. Cambridge: Cambridge University Press.

Buhl, F. 1906. "Ein paar Beitrage zur Kritik der Geschichte Muhammeds." In *Orientalische Studien Theodor Noldeke . . . gewidmet*, 7-22. Giessen.

_____. 1955. *Das Leben Muhammeds*. Heidelberg: Quelle U. Meyer.

Caetoni, L. 1909-12. *Annali dell'Islam*. Milan.

Carra de Vaux, B. 1953. "Wali." In *Shorter Encyclopaedia of Islam*, edited by H. A. R. Gibb et al. Ithaca: Cornell University Press.

Cheyne, A. 1979. *Succession to the Rule in Islam*. London: Luzac and Co., Ltd.

Chittick, W. C., ed. and trans. 1981. *A Shiᶜite Anthology*. Selected by A. Tabataba'i, with an introduction by S. H. Nasr. Albany: State University of New York Press.

Cook, M. 1983. *Muhammad*. Oxford: Oxford University Press.

Corbin. H. 1964. *Histoire de la Philosophie Islamique*. Paris.

Corbin, H., and Y. Osman. 1969. *La Philosophie Shiᶜite*. Tehran and Paris: Bibliotheque iranienne.

Crone, P. and M. Hinds. 1986. *God's Caliph: Religious Authority in the First Centuries of Islam*. Cambridge: Cambridge University Press.

Dawood, N. G. 1956. *The Koran*. London: Penguin Books.

Dekmejian, R. H., and M. J. Wyszomirski. 1972. "Charismatic Leadership in Islam: The Mahdi of Sudan." *Comparative Studies in Society and History* 14 (March): 193-214.

al-Dinawari. 1967. *al-Akhbar al-Tiwal*. Edited by Sadiq Nashát. Tehran: Bunyad-i Farhanq-i Iran.

Donaldson, D. M. 1933. *The Shiᶜite Religion*. London.

Eliash, J. 1969. "The Ithna ᶜashari-Shiᶜi Juristic Theory of Political and Legal Authority." *Studia Islamica* 29:17-30.

Fakhry, M. 1983. *A History of Islamic Philosophy*. New York: Columbia University Press.

Fuck, J. 1936. "Die Originalitat des arabischen Propheten." *Zeitschrift der deutschen morganlandischen Gesellshaft* 90:509-25.

Gardet, L. 1961. *La Cite' masulmane: vie sociale et politique*. Paris.

———. 1979. "Karama." In *The Encyclopedia of Islam*, edited by H. A. R. Gibb et al. Leiden: E. J. Brill.

Gaudefroy-Demombynes, M. 1957. *Mahomet*. Paris: Albin-Michel.

Gibb, H. A. R. 1962. *Studies on the Civilization of Islam*. Princeton: Princeton University Press.

Gibb, H. A. R., et al., eds. 1953. *Shorter Encyclopaedia of Islam*. Ithaca: Cornell University Press.

———. 1979. *Encyclopaedia of Islam*. new ed. Leiden: E. J. Brill.

Goitein, S.D. 1966. *Studies in Islamic History and Institutions*. Leiden: E. J. Brill.

———. 1968. "Attitudes towards Government in Islam and Judaism." In *Studies in Islamic Religions and Political Institutions*, 149-67. Leiden: E. J. Brill.

Goldziher, Ignaz. 1971. *Muslim Studies*. Edited by S. M. Stern. Chicago: George Allen and Unwin.

———. 1981. *Introduction to Islamic Theology and Law*. Princeton: Princeton University Press.

Henninger, J. 1981. "Pre-Islamic Bedouin Religion." In *Studies on Islam*, translated and edited by Merlin L. Swartz, 3-22. Oxford: Oxford University Press.

Hitti, P. 1970. *History of the Arabs*. New York: St. Martin's Press.

Hodgson, M. 1974. *The Adventure of Islam*. Chicago: University of Chicago Press.

Holt, P. M., et al., eds. 1970. *The Cambridge History of Islam*. 4 vols. London: Cambridge University Press.

Hourani, G. 1964. "The Basis of Authority of Consensus in Sunnite Islam." *Studia Islamica* 21:13-60.

Huart, I. 1979. "ᶜAli." In *Encyclopedia of Islam*, edited by H. A. R. Gibb et al. 30-32. Leiden: E. J. Brill.

Ibn al-Athir. 1851-76. *Kitab al-Kamil*. Edited by C. J. Tornberg. Leiden: E. J. Brill.

Ibn Hisham. 1955. *Sirah Rasul Allah*. Translated by A. Guillaume. Oxford: Oxford University Press.

_____. 1974. *al-Sira al-Nabawiya*. Edited by T.A. Saᶜd. Cairo.

Ibn Qutaiba, Abdullah ibn. 1969. *Kitab al-Maᶜari*. Edited by T. ᶜUkasha. Cairo.

Ibn Rusta, Ahmad ibn ᶜUmar. 1892. *al-Aᶜlaq al-Nafisa*. Edited by M. J. de Goeje. Leiden: E. J. Brill.

Jafri, S. H. M. 1979a. "Conduct of Rule in Islam (in the Light of a Document of 38/658)." *Hamdard Islamicus* 11:3-34.

_____. 1979b. *The Origins and Early Development of Shiᶜa Islam*. New York: Longman.

Khan, Bakher ᶜAli. 1981. *Islam-Shiah Point of View*. Madras.

Lambton, A. K. S. 1981. *State and Government in Medieval Islam: An Introduction to the Study of Islamic Political Theory: The Jurists*. Oxford: Oxford University Press.

Lammens, H. 1924. *La Mecque a la veille de l'hegire*. Beyrouth.

Laoust, H. 1961. "La classification des sectes dans 'Le Farq' d'al-Baghdadi." *Revue des etudes islamique* 29:19-59.

_____. 1962. "Le role de ᶜAli dans la chiite." *Revue des etudes islamique* 30:7-26.

_____. 1965. "La classification des sectes dans L'heresiographie ashᶜarite." In *Arabic and Islamic Studies in Honor of H. A. R. Gibb*, 377-86. Leiden: E. J. Brill.

Lapidus, I. M. 1975. "The Separation of State and Religion in the Development of Early Islamic Society." *International Journal of Middle East Studies* 6:363-85.

Lecky, W. E. H., 1878-1890. *History of England in the Eighteenth Century*.

Levi della Vida, G. 1934. "Pre-Islamic Arabia." In *The Arab Heritage*, edited by N. Faris, 25-57. Princeton: Princeton University Press.

_____. 1953. "ᶜUmar." In *Shorter Encyclopaedia of Islam*, edited by H. A. R. Gibb and J. H. Kramer. Ithaca: Cornell University Press.

_____. 1953. "Kharijites." In *Shorter Encyclopedia of Islam*, edited by H. A. R. Gibb et al., 246-49. Ithaca: Cornell University Press.

Lewis, B. 1953. "Some Observations on the Significance of Heresy in the History of Islam." *Studia Islamica* 1:43-63.

_____. 1970. "On the Revolutions in Early Islam." *Studia Islamica* 32:215-31.

_____. 1972. "Islamic Concepts of Revolution." In *Revolution in the Middle East*, edited by P. J. Vatikiotis, 30-40. London.

_____. 1974. *Islam: From the Prophet Muhammad to the Capture of Constantinople*. New York: Harper & Row.

Lings, M. 1983. *Muhammad: His Life Based on the Earliest Sources*. London: George Allen and Unwin.

Macdonald, B. 1953. "Karama." In *Shorter Encyclopaedia of Islam*, edited by H. A. R. Gibb et al. Ithaca: Cornell University Press.

al-Maqdisi, Mutahhar ibn Tahir. 1899. *al Bada' wa Ta'rikh*. Edited by C. Huart. Leiden: E. J. Brill.

Margoliouth, D. S. 1922. "The Sense of the Title *Khalifah*." In *A Volume of Oriental Studies Presented to E. G. Browne*, edited by T. W. Arnold and R. A. Nicholson, 322-28. Cambridge: Cambridge University Press.

al-Mas^{c}udi. 1977. *Muruj al-Dhahab wa al-Ma^{c}adin al-Jawhar*. Tehran.

Mashkur, M.J. n.d. *Tarikh-i Shi^{c}ah va Firqehhay-i Islam*. Tehran: Ishraqi Publications.

Meddin, J. 1976. "Human Nature and the Dialectics of Imminent Sociocultural Change." *Social Forces* 55 (December): 382-93.

Mottahedeh, R. P. 1980. *Loyalty and Leadership in an Early Islamic Society*. Princeton: Princeton University Press.

Muir, W. 1975. *The Caliphate: Its Rise, Decline, and Fall*. New York: AMS Press.

al-Nasafi, Aziz al-Din. 1962. *Kitab al-Insan al-Kamil*. Tehran.

al-Nawbakhti, Abu Muhammad. 1963. *Firaq al-Shi^{c}ah*. Najaf.

Nuri ^{c}Ala', Isma^{c}il. 1978. *Jami^{c}ah Shinasi-i Siyasi-i Tashayyu^c-i Ithna ^{c}Ashari (The Political Sociology of the Twelve-Imami Shi^{c}ism)*. Tehran: Quqnus Publications.

O'Leary, D. 1927. *Arabia before Muhammad*. London.

Parsons, T. 1951. *The Social System*. New York: Free Press.

_____. 1969. *Politics and Social Structure*. New York: Free Press.

_____. 1973. *The Structure of Social Action*. New York: Free Press.

Petersen, E. 1959. "^{c}Ali and Mu^{c}awiyah: The Rise of the Umayyad Caliphate, 656-661." *Acta Orientalia* 23:157-96.

Petroshevsky, I. P. 1971. *Islam Dar Iran (Islam in Iran)*. Tehran: Payam.

Pickthall, M. 1976. *The Glorious Koran*. London: George Allen and Unwin.

Rahman, Fazlur. 1966. *Islam*. Chicago: University of Chicago Press.

Rieff, P. 1959. *Freud: The Mind of the Moralist*. Chicago: University of Chicago Press.

_____. 1966. *The Triumph of the Therapeutic: Uses of Faith after Freud*. New York: Harper & Row.

_____. 1972a. *Fellow Teachers*. New York: Delta Books.

_____. 1972b. "Toward a Theory of Culture: With Special Reference to the Psychoanalytic Case." In *Imagination and Precision in the Social Sciences: Essays in Memory of Peter Nettl*, edited by T. J. Nossiter, 90-108. London: Faber and Faber.

_____. 1981. "By What Authority?" In *The Problem of Authority in America*, edited by John P. Diggins and Mark E. Kahn, 225-55. Philadelphia: Temple University Press.

Roth G., and W. Schlechter. 1979. *Max Weber's Vision of History: Ethics & Methods*. Berkeley: University of California Press.

Saunders, J. J. 1965. *A History of Medieval Islam*. London: Routledge and Kegan Paul.

Scarrilla, N. 1974. "The Persistence of Charisma: A Re-interpretation of Routinization." *Review of Social Theory* 2 (May):91-108.

Schacht, J., and C. E. Bosworth, eds. 1979. *The Legacy of Islam*. Oxford: Oxford University Press.

Sellheim, R. 1965-67. "Prophet, Caliph und Geschichte: Die Muhammed-Biographie des Ibn Ishaq." *Oriens* 18-19:33-91.

Shaban, A. 1971. *Islamic History: A New Interpretation*. 2 vols. Cambridge: Cambridge University Press.

Shahid, Irfan. 1970. "Pre-Islamic Arabia." In *The Cambridge History of Islam*, edited by P. M. Holt et al., 1:3-29. Cambridge: Cambridge University Press.

al-Shahrastani. 1979. *al-Milal wa al-Nihal*. Tehran.

Swartz, M. L., ed. and trans. 1981. *Studies on Islam*. Oxford: Oxford University Press.

Smith, S. 1954. "Events in Sixth Century Arabia." *Bulletin of the School of African and Oriental Studies* 16:425-68.

Sourdel, D. 1970. "La classification des sectes islamiques dans 'Le Kitab al-Milal' d'al-Shahrastani." *Studia Islamica* 31:239-47.

al-Tabari, M. J. 1879-1901. *Ta'rikh al-rusul wa al-muluk*. Edited by M. J. de Goeje. Leiden: E. J. Brill.

Tabataba'i, A. S. M. H. 1969. *Zuhur-i Shiᶜah (The Appearance of Shiᶜism): The Collection of Interviews with Professor Henri Corbin*. Tehran.

_____. 1975. *Shiᶜite Islam*. Translated from the Persian and edited with an introduction and notes by S. H. Nasr. Albany: State University of New York Press.

Toth, M. A. 1972. "Toward a Theory of the Routinization of Charisma." *Rocky Mountain Social Science Journal* 9 (April): 93-98.

Turner, B. S. 1974. *Weber and Islam*. London: Routledge and Kegan Paul.

Von Grunebaum, G. E. 1946. *Medieval Islam: A Vital Study of Islam at Its Zenith*. Chicago: University of Chicago Press.

_____. 1963. "The Nature of Arab Unity before Islam." *Arabica* 10:5-23.

_____. 1970. *Classical Islam: A History, 600 A.D.—1258 A.D.* Chicago: Aldine.

Wach, J. 1944. *Sociology of Religion.* Chicago: University of Chicago Press.

Wallace, R. 1976. "Process in the Development of Social Movements." *Scottish Journal of Sociology* 1 (November): 81-93.

Wansborough, J. 1978. *The Sectarian Milieu: Content and Composition of Islamic Salvation History.* Oxford: Oxford University Press.

Watt, W. M. 1951. *Muhammad at Mecca.* Oxford: At the Clarendon Press.

_____. 1956. *Muhammad at Medina.* Oxford: At the Clarendon Press.

_____. 1961. *Muhammad: Prophet and Statesman.* Oxford: Oxford University Press.

_____. 1962. *Islamic Philosophy and Theology.* Edinburgh: Edinburgh University Press.

_____. 1968a. *Islamic Political Thought.* Edinburgh: Edinburgh University Press.

_____. 1968b. *What Is Islam?* New York: Longman.

_____. 1969. *Islam and the Integration of Society.* London: Northwestern University Press.

_____. 1973. *The Formative Period of Islamic Thought.* Edinburgh: Edinburgh University Press.

_____. 1974. *The Majesty That Was Islam.* London: Sidgwick & Jackson.

Weber, M. 1946. *From Max Weber: Essays in Sociology.* Translated, edited, and with an introduction by H. H. Gerth and C. Wright Mills. New York: Oxford University Press.

_____. 1968. *On Charisma and Institution Building.* Edited by S. N. Eisenstadt. Chicago: University of Chicago Press.

_____. 1978a. *Economy and Society: An Outline of Interpretive Sociology.* Edited by Guenther Roth and Claus Wittich. 2 vols. Berkeley: University of California Press.

_____. 1978b. *Gesammelte Aufsatze zur Religionssoziologie.* 3 vols. Tubingen: J. C. B. Mohr (Paul Siebeck).

_____. 1980a. *Gesammelte Politische Schriften.* Tubingen: J. C. B. Mohr (Paul Siebeck).

_____. 1980b. *Wirtschaft und Gessellschaft.*Tubingen: J. C. B. Mohr (Paul Siebeck).

Wellhausen, J. 1927. *The Arab Kingdom and Its Fall.* London: Curcon Press.

_____. 1961. *Reste Arabischen Heidentums.* Berlin.

Wensinck, A. 1932. *The Muslim Creed.* Cambridge: Cambridge University Press.

Williams, J. A., ed. 1971. *Themes of Islamic Civilization.* Berkeley: University of California Press.

Wolf, E. 1951. "Social Organization of Mecca and the Origins of Islam." *Southwestern Journal of Anthropology* 7:329-536.

al-Yaᶜqubi. 1883. *Ta'rikh.* Edited by M. Th. Houtsma. Leiden: E. J. Brill.

Zarrinkub, A. 1951. *Du Qarn Sukut (Two Centuries of Silence)*. Tehran: Javidan.

Index

Abbasyds, 92
Abd al-Dar, 23–24
Abd al-Rahman ibn Awf, 68
Abd Manaf, 23–24
Abd Shams, 20, 24
Abrahah, 28
Abu Bakr, 4, 10, 65–67, 75, 101; election as Muhammad's successor, 83–85, 89
Abu Sufyan, 21
Abu Talib, 53, 95, 102
Abyssinian migration, 53
Ahl al-bayt, 102–103, 107, 108–109
Ali, 5–6, 9–10, 62; charismatic authority of, 110–112; Kharijite opposition to, 122–123; as Muhammad's successor, 95–120; Muslim opposition to, 86–87; refuses allegiance to Abu Bakr, 67
Allah, 2, 8–9, 56–60, 63, 150
Al-muhillun, 31
Al-muhrimun, 31
Anbiya', 9
Ansar, 53. 58, 65–66
Arabs, 6–8, 77; Kharijite opposition to, 137–139; pre-Islamic culture, 17–32, 106–108, 149
Arberry, A.J., 39
'Asid ibn Hudayr, 65–66
'Aws tribe, 65–66
Azraqites, 124–125, 130–131, 139, 144

Baghdadi, al-Abu Mansur, 101, 106, 113, 122, 124, 128, 132, 144
Banu Abd Shams, 19–21, 24
Banu Hashim, 19–21, 24, 107
Barnes, D.F., 149
Barthold, W., 97
Basrah Kharijites, 133–134
Battle of Badr, 86–87
Battles, 54–55, 86–87
Bayah, 89
Bendix, R., 84, 91, 114, 117

Blood relationship, 19
Book of the Perfect Man (Nasafi), 37–38
Brockelmann, Carl, 19
Browne, E.G., 107–108

Caliphate, 88–93
Carra de Vaux, B., 41
Charisma: charismatic community, 141–142; leadership attributes, 149; personal v. official, 105; routinization of, 68–70, 76, 119; sociological definition of, 33–34
Commerce, 26–28
Constitution of Mecca, 8
Constitution of Medina, 54
Corbin, H., 116–117
Cultural revolution, 152
Culture, 147–149

Dar al-Nadwah, 20, 21, 25–26
Dawood, N.G., 39
Dekmejian, R.H., 103
Dinawari, al-, 130
Divine origin, 34
Divine right, 109

Fakhry, M., 106
From Max Weber: Essays in Sociology (Weber), 141
Fundamentalism, 126–135

Ghadir Khum, 98–99, 110
Gibb, H.A.R., 79–80, 87–88, 138
Goldhizer, Ignaz, 13, 15, 87, 90, 138; on Shiite origins, 96–97

Hadith, 4–5
Haji, 76
Halif, 23
Haram, 28, 30–32
Hashim, 19, 20, 24
Hejira, 53–55

JA 15 '02

DATE DUE

JUN 1 3 2003		

GAYLORD   #3523PI   Printed in USA